NIAGARA'S WINE VISIONARIES

NIAGARA'S WINE VISIONARIES

Profiles of the Pioneering Winemakers

LINDA BRAMBLE

JAMES LORIMER & COMPANY LTD., PUBLISHERS
TORONTO

James Lorimer & Company Ltd., Publishers acknowledge the support of the Ontario Arts Council. We acknowledge the support of the Government of Canada through the Book Publishing Industry Development Program (BPIDP) for our publishing activities. We acknowledge the support of the Canada Council for the Arts for our publishing program. We acknowledge the support of the Government of Ontario through the Ontario Media Development Corporation's Ontario Book Initiative.

Cover design by Meghan Collins

Library and Archives Canada Cataloguing in Publication

Bramble, Linda
Niagara's wine visionaries : profiles of the pioneering winemakers / Linda Bramble.

ISBN 978-1-55277-429-8

1. Wine and wine making—Ontario--Niagara Peninsula.
2. Wineries—Ontario—Niagara Peninsula. 3. Wine industry—Ontario—History. I. Title.

TP559.C3B74 2009   663'.200971338   C2009-904185-5

James Lorimer & Company Ltd., Publishers
317 Adelaide Street West, Suite 1002
Toronto, Ontario
M5V 1P9
www.lorimer.ca

Printed in Canada

To Ben

CONTENTS

1 SUBLIME MADNESS: MAKING FINE WINE IN ONTARIO

"We are all mortal until that first kiss and the second glass of wine."
—*Eduardo Galeano*

Why do they even bother to grow grapes to make fine wine in Ontario? The climate is marginal. The places where premium grapes do grow are small, and the memory of an old industry with abysmal quality lingers. The system supporting Ontario wines is one of the most controlled in the world. Yet the men and women of 133 grape wineries in Ontario persist.

They know that wine grapes do best at the coolest limits of their range. In warmer climates, the ripening of grapes occurs early. Under the hot conditions of mid-July, sugars develop rapidly and acids drop before giving the grapes time to accumulate the flavour compounds that add distinction. In cooler climates, especially in autumn when the flavour constituents are developing, the warm days and cool nights allow development at a slower rate. The longer the grape clusters can stay connected to their roots, the more time they have to develop physiological ripeness and personality.

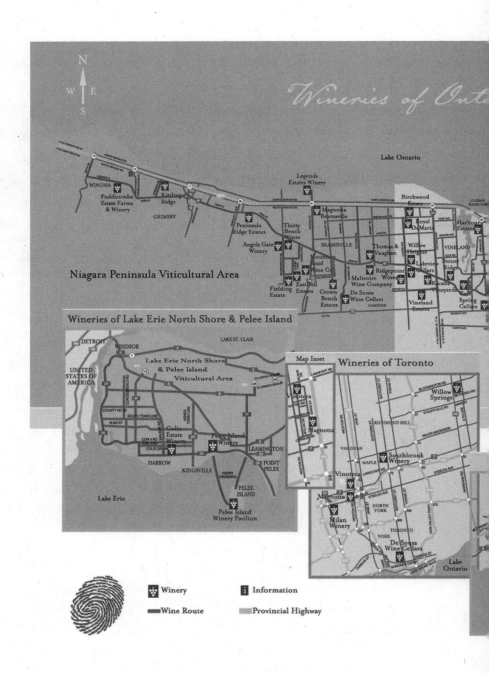

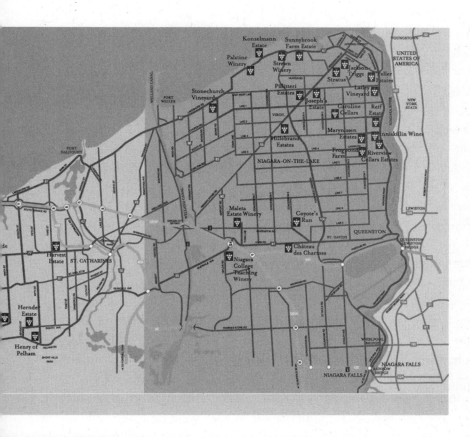

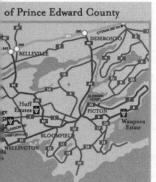

of Prince Edward County

Wine Route (TM) is a registered trademark and property of the Wine Council of Ontario. This map can not be reproduced without permission. All rights reserved. The Wine Council of Ontario urges all visitors not to drink and drive and suggests the use of a designated driver.

Wines of Ontario

AS MUCH CHARACTER AS THE PEOPLE WHO MAKE THEM

Estimated Driving Times:

Toronto–Niagara:	1 to 1-1/2 hours
Buffalo–Niagara:	1/2 hour
Toronto–Lake Erie North Shore:	4 hours
Detroit–Lake Erie North Shore:	1/2 hour
Toronto–Pelee Island:	4 hours, PLUS 1-1/2 hour ferry ride or 20 minutes on the hydrofoil
Toronto–Prince Edward County:	2-1/2 hours

The pests and diseases that plagued the vines of early cool-climate growers were difficult to control. These growers didn't know until the early part of the twentieth century that the greedy and vine-suffocating phyloxxera louse could be starved by grafting tolerant North American rootstock onto *vinifera* vines.

Cool climate seems to be an oxymoron in the summer, when Ontario temperatures can rise above the 30°Celsius (86°Fahrenheit) mark and the long hot days of summer rival those anywhere in more southerly growing areas. The length of the growing season in Ontario's wine regions can equal that of the best regions in the world — Bordeaux, Tuscany, Burgundy, the Loire or Champagne. What those regions don't have, however, is the killing temperatures of winter. When temperatures fall below −15° or −20°Celsius (5° or -4°Fahrenheit), certain varieties of vines can be damaged or even die. That's the rub.

Many producers address the problem with winter management techniques such as burying vines, delaying pruning, managing the canopy, establishing multiple trunks, reducing crop load, using wind machines or even lighting candles to get through a really chilling spell. They spend the money and the time because they know that, if they can keep the vines alive, the results could be delicious come harvest. That's sublime.

But it's madness when you consider all the other factors that could limit ripening: hail, humidity, too much rain at the wrong time, too little rain at a necessary time, too-hot temperatures and the vines shut down, too-cold temperatures and the vines die, pests such as lady beetles of the Asian kind or berry moths of the Canadian kind. Yet the valiant wine producers of Ontario persist — so much so that between 1997 and 2005, according to Statistics Canada, the real gross domestic product of the wine industry increased at an average annual rate of 7.1 percent, more than double the 3 percent rate of national growth.

Vines for wine can grow in temperate climate zones across the world in a band roughly between 30° and 50° north and south of the equator. At these latitudes, they receive enough sunlight for photosynthesis to occur. Ontario's wine country lies on either side of 43°N, smack dab in the middle. Two of the five Great Lakes — Erie and Ontario — also play a key role in moderating the weather patterns by staying cold enough in the late spring to prevent frosts from killing early buds, helping acclimatize them to withstand the spring frosts, and staying warm enough in the fall to extend the growing season. Because Ontario wine production is situated in the middle zone of North America, tropical and polar air masses meet, creating variable and often unexpected weather conditions. This adds to the mystique. Right — tell that to a young Niagara bride planning an outdoor wedding in June or a grape grower waiting for the winter temperatures to go low enough in January so he can pick his Icewine crop before it all deteriorates.

Most of Ontario's wine country is located within the famous Carolinian zone, named after the same habitat that extends as far south as the Carolinas, containing more rare species of plants and animals than any other place in Canada. In 1990, the United Nations Educational, Scientific and Cultural Organization (UNESCO) designated Ontario's Niagara Escarpment as a World Biosphere Reserve for its internationally significant ecosystem and special environment. Biosphere reserves, such as the Galapagos Islands, Africa's Serengeti and the Florida Everglades, are heavily protected lands that are monitored to maintain a balance between conservation and development. Wine country is alluring no matter where you go in the world. Ribbons of vines rhythmically rolling across a landscape form a peaceful, unadorned beauty like no other. Ontario's wine country is no exception.

The soils in the grape-growing regions of Ontario are a mosaic of sandy loam, limestone, gravel and clay, dropped by the same glacier that carved out the Great Lakes. These soils provide the necessary drainage needed to grow classic vines. Mind you, to be on the safe side most growers still install drainage tiles to carry away surface water.

There are 15,006 acres (6,004 hectares) of vines presently growing in four areas capable of producing finer quality grapes: the Niagara Peninsula, Pelee Island, Lake Erie North Shore and Prince Edward County. These are Ontario's appellations, so named by the Vintners Quality Alliance.

The Niagara Peninsula is the largest grape-growing region in Canada. Seventy-five percent of domestic wine grapes are grown here. The arable land for grapes is about the same size as Napa (54,000 acres, or 21,853 hectares). Only about one-quarter of that is currently being farmed. This area played a pivotal role in the development of early Canada, serving as a crossroads for trading and warring Aboriginal peoples, traders from Quebec who came by water, the French, who established the first permanent European settlement in the region, and the British, who conquered it.

When the Americans revolted against the British, those Americans loyal to the Crown moved northwards to this safe haven, where they settled, unmolested by angry patriots. Among other early settlers were soldiers who were rewarded for their service with tracts of land. Many of their descendants still farm those same Crown grants. Three natural features define Ontario wine country's boundaries: Lake Ontario to the north, the Niagara River to the east, and the Niagara Escarpment, its most prominent feature, to the south. The Niagara Escarpment is the same 335-metre (575-foot) ridge over which the Niagara River plummets into Niagara Falls. Even though the Falls section of the ridge has been pushed farther upstream towards Lake Erie through erosion, it is still part of the ancient shoreline of the once-mammoth Lake Iroquois.

The Niagara Escarpment begins in Rochester, New York, crosses the Niagara River and continues through the Niagara Peninsula, winding its way for 725 kilometres (450 miles) to Tobermory. In Niagara, the Escarpment acts as a rampart against lake winds, circulating them back to the lake and keeping the vines planted along its leeward base fresh and invigorated. Two ridges or benches serve as gentle ramps that parallel the "mountain" — the Beamsville Bench and the Queenston Bench. Several vineyards and wineries are located along each bench. Niagara-on-the-Lake, at the spot where Lake Ontario and the Niagara River meet, has sandier soils and weather moderated by the waters' influence. Iroquois-speaking tribes who lived in Niagara recognized it as a favoured place. It was easy to see why they settled there and named it *Onguiaahra,* meaning "strait," or in some, more evocative, translations, "place of thundering waters."

It was also easy to understand why the pioneering men and women of early Ontario tried to grow wine grapes. Settlements were scattered, life was rough and rural, and grapes grew wild. Johann Schiller, a retired German soldier who had fought for the Crown in the early years of the nineteenth century, was the first to domesticate the wild vines that grew along his Crown-granted property. He farmed along the banks of the Credit River in Cooksville, Ontario, near York (soon to be Toronto). By 1811, he had supplemented his vines with American hybrids from Pennsylvania, making enough wine for himself and to sell to his neighbours. Schiller is considered the father of commercial winemaking in Canada.

He sold his place in Cooksville to Count Justin M. de Courtenay, who doubled the size of the vineyard in 1864 by planting Clinton and Isabella grapes, also American hybrids. He labelled his wines Clair House, which soon became the largest brand in Ontario. There were other "brands." Porter Adams, seventy kilometres (forty-three miles) away in Niagara, had a farm in Queenston, not far from today's Château des Charmes. He shipped his surplus grapes to Toronto for the home winemaking market. John Killborn, even more enterprising, proudly made his own wine and sold it locally for $1.75 a gallon (3.8 litres) from his Beamsville property, now the site of Peninsula Ridge Estates.

In 1873, George Barnes built his winery in St. Catharines along the banks of the old Welland Canal. Until the late 1980s, Barnes Wines was known as Canada's oldest continuously run winemaking operation, even though George sold his interests in 1932 to Grimsby Wine, Ltd., who in 1966 sold their interests to Parkdale Wines, who were soon acquired by Labatt Breweries. And so the lineage goes.

Thomas Bright and his partner F.A. Shirriff opened the Niagara Falls Wine Company in 1874, moving to Niagara sixteen years later to be closer to the grapes. Novel idea! On the purchase of Vincor in 2007, the Bright's lineage became part of the largest wine company in the world, American-owned Constellation Brands.

The many mergers and acquisitions are easy to understand. Growing grapes to make wine in Ontario is hard. The native grapes that grow here and in other parts of the northeast come from a species of vine called *Vitis labrusca*. What they gain in cold-weather brawn they lose in flavour to a compound called methyl anthranilate. This gives the grapes a "foxy" taste — a descriptor thought to have been derived from a farmer's familiarity with fox urine. (This story was proven apocryphal by a group of courageous agriculture students from the University of Guelph. Goodness knows what their sensory testing entailed.) With water, sugar and alcohol added, even foxy wines were palatable, but hardly fine.

As hard as they tried to grow the European varieties, which come from a tastier branch of the vine family called *Vitis vinifera*, they could not succeed. The plants might live for two or three years, then wilt and die, their lives sucked out of them by phyloxxera. Or they would collapse under the infections of fungal diseases, or freeze to death in winter. So the *labrusca* varieties and their crosses or hybrids survived and formed the basis for the early industry. In spite of all this, there were 5,000 acres (2,023 hectares) of grapes in Niagara supporting ten fairly healthy wineries by 1914. Although none of the wineries that were operating before the First World War exist today, their ghosts are all rattling around present-day companies that still use the early wineries' licences, acquired in one way or another, to sell wine.

Lake Erie's Pelee Island, the second appellation in Ontario, is just a short boat ride away from American and Canadian shores. It is Canada's most southerly point — it is closer to the equator than Rome! The growing season for Pelee Island vines begins almost two weeks earlier than in the Niagara Peninsula and lasts longer in the fall because of the expansive surface of the lake holding summer heat. Lake Erie is shallow, however, and its winter deep-freezes can wreak havoc on the vines.

Settlers from the United States began growing grapes here in the 1850s, and it soon became one of the major growing areas in the province. In 1866, after the Civil War, two Kentuckians, Thaddeus Smith and Thomas S. Williams, travelled north. Whether too proud to live under Yankee rule or too entrepreneurial to pass up a good thing, they planted twenty-five acres (ten hectares) of grapes the first year, then another thirty the next. Their third partner, J.D. Williams, lived in Windsor and had been encouraged by the owner of the island to invest. By 1871, the three gentlemen opened their winery, Vin Villa, selling much of their inventory to thirsty island tourists and American consumers in Sandusky, Ohio. To distribute their wines in Ontario, they hired a grocer from Brantford, J.S. Hamilton, as their agent. Hamilton also sold for other Pelee Island wineries. The enterprising grocer not only found markets for Pelee Island wines, but also generated one of his own, the Pelee Island Wine and Vineyard Company. This winery had facilities on the mainland and on the island, where by 1888 Hamilton had built a three-storey winery from local stone. From the winepress on the top floor, juice was gravity-fed to one of eighteen 1,000-gallon (3,785-litre) vats on the lowest level.

When the available land on Pelee Island became covered with grapes, growers turned to the mainland around Leamington, which had a similar climate to Pelee Island, and to Essex County around the town of Sandwich. Near the beginning of the twentieth century, the grape industry was well established in southwestern Ontario, but its predominance was short-lived. The lure of better cash crops was too tempting. Local Aboriginal populations and early pioneers had carried on the growing of tobacco for many years. When protective duties on imported leaf were imposed in 1897, tobacco prices rose, making it a more lucrative enterprise than wine.

When Hamilton moved his winery off the island to Brantford, he renamed his operation the J.S. Hamilton Wine Company and continued the business until 1949, selling his assets to The London Winery. By that time, nearly all the wineries in southwestern Ontario had closed down, with the exception of The London Winery, which the Knowles family had established in 1924. Unlike most of the other winery operators of the period, Joseph Knowles actually knew how to make wine.

In 1890, twenty-three of the forty-one wineries operating in Ontario were located in southwestern Ontario. Of these twenty-three, The London Winery was the only one left in 1977, when grape grower Alan Eastman opened Charal Winery and Vineyards in nearby Blenheim. Eastman and his father had made test-plots they had been farming since 1968. Although Eastman's winery was not successful, his enterprise renewed interest in growing grapes in southwestern Ontario. Land was cheaper there than in Niagara, so several other growers followed. Ron Moyer, chair of the Grape Growers Marketing Board, planted there in 1974, and Austrian winemaker Walter Strehn invested and formed Pelee Island Winery by 1979. Bright's also planted an experimental vineyard not far from Moyer's farm.

This third appellation along the old Windsor corridor became known as the Lake Erie North Shore. Today there are twelve wineries with more than five hundred acres (two hundred hectares) altogether of grapes growing along the bow-shaped shoreline of Lake Erie from Amherstburg to Leamington. Like Pelee Island, this area has an abundance of sunshine and enjoys one of the longest growing seasons in Canada. Many argue that this is where the smart money is being invested today. Distance from markets, lack of infrastructure and a sparse population base has limited its growth, but for grape-growing it is ideal. The leading light of this appellation is Colio Estate Winery, which had its first crush in 1980 with Carlo Negi, a young Italian winemaker from San Michelle Adige in northeastern Italy. Two investors whose families came from Friuli enticed the thirty-eight-year-old Negi to come to Canada. When he discovered he had only hybrids from which to make wine, he almost despaired, "What have I done?" Eventually, he did accept the challenge. His wine, at the least, would be better than what he had tasted of the local wines.

For the first decade, Colio didn't own their own vineyards and had to make do with whatever Jordan's, Bright's, Chateau Gai, London and the other wineries didn't need or want. By 1984, Carlo Negi had developed a Bianco Secco and a Bianco Rosso, with a whopping twenty-five thousand cases headed for the Liquor Control Board of Ontario (LCBO), soon to become the best-selling white and red wines in the province. Little by little, they started to buy their own land with the aim of eventually becoming self-sufficient. Taking advantage of the turbulence from the new Free Trade Agreement, Colio developed a retail store system, ending up with fourteen retail locations throughout the province. The ever-modest Negi went on to win dozens of prizes for his wine, including Winemaker of the Year and Winery of the Year. Jim Clark, the winery's current president, recognizes the leadership role Colio took on in the industry: pioneers from day one who developed the business in all channels and created a well-integrated operation.

Travelling east by water to the end of Lake Erie, then through the Welland Canal in Niagara and east again past Toronto to Lake Ontario's north shore, we arrive at Prince Edward County. There are currently thirty-two growers and fourteen wineries in the county with more than $30 million invested. The county's been gussied up as a culinary getaway to attract Toronto's urban market. According to wine and food writer James Chatto, senior editor of the LCBO's *Food & Drink* magazine, Prince Edward County is "uncannily similar to Burgundy's Côte d'Or," and its Pinot "could be Canada's next great wine success story." High praise for Ontario's newest appellation.

Ontario's wine industry is lucky compared to other wine regions of the world. It is equidistant to the largest domestic market in Canada, the Greater Toronto Area, and to the U.S. border at Buffalo and Detroit. There are other factors, however, that have tended to temper that good fortune and inhibit its growth.

Even though the Ontario wine industry evolved to serve its market, the market resisted. Toronto became a "sophisticated" urban market and for many years refused to change its mind about the palatability of domestic wines, even as those domestic wines became more sophisticated and won the prizes to prove it.

Unlike any other wine jurisdiction in the world, Ontario's producers are controlled by a liquor-control board that is also the largest purchaser, distributor and retailer of wines in the world and a Crown business operating under the jurisdiction of the Province of Ontario. The Liquor Control Board of Ontario (LCBO) provides wines throughout their network of six hundred stores. If a winery's volume is too small, it presents a very difficult challenge for the LCBO. This, in turn, creates a problem for producers, since there are only two other places where a bottle of domestic wine can be sold: through a restaurant or at a winery retail store.

Another differentiating factor is the way in which grapes are sold. Similar to the situations with milk or wheat, there is a board that markets all grapes grown and sold in Ontario. Even if a winery has its own grapes, it must comply with the price negotiated between the Wine Council and the Ontario Grape Growers Marketing Board. One price fits all. If one grower is conscientious and tends his vineyard with assiduous care and produces grapes of uncommon quality, he will get the same price as the grower whose grapes come in at lesser quality. This has been an inhibiting factor to improvement for many, many years. Wineries can, and do, contract with selected growers and give them incentives over and above the base price. Quality is achieved, but there is a cost.

The story of the Ontario wine industry and the entrepreneurial men and women who shaped it is a story of fortitude and futility, heartbreak and exhilaration, annihilation and, finally, rebirth. Like a slowly turning helix, it has evolved, reconciling opposing forces. In so doing, it has created one of the most intriguing success stories of modern Canadian culture and business.

2 HARRY HATCH'S BRIGHT AMBITION

"Entrepreneurs are simply those who understand that there is little difference between obstacle and opportunity and are able to turn both to their advantage."

— *Machiavelli*

Ten-year-old John Ghetti was working in his father's Niagara-on-the-Lake vineyard when he heard an unfamiliar motor humming through the adjacent laneway. When he peeked through the vines, he saw a brand-new 1935 Cadillac sedan, so black and sleek it seemed to vibrate in the sun. As it approached, the outstretched winged ornament on the hood warned anyone or anything in its path to step aside. John knew there had to be someone larger than life inside, someone who defied conventionality. To drive a Cadillac through a grapery was one thing, but it was the middle of the Great Depression. Who had such wealth and such defiance?

John Ghetti would learn that the man inside was Mr. Harry C. Hatch, who, in 1933, only two years before driving through the vineyard, had purchased T.G. Bright and Company, the Niagara Falls winery where John's father sold his grapes. What John couldn't have known that day was that within little more than a decade, with agricultural school behind him,

Harry Hatch, CEO, T. G. Bright and Company, 1933–1945

he would become the fieldman in charge of 1,300 acres (526 hectares) of experimental vines begun by Hatch in his quest to improve Bright's wines.

What few could understand was why a wealthy man such as Hatch would buy the largest winery in Canada in 1933? What could possibly motivate paying $1.5 million to the founder's son, William Bright, a Scotch-drinking man who bragged about never drinking his own wines? Although the wine business had been profitable during Prohibition, sales had plummeted with its repeal in 1927. When American Prohibition ended six years later, sales declined even further. It was the height of the Great Depression, and Canada had been hit extremely hard. Unemployment was 27 percent. The gross national product had dropped to 43 percent. Businesses had closed as corporate losses spiralled downward. Exports shrank drastically.

Harry Hatch had to have been aware that severe changes in wine standard compliance were imminent. Before Prohibition, the only aspect of winemaking that was regulated was the issuance of a licence to manufacture through a provincial board of commissioners. Once a proprietor had a licence, it was up to him to monitor his wines' safety, quality, distribution and sale. Repeal had come, but at a cost. Part of the agreement the government made with the electorate, which was still comprised of a good portion of temperance supporters, was a promise to control all beverage alcohol in the province, from licensing, production and standards to auditing, distribution and sale. For so long, Hatch had disdained repressive temperance attitudes toward alcohol. He had to have realized that things in the wine industry would become even more controlled. The industry had suffered a severe setback. No one knew how long it would take to turn around.

Yet, in the face of all these dislocations and obstacles — economic, political and social — he bought a huge winery, the largest in Canada, and dedicated his resources to revolutionizing it. Consequently, he changed the course of the entire wine industry of Ontario.

* * *

Harry Hatch was born in 1884 in Ameliasburgh, Ontario, a hamlet in Prince Edward County, where his father, Bill Hatch, had a hotel business. Harry and his brother Herb apprenticed in the liquor business, working for their father as bartenders. When Harry was twenty-seven and newly married, he struck out on his own and opened a liquor store in Whitby, Ontario. Undaunted by the meagre $8.40 he made the first day open, he soon prospered. By 1913, two years later, he and his brother opened another store in Toronto at 433 Yonge Street. Business was good, despite the constant agitation of temperance forces. Fundamentalist Protestant groups and organizations such as the Women's Christian Temperance Union (WCTU) held rallies on the alarming extent of intemperance, warning that its evil effects would be the end of society. As one pamphlet pronounced, drinking was the cause of "the loss of labour, vice, sickness, premature death, criminal prosecutions and jail confinement, plus the deterioration of property value."

There was little doubt that high-potency alcohol dominated the Canadian experience in the early 1800s and 1900s. Storage and transportation gave whisky an advantage over easily spoiled beer or wine. For those who drank, the pattern of drinking was periodic — heavy but recreational.

Daily drinking was rare. Ontario was wild, agrarian and unsettled. Life was harsh. Release from stress with alcohol, particularly at social occasions, made lives more bearable. When people did drink in saloons, the unsavoury nature of the establishments themselves fuelled temperance sentiments. Imagine the stench: mud, spittoons and sawdust on the floors, thick smoke in the air and, running under the brass footrails along the base of the bar, urinal troughs.

Early temperance leaders had encouraged moderation, but as time went on their tone changed. As the movement gathered momentum, they started asking for pledges of total abstinence. In 1898, the lobby succeeded in getting a national plebiscite placed before the voters, asking: "Are you in favour of passing an Act prohibiting the importation, manufacture, or sale of spirits, wine, ale, cider and all other alcoholic liquors for use as a beverage?" Temperance leaders in Ontario and the Maritimes had landslide victories. In Quebec, five times as many voted against Prohibition as for it. Across the country, 52.5 percent were in favour of Prohibition. Prime Minister Wilfrid Laurier was able to avoid acting on the results by stating that, since only 44 percent of the voters had turned out, "it did not justify the introduction by the Government of a prohibitory measure." A close call. Prohibitionists would never again make the same mistake of not getting a clear statement that a simple majority of those voting was sufficient to bring about Prohibition. The people had been indoctrinated with the idea that the "trafficking of liquor" had to be destroyed; it was only a matter of time before it would be banished from Canadian life.

When the First World War broke out in 1914, the temperance lobby encouraged the provincial government to pass an act to prohibit the manufacture and sale of all alcoholic beverages. Their campaign shifted from the inherent evils of demon rum to one of patriotic duty. After all, they reasoned, it was the least a citizen could do. Our boys were sacrificing their lives; the electorate could sacrifice its booze. Since alcohol was needed in the manufacture of munitions, it was a convenient way for the government to satisfy a very strong lobby. Ontario passed the Ontario Temperance Act, bringing Prohibition into force in April 1916. After the war, it would be subject to a referendum to determine whether the statute should be permanent. By 1917, every province in Canada was dry except Quebec. In 1918, the federal government stepped in and required it to comply.

The Ontario Temperance Act stipulated that no alcohol could be sold in the form of drink in Ontario. Some of the "wets" were incredulous at its passage. One Toronto journalist asked in 1919: "Did somebody slip something over us while the casualty lists blinded our eyes with tears? ... Did we give up drink because giving things up was the fashion? ... And when we did, did we mean it?"

Wine, in Ontario, was included in the ban, until the grape growers protested that their livelihood was at stake. The act was amended to exclude domestic wine. There were six established wineries at the time of its passage: Barnes (1873), T.G. Bright and Co. (1874 — the company Harry Hatch would buy in 1933), Jules Robinet and Sons (1882), National Wine Company (1894), Turner Wine Co. (1885) and Stamford Park Wine Co. (1890). In a convoluted anomaly that only a bureaucrat could devise, the buyer had to go to the winery to purchase his wine and was compelled by law to buy two cases or five gallons (nineteen litres) at a time. The wine had to be made from *labrusca* grapes native to Ontario; no imported blends were allowed. Was it any wonder that adventurous entrepreneurs, mostly new European immigrants with a history of making wine at home, flooded the newly created Board of License Commissioners with applications to open a winery — which the commissioners issued with no investigation into the competence, capital or credibility of the applicant to make or sell wine?

Another part of the act gave early meaning to "cross-border shopping." Although it was illegal to drink beverage alcohol in public, it wasn't illegal to manufacture and sell to international markets. Boatloads of Canadian booze, which included beer, wine and spirits, left border ports such as Niagara and Windsor with cargo ostensibly addressed to customers in Cuba or Mexico. Strangely, they made it only to the border cities in the United States. And from there it was anybody's guess where they were destined. The particularly enterprising shippers would divert a shipment back to Canadian shores to waiting bootleggers and "blind pigs," which were rooms in a family household, the Canadian equivalent to speakeasies. More serious was the rise in convictions of Canadian moonshiners who sold illicit whisky that bordered on being, or indeed was, lethal.

The act had many loopholes. Alcohol could be produced for medicinal, sacramental, industrial or scientific reasons. To meet that need, government dispensaries were set up throughout the province to fill such orders. The Ontario government was so flooded with "prescriptions" from physicians and druggists that by 1923 it had sold nearly $5 million worth of alcohol by prescription. Those physicians and druggists who were found to be too compliant with their patients' requests were found guilty of flagrantly trafficking in alcohol and were subsequently fined or arrested. Humorist and anti-prohibitionist Stephen Leacock, in describing the law's folly, wrote about the ease with which one could get a drink: "It is necessary to go to a drug store," he wrote, "and lean up against the counter and make a gurgling sigh like apoplexy. One often sees these apoplexy cases lined up four deep."

When the Temperance Act was enacted, saloons, hotels and all private retailers were immediately shut down. But Herb and Harry Hatch were not to be denied. Although like other private retailers they were put out of business and their entire stock confiscated by the government (which it sold to its own dispensaries for a sizeable profit), the brothers Hatch thought of a new way to recoup their losses. Harry had previously negotiated the right to handle Watson's scotch whisky, an imported blend, so the nimble boys moved to Montreal, where Prohibition had not yet become law, and opened a shop in the mail-order business. There were enormous profits to be made selling liquor through the mail to the thirsty residents of Ontario.

That business lasted until 1918, when the federal government used its emergency powers to extend Prohibition to Quebec. That was the same time the feds also banned the interprovincial sale of alcohol, a law that would take ninety years to redress. Quebec endured Prohibition as a war measure imposition but quickly dispensed with it as soon as peace returned. In October 1920, Quebec and British Columbia held referenda that ended Prohibition in both provinces, with the proviso that their respective provincial governments would take over the control of alcohol. Going back to the days of the private sale of liquor was not even an option.

A referendum held in Ontario the same year had very different results. By a whopping margin of four hundred thousand votes, the electorate of Ontario, which included the newly franchised women's vote, decided to keep in force the Ontario Temperance Act of 1916. Ontario would stay dry. Another referendum in 1921 resulted in ending the private import of liquor from outside the province. The net had been tightened. Beverage alcohol still couldn't be sold, but in Ontario the manufacture of it was never forbidden. Brewers and distillers continued to make substantial profits selling to the United States. Ontario would stay dry. Even without the wartime sentiment of self-sacrifice, Ontarians chose to abstain. From that point on, however, the history of beverage alcohol — wine, beer and spirits — would be tightly bound to the fortunes of Prohibition, begotten and misbegotten.

In the meantime, young Harry Hatch caught the eye of Sir Mortimer Davis. Davis, a wealthy Montreal businessman, owned the Belleville distillery Corby's, which like so many was suffering under the continuing Prohibition. He hired Harry, who had a scheme involving his relative Maudie Hatch of Whitby to bring life back to Corby's liquor sales. Maudie had loaned money to local fishermen, taking their boats as surety. Now, most of the loans were in default. This leverage, plus the attitude of the "wets" that Prohibition was "a law that did not deserve to be obeyed," enabled Maudie to recruit the fishermen to run Corby's liquor across the lake to be sold, all legally manufactured in Canada but dangerously slippery in the United States. "Harry's Navy" was launched, and Corby's made a tidy profit.

Harry wanted in. He wanted his own distillery to make his own whisky, to call his own shots. Sir Mortimer Davis was not pleased. His star salesman jumped ship, so to speak, taking with him his navy and the list of American bootlegging contacts. Harry had been eyeing a prestigious but inactive distillery in Toronto, Gooderham and Worts, which had loyally stopped producing alcohol unless for the war effort. It was near downtown, on sixteen acres (six and a half hectares) of land, idle for nearly a decade, with antiquated equipment. Harry discovered a $500,000 mortgage with payments due. The aristocratic Gooderham might just sell.

In 1923, Harry got $1.5 million together to buy the distillery lot, stock and barrels, plus the venerable Gooderham and Worts name. With his own distillery, Harry could serve the parched American market. But there was a snag. Under Canadian law, whisky had to age for two years before sale. There was nothing in his barrels. He went to the federal government to ask for an exemption. He reasoned that the government had granted distillers an exemption in 1920; why not give him one now, only three years later?

His request just happened to be accompanied by a generous gift to the bagman of the Liberal Party. He got an Order-in-Council for the next six months, just enough time to fill outstanding orders from both Canadian and American bootleggers. Americans were dependent on Canadian distillers for premium product. Even if it wasn't barrel-aged, at least it was sound. Montreal's Bronfmans, Sir Mortimer Davis and Harry Hatch made sure their supply was safe and mellow.

In 1926, Harry Hatch bought Hiram Walker in Walkerville, Ontario, for the astronomical figure of $14 million. He had become one of the wealthiest and most successful men in Canada. His success, in large part, was due to his uncanny ability not only to read the market, but to respond. When he merged his two companies, the *Toronto Star* called him the "King of Canadian Distillation."

*　*　*

Harry's wealth was just one indication that Prohibition had failed. The absence of "demon rum," a category that included anything alcoholic, did not meet the expectations of the temperance leaders. It did not bring peace, happiness and salvation, nor did it rid the province of poverty, venereal disease, lunacy and prostitution. Rather, it nurtured gangsters, racketeers, venal judges, corrupt police, crooked politicians and a colluding citizenry. The law, on both sides of the border, was simply unenforceable. Moderation leagues championed an image of respectability and true temperance. They also argued that Prohibition was un-British. Red-blooded Britons and their colonials were not afraid of temptation; besides, to prohibit anything was so "Yankee"! They proposed a "sane, moderate compromise," as Quebec and British Columbia had done a few years before — government control and sale of liquor. The Canadian way of compromise proved to be a win-win solution. Ontario ended Prohibition on April 5, 1927, eleven years from the month of its original enactment. The Ontario government would get a lucrative windfall of revenue in return for a guarantee to control the products it offered. Once again, the consumer could buy a drink, legally.

A board of directors for the newly established Liquor Control Board of Ontario was sworn in the following day, drafted to tackle the enormous job of opening for business. Regulations had to be considered, staff hired and trained, premises rented, stock selected and shipped, selling systems determined and permits sold. Within a miraculous two months, the government liquor stores were ready.

Their ostensible mandate was to discourage consumption, so these early merchandisers intentionally designed the buying experience to be a dreary one. A purchaser, before receiving his order, had to buy a permit, sign his name, give his address, and list the liquor he wanted to buy. By law he had to go directly home with his brown paper bag before opening the bottle concealed inside. But the government was also benefiting from the sales. They were in business, and liquor taxes were feeding their empty coffers. This contradictory mandate helps explain the limits placed on the holder of the permit: one quart (nearly one litre) of spirituous liquor, two gallons (7.5 litres) of beer and one gallon (3.8 litres) of wine per day. The store manager could choose to refuse to sell to a person he suspected of excessive drinking. Special permits were given to druggists, physicians, clergymen and hospitals to make purchases in connection with their work.

The general functions and duties of the LCBO were to import, buy and sell alcoholic beverages, to establish and manage liquor stores, to control the possession, sale, transport and delivery of liquor within the province, to maintain inspection staff, and to assist the police in enforcing the act. The first chief commissioner of the board was D.B. Hanna, the former president of the Canadian National Railways. He would orchestrate the buying of real estate for new stores, supervise the stocking and training of personnel and see to it that this first business of the government was as efficient and smoothly run as the railway. He was a fit man for the job. He made sure that entering a store was like entering a train station — each detail designed to make the customer stay on track, no diversions, no desire to linger. In and out.

On June 1, 1927, the LCBO opened sixteen stores. As Hanna's first annual report stated, within six months they had added eighty-six more, plus four warehouses and eighty-six breweries. The board invoked measures of cleanliness on wineries and strictly regulated their hours of operation, as well as setting limits on the amount of wine they sold. What wasn't in the report was the understanding the government had reached with the larger, more established, wineries.

The wine industry was in severe trouble due to the proliferation of small wineries during Prohibition. Before Prohibition, there were six wineries. By the end, there were fifty-one, some legitimate, many not. When wine is made in the back of a barn, in the pigshed or in a mould-covered cellar under conditions less than sanitary, deleterious microbes abound. Prior to Prohibition, each winery was allowed one on-premise retail outlet. Now the government promised that, if the more established wineries bought out the smaller and more precarious ones, they could keep the retail licence of the winery purchased. Further proliferation of dubious operations would be curbed and the legitimate enterprises could extend their reach beyond their cellar doors. Once consolidated, the industry could get on a more stable footing. A moratorium was placed on the authorization of any new licences. It would last for the next forty-seven years.

With more wine available through the government stores, calls came in complaining of vinegary wines, exploding bottles, strange insect-ridden sediment and other foreign matter in the wines. To correct the quality problem, R.A. Bonham, the provincial chemist from the Department of Health, conducted a lab analysis on wine quality of all commercial wines in Ontario. In his first report in 1928, he gave violators severe warnings. They had two years to clean up their wines. A follow-up report saw some improvement, but there were still too many wineries using carcinogenic cold tars and high amounts of preservatives. The wines continued to contain excessive levels of volatile acidity or vinegar. To address this and other winemaking fiascoes, Bonham held winemaking classes. Some attended, but many never did. The classes were given in English. Many of the immigrant entrepreneurs, who made up most of the winemakers, couldn't understand.

For those whose operations were sketchy at best, compliance with the new regime of wine standards was next to impossible. If the wines didn't comply, they could not be sold through the government stores, only at the winery. These wineries weren't exactly market-ready for wine tourists. Sterner measures would follow. The medicated and tonic wine business — which produced big sellers for pharmacies — was checked by requiring an additive to be put in their "wine" that would induce vomiting if taken in large quantities. Within months those businesses shut down. In time, the licences of only six wineries remained, differently configured from the pre-Prohibition original six, the result of the incremental process of consolidation.

* * *

Consolidation was big on Harry Hatch's agenda. By 1940 Hatch's winery, Bright's, had acquired fourteen stores. All had been purchased not for the equipment or the brand, but for the attached retail licences. In most cases the wine stocks were sent to the distillery to make grape spirit. Legislation soon followed to allow the purchaser to transfer the retail licence to a larger urban centre for greater market penetration. Within the next fifty years, these additional retail licences, plus more than a hundred more, would cause great dissension among the have-not wineries.

And there was a market to fight over. Whether it was human perversity or the times, wine consumption had soared during Prohibition. Before Prohibition, in 1921, total consumption of domestic wine in Canada was a modest 221,985 gallons (840,304 litres). By 1930, total consumption in Ontario alone exceeded 2 million gallons (7.5 million litres), yet the domestic wine industry wasn't seeing the benefits. In Ontario, there was a combination of competing imports, poor quality and a severely depressed economy. Grape growers were on the edge of bankruptcy. Some would drive two hundred to three hundred miles (three hundred to four hundred kilometres) from their farms with truckloads of grapes, hoping to sell their harvest to home winemakers for as little as $12 a ton. Others sent their surplus directly to the distillery to be made into grape spirit.

Harry's distillery, and those of his Canadian competition, relied heavily on the U.S. market, but by 1933 there were murmurings that the United States was about to end Prohibition, which would open the market back up to U.S. distillers. Harry began constructing a huge Hiram Walker distillery in Peoria, Illinois, capable of producing 50 million gallons (189 million litres) of whisky a year, making it the world's largest distillery. Harry would be the first to supply the legal American market.

The year 1933 was a busy one for Harry. He acquired the declining Canadian winery T.G. Bright and Co. for 1.5 million. He applied the same determination to his winery venture that he had to his other enterprises. He hired the best quality-control people available and gave them a free hand to develop the best wines that could be made from the grape varieties available. And if the grapes weren't available, he would have them test to find new ones. International events, beyond even Harry's control, made this a much longer process than anticipated.

His winemaker was microbiologist Dr. John Ravenscroft Eoff III, a southern gentleman who had been involved in the development of the U.S. Food and Drug Administration, and who had considerable background in the California wine industry. It was Eoff who introduced microbiological control to the Canadian wine industry. He showed producers how to institute quality control and sanitation procedures. The result was an observable improvement in the quality of Ontario wines.

One of the young microbiologists that Eoff hired was Adhemar de Chaunac, a microbiologist originally from France who had been working on yeast production with the Lallemand Yeast Company in Montreal. Hatch soon realized that Eoff and de Chaunac could not make quality wines with poor grapes. In 1934, he began purchasing land on which to conduct large-scale research with new varieties. Once he could guarantee which varieties were reliable, he would drive his brand-new 1935 Cadillac sedan around the Niagara area finding growers to plant them, growers such as John Ghetti's dad.

The quest was to develop a viable and delicious dry table wine. The portfolio of wines up until then were fortified sweet port and sherry-style wines made from basically only two grape varieties: Concord and Niagara, neither of which could produce an acceptable dry table wine. In 1938, de Chaunac was the first to introduce to Canada *vinifera* hybrids such as Maréchal Foch and Baco Noir. He planned to continue experimenting with the premium *vinifera* vines of France, Germany and Russia. But 1939 saw the outbreak of the Second World War, which brought his project to a halt. Sourcing vine stock became impossible.

With the war came rationing — rationing of wine for the consumer and rationing of products for the producer. Sugar, for instance, a legal addition to wine before fermentation and used to boost the level of alcohol, was rationed and just about doubled in price. With farmhands on the war front, labour for fieldwork was scarce.

Finally, with the war's end, de Chaunac ordered thirty-five French hybrids and four *vinifera* varieties from France, including Chardonnay, Riesling, Pinot Noir and Gamay. When the vines arrived in 1946, Harry Hatch, the man behind the vision who by now had invested nearly $1 million in the Bright's viticulture program, died suddenly. He was sixty-two. If he had lived to see 1949, he would have tasted the first commercial sparkling wine made in the traditional method. By 1955, he would have been proud of his wines made from French hybrids Maréchal Foch, Baco Noir and the first *vinifera* wine in Canada, a 100 percent Chardonnay — a signal of a new era to come.

Over the course of thirty years, Bright's would test six hundred grape varieties with fifty selected for commercial production. When de Chaunac died in the 1960s, his assistant George Hostetter became the new director of their vineyard research division. Hostetter received many awards for the work he continued, including the Order of Canada. The men who did the fieldwork, however, seldom receive the same recognition. Hostetter's viticulturist Art Neff and his fieldman John Ghetti made it all happen. Art and John shared their experience with the Bright's growers throughout the peninsula through Neff's meticulous records and handbooks, giving them current insights on how to raise the new cultivars. Ghetti, who had monitored the experiments, was on-site to respond to growers' questions.

A few years later, in 1978, Dr. John Paroschy, a young assistant in the Bright's lab, would be the first to test the use of Vidal for icewine. Had it not been for the unseemly theft of his research wines, Paroschy would have been credited today as the first to introduce icewine to Canada. After Bright's, Paroschy joined Paul Bosc at Château des Charmes and conducted some of the most forward-looking viticulture trials in Ontario. Long after Harry Hatch's death, the wine industry benefited from his insightful hiring and nurturing of these extraordinary people.

Extraordinary talent was needed. The introduction of new varieties required a quantum leap in education. No one, including Adhemar de Chaunac, George Hostetter, Art Neff, John Ghetti or John Paroschy, really knew at the time how to grow the more vulnerable *vinifera* varieties under Niagara's growing conditions. Winters were colder than they are today. Methods of growing native varieties were diametrically opposed to those needed to grow *vinifera* and hybrids. Local stories abound about the discouraging advice that well-meaning scientists at the local horticultural station gave to growers who wanted to branch into *vinifera* varieties. One story may be apocryphal, but since it rings true it has survived. In response to a grower's question on how he should prune *vinifera*, the local scientist is said to have illustrated his answer by approaching a Chardonnay vine and dramatically cutting it off at the trunk, effectively killing it.

Bright's experiments paved the way for a new industry, but the accomplishments of the Horticultural Research Institute of Ontario (HRIO), more commonly referred to as the Vineland research station, should not be overlooked. Its focus was different. The scientists at the station were more interested in breeding new varieties that could survive the cold winters and the hot summers of Niagara's fickle semi-continental climate. They concentrated on improving the varieties that the growers had in the ground in order to make those vines more productive and easier to grow.

From its inception in 1906 until 1960, the research station tested eighty thousand seedlings. Those with more acceptable results were subjected to second and third generations of study. Each was based on a native *labrusca* type; the goal was to produce cultivars that had fewer *labrusca* characteristics and features closer to *vinifera* varieties. The names given to results all started with V — Vincent, Veeport, Veeblanc, Vivant — but none of them received much attention from wineries or growers.

They experimented with *vinifera* hybrids as well. In 1946, Ollie Brandt, planter breeder with the HRIO, contacted de Chaunac and asked for his assistance in selecting a list of *vinifera* hybrids for planting on their new vineyard in Vineland. The development of these two sites, Bright's experimental 1,300 acres (526 hectares) of vineyards in Niagara-on-the-Lake and HRIO's in Vineland, provided valuable data for growers.

Perhaps one of the greatest contributions HRIO made was the role it played in establishing improved wine standards. The stigma of Prohibition was still prominent in the consumer's mind. Imported wines, by definition, had to be better. In the 1970s, new, dry table wines were introduced. The industry had to change the mind of the consumer. Ontario wines needed to be recognized to be as good as the imported brands.

To address this problem, the HRIO brought together panels of six wine experts who met bi-weekly. The members of the panels were drawn equally from the wineries, the LCBO and HRIO staff. In blind tastings, they would compare domestic wines to comparable imported wines according to colour, clarity, aroma, taste and appeal. The tabulated results would be returned to the LCBO and the Wine Council, the trade organization of member wineries. If a wine was found less than acceptable, the LCBO would conduct further tests, and steps would be taken to advise the producer. The program would continue until 1986, after which time the Vintners Quality Alliance took over the tasting program.

Bright's had demonstrated in 1955 that credible, premium varieties such as Chardonnay could be grown in Niagara. Why did it take another thirty years before their presence was more prevalent in Niagara vineyards and on Ontario tables?

A paradigm shift takes a long time to occur. Dr. Helen Fisher, a senior scientist at the HRIO, reasoned that two things happened. First, the wineries decided to pay more for the premium varieties — it cost more to grow them — pushing up the cost to the consumer. Second, European money started to be invested in Ontario, creating a base of knowledge that Niagara's growers didn't have. It was driven at first by the Europeans who understood cool-climate growing, such as Herman Weis, Martin Scheule, Roman Prydatkewycz, Ewald Reif, Joe Pohorly, Albrecht Seeger and Herbert Konzelmann. This not only changed the investment market, it also changed the way local growers perceived what was possible. If they looked over the fence and watched their neighbour doing something interesting and profitable, they started to believe that they could do it too. They needed to see it first.

Harry C. Hatch had been the first to show the way. His leadership and investment began the transformation of the wine industry. Had he not bought T.G. Bright Wines in 1933, Niagara's wine landscape might have looked very different today. What prompted the King of Distillation to buy? Maybe it was as simple as the opportunity to diversify and create another profit centre supplying grape spirit for the fortification of Canadian ports, sherries and brandies. But that would have been a very small portion of the business. Perhaps he had once again read the market, sensing the comparative advantage a winery would soon provide as the government curbed the use of more "ardent spirits." Or could it have been to redeem himself from the darker side of his "kingly" past, to provide a nobler legacy for his children?

The Ontario wine industry was out of step with the times and it was Harry Hatch's ambition to change that. Whatever his reasons, he brought his resources to bear in his quest to make better wines. Harry's ambition inspired the turnaround of the Ontario wine industry.

3 DONALD ZIRALDO'S ZAP

"Our awareness presents itself to us as immediate and unmistakable, yet there is always much more than we see."
— *Thich Nhat Hanh*

K arl Kaiser vowed to his young Canadian wife, Silvia, on their first visit back to see her parents, that he would never, absolutely never, immigrate to Canada. At age twenty-seven, he was happy at home in Austria, teaching bookkeeping and civics at a vocational high school.

Never mind the Hamburger Helper, Jell-O salads, fruit cocktail and tinned peas that seemed to define Canadian cuisine in 1968. He could tolerate that. Even the long hot summer's endless beer strike that forced him to drink homemade Concord wine made by a friend of his father-in-law was more tolerable than the thought of immigration. His decision was solidified the day the whole family — in-laws, wife and baby — went to a little tavern in St. Catharines for lunch and the owner wouldn't let them bring their baby into the same room where alcohol was being served. That day Karl swore to himself that absolutely never would he move to Canada. Never. The monastery where he had been educated as a boy was more liberal than this small, conservative, southern-Ontario town.

That day it would have been inconceivable that he and Donald Ziraldo would someday be regarded in the evolving wine industry of Ontario as critical to the ushering in of new and irreversible change. Within six years of his adamant pronouncement, the serendipitous story of the intersection of two like-minded individuals began to unfold — their dreams, their unbounded ways of seeing and their uncompromising dedication to the possible.

Despite Karl's first impressions of life in southern Ontario, the economy in Canada was experiencing a period of prolonged buoyancy. Working people had regular employment, with more leisure time and the disposable income to enjoy it. There was a vibrant awareness that everyday life was changing. An old order was being actively challenged by the remnants of the counterculture of the 1960s that sought an end to the authoritarianism and inequalities of the 1950s. Social institutions, such as education and the church, and cultural assumptions — the rights of women and gays, tenants' rights — were being upended. Even the way in which liquor was sold and controlled was being challenged.

As in any period of social change, the vestiges of the past were still curiously threaded among the new. Although it was now considered acceptable that women could drink in public without igniting moral outrage, they still couldn't enter a bar through the front door by themselves. They were relegated to the side door for "Ladies and Escorts Only." The personal permit required for all liquor purchases had been abandoned and public drunkenness decriminalized, yet liquor stores throughout the province were the same bleak government-run warehouses. Customers still had to write out their liquor order on a small form with a stubby yellow pencil attached to the table by a short chain. Once the form was completed and submitted, one of the men behind the counter would disappear to the back and retrieve the order, never to be touched by the customer's hand prior to purchase. Self-service, although being tested in some parts of the province, would not be introduced in Niagara for another several years.

The trip back to Austria for Karl and Silvia was a nightmare. Travelling with a five-month-old was difficult enough, but then a massive thunderstorm out of New York's Kennedy airport delayed them for several agonizing hours. When they finally arrived in Vienna, they learned that the Russians had just invaded and occupied Czechoslovakia. This unexpected homecoming thrust their young lives into another storm of uncertainty. The school where Karl taught was on the Czech border. Would the Russians just keep on going and invade Austria as well? Despite the questions, school started within a few weeks and Karl returned to his vocational-high-school students and the pleasure of a decent glass of wine with supper. Wine in his home, as in most European households, was considered a normal part of family life. Karl had been teaching in a wine-growing area, and started to get interested in helping to make wine with his wife's grandfather, a vintner.

Fall turned to winter, yet the political threat of a Russian invasion remained unabated. Karl's mother-in-law kept writing letters about how "golden" things were in Canada. She insisted that he could easily get a job teaching there. Finally, maybe inevitably, on the spring night of Silvia's birthday, just after midnight, he relented. Yes, they could move to Canada. Admitting later that he was "half-loaded" at the time, he kept his promise and the same night they called to say that they were coming home.

Karl, looking forward to getting a job teaching, enrolled right away in a course to learn English as a second language, studying by day and working in a gas station at night. They were living with Silvia's parents in a rented house in St. Catharines. Karl helped around the house as much as possible, and one job was repairing the fence in the backyard. When the repairs were done, he thought it would be nice to plant a few rows of grape vines so he and his father-in-law could eventually have grapes of their own to make wine. He had tasted the local commercial products and knew he could make better wine himself. But to begin with, he needed good grapes.

In 1970 there were seven wineries: Andrés, just new in town, Barnes, T.G. Bright, Jordan, Chateau Gai, Parkdale and The London Wine Company. Karl would learn that unlike Europe, where wineries were small operations owned by the farmers who grew the grapes, in Niagara, where 90 percent of the grapes in Canada were grown, growers were not usually winemakers. Bright's, an exception, farmed 1,300 acres (526 hectares) of its own vineyards, with some serious experimental *vinifera* and French hybrids in viticulture trials, but those vines were not for sale. Independent growers were contracted to the other wineries, but most were growing domestic grapes from *labrusca* or *labrusca* crosses such as Concord, Niagara, Delaware and Catawba. Karl didn't want these varieties because the wines they made had the musty flavour caused by methyl anthralilate, a compound not found in other varieties. When the wines were sweetened, diluted and fortified to produce a sherry- or port-style beverage, the unbecoming flavour could be masked, but not so with drier table wines.

French hybrids, on the other hand, whose parents were a mix between *Vitis vinifera* and *Vitis riparia* or *Vitis rupestris* species, had gone through more breeding iterations to select out the foxiness of the *labrusca* while breeding in their winter hardiness and disease resistance. Although never quite as good as the *vinifera* parent for flavour, these grapes were capable of making a tastier table wine than the *labrusca* alone. Karl decided he would plant French hybrids in their little backyard plot. By asking around, he learned of a small nursery in St. Catharines that specialized in tender fruit and French hybrids run by an Italian family by the name of Ziraldo.

In 1970, only 5,000 tons of French hybrid grapes were harvested from a total harvest of 51,300 tons of *labrusca*-based varieties. The prevailing research paradigm was not designed to replace *labrusca* but to harvest more of them at a lower cost. At the Horticultural Research Institute of Ontario (HRIO), director, Dr. John Archibald, and breeder, Ollie Brandt (who had used Harry Hatch's resources in the selecting of *vinifera* hybrids for planting in Vineland), told an audience of Ohio grape growers that he and his scientists were conducting spacing trials with three grape varieties at spacings of six feet by six feet (two metres by two metres), eight feet by eight feet (two and a half metres by two and a half metres) and ten feet by ten feet (three metres by three metres) to determine which distance could yield the most crop. In another trial they compared different training systems, Geneva Double Curtain and Kniffen, to see which had the better yield. The results showed that the Concord planted on the Kniffin system produced eight tonnes per acre compared to eleven tonnes per acre under the Geneva Double Curtain. Quantity of yield was their main concern, as well as spacing that could allow harvesting machines to do the mechanical harvesting and avoid the high costs of labour. Ultimately, the quality of the grape that the vine produced was not part of their research equation.

When new varieties were bred, Brandt used *labrusca* for the crossing to assure their hardiness against winterkill and summer diseases. If the *vinifera* vines couldn't be grown in the same way as the *labruscas*, the results were usually discarded.

This was not to say that Brandt and his colleagues didn't conduct any *vinifera* trials. They did. However, there seemed to be an incomplete understanding as to how to·treat them. They did little grafting onto proper rootstock, nor did they use any spraying regimes to protect the more vulnerable plants from disease, particularly powdery and downey mildew, nor was the land underneath the vine drained — all established practices by now. Growers got paid by the tonne, not by the quality of the grapes they harvested. Brandt was serving his stakeholders. If you had told a grower in those days to cluster-thin ripening fruit in order to concentrate the vine's energy into fewer clusters, he would have laughed at the prospect of making less money for the sake of more concentrated fruit. Plus, there would have been no reason to do this for *labrusca* varieties. There was little acceptance of the idea that perhaps *vinifera* plants would have to be treated and managed differently. It was no wonder that their *vinifera* trials let them down.

The hybrid experimental efforts that Adhemar de Chaunac at Bright's introduced in the 1940s served as a stepping stone in the transition from *labrusca* to *vinifera*. However, there were also other personalities in the research community that discouraged, with a strange contempt, any planting of *vinifera* in Ontario. One influential scientist from Bright's was later reported to have dismissed growing *vinifera* entirely by saying at a meeting of growers, "A *vinifera* vine is like a sexy woman: take her to bed with you but never marry her."

* * *

When Karl drove up to the entrance of Ziraldo Nurseries to buy the vines for his backyard plot, he was greeted by an effervescent woman who invited him in and, like most Italian mothers, graciously offered him a glass of wine — a wine her son Donald had made from Verdelet, French hybrid grapes from their vineyard in the nursery. Donald, then a student at the Ontario Agriculture College at the University of Guelph, used to bring his homemade wine back to his football buddies. They called it "Ziraldo Zap." Karl found the Verdelet a welcome relief from the *labrusca*-based products he had tasted up until then. Mrs. Ziraldo explained that her husband had died when Donald was fifteen years old, and now he and his younger brother Bobby were running the farm. On that day Donald was away at school, but Mrs. Ziraldo encouraged Karl to return. "Why don't you come back to meet Donald when his university classes are over in the spring?"

Donald Ziraldo had been born on this sixteen-acre mixed-fruit farm in

St. Catharines where his forward-looking father from Friuli, in the cooler northeast part of Italy, had planted French hybrids — de Chaunac Seibel 9549 (a tribute to Adhemar de Chaunac in 1965), Verdelet, Seibel 9110 and Chelois, most of which they sold to Chateau Gai. Donald used to go with his dad to deliver grapes to the winery, standing on the truck for eight hours at a time waiting for their harvest to be unloaded. Now responsible for running the farm, he started to think of better ways to propagate French hybrids, as well as *vinifera*. He turned to the Horticultural Research Station at Vineland for advice.

"Don't bother, son," the scientists said. "They won't grow here. It's too cold." They proceeded to walk him through their trials. "Look here at this Riesling vine and compare it to this Catawba." Where the Riesling was frail and mildew-infested, the Catawba was strong and vigorous. Donald could only agree in the face of such overwhelming evidence. Then he thought about it. They sprayed them the same. The Catawba was more resistant to mildew than the more vulnerable Riesling. What the mildew didn't get, the winter did.

Donald knew about winter cold. While at Guelph he had developed a growth chart as a two-year research project. His professor had asked the class to take construction plans and apply them to farming. Donald suggested to the professor that grapes couldn't work that way: "You've got to make a growth curve based on the plant and its growing season, not an arbitrary construction date." Donald received an award for his project at their annual exhibition on wine and grapes in his last year at university, and later inserted that same growth chart, which had proven itself over time, into a book he wrote twenty-five years later, *Anatomy of a Winery.*

Donald's mother might have attested to even earlier signs of his stubborn resistance to accept things as they were without first questioning why, and this challenge to conventional wisdom wouldn't be his last. The more he travelled to Europe on plant-buying trips, the more convinced he became of the untapped potential in Niagara. There were peaches and apricots in the cool parts of France, Italy, Germany and Switzerland, and they grew the better *vinifera* grapes there too. Why not here?

In 1971, the same year he graduated, he bought the Dawson farm in Niagara-on-the-Lake. It had deep, beautiful soil, and he intended to continue the family's tender fruit nursery. But he soon began propagating more and more plant material from European grape varieties. In 1974 he bought the Jeffries farm on Line 3 on which he planted thirty thousand *vinifera* grape vines that were left over from the nursery, vines no one would buy. This vineyard was directly across the road on Line 3 from the Brae Burn farm, a site he would buy in 1978 and which would later become the site of the winery.

The original Dawson farm was Crown land granted to a Colonel Cooper, who had served as a member of the Inniskillin Fusiliers, which had fought in the War of 1812. Many of the other farmers in Niagara called him naive, even crazy, but Ziraldo didn't care. He continued his field trials, risking family money on plants, many of which died because they were experimental. There was no profit in those losses other than knowledge.

Karl Kaiser also found the pursuit of knowledge, initially, unprofitable. After receiving his English-language certificate and doing very well, he was ready to teach, but contrary to his mother-in-law's visions, the opportunities in teaching were not that "golden" after all. Rather than languish in non-professional jobs forever, Karl enrolled in Brock University to earn a degree in chemistry, a subject that had always intrigued him and for which he was confident he had an aptitude. For personal interest, he took all his electives in subjects that could possibly be useful in winemaking.

During Karl's second summer in Canada, he had a distant encounter with Donald. Karl worked for a rental equipment business where the manager was married to a grape farmer's daughter on Louth Street. The grape farmer, Ron Moyer, was one of the few growing French hybrids and happened to grow two varieties that he had bought from Donald's father and was willing to sell — de Chaunac and Chelois. Karl's vines were still too young to produce fruit, so in the fall of 1970 he bought some Chelois from Ron Moyer and made a fruity rosé.

When university was out in the spring of 1971, Karl took Mrs. Ziraldo's advice and returned to meet Donald. This time he brought a bottle of his own wine to share. The Ziraldos were impressed with Karl's winemaking skill. Encouraged by Donald's positive reaction to his wine, Karl started thinking that perhaps he might find work in a winery. Since Donald's network in the grape industry was extensive, perhaps he could ask his friend at Andrés, Larry Gibson, who procured grapevines for Andrés' growers, if they still had an opening in the cellar?

Donald inquired, but regrettably had to tell Karl that they had already hired someone else. Karl's next wistful comment was more like wishful thinking than anything else. "It would be nice to have a winery of our own," he said. The next thing Karl knew, Donald had taken the idea with all the paperwork it required and had gone to the Liquor Control Board of Ontario (LCBO) to apply for a licence. After nearly five decades of upholding a moratorium on the granting of new winery licences, Karl felt that applying was "like asking for a ticket to the moon." At first he wasn't far from wrong.

"You want a what?" was the response Donald received from an incredulous Mr. Harris, the LCBO vice-president in charge of new authorizations. Then he pointed to an application on his desk from Corby Distilleries to establish a winery in Niagara. Corby's stood no chance either, Harris explained. Once again Donald had to face Karl with disappointing news: "No luck with the licence application. Sorry, Karl."

By the end of the 1960s, more and more Canadians were incorporating wine into their lives. Although Canadians were drinking as they had before Prohibition, most of it was enjoyed at home, and often made there. This contributed to a serious decrease in revenue the LCBO was able to turn over to the provincial treasury. In 1942, profit from the board had represented a hefty 20 percent of the provincial budget, based mostly on beer and spirits sales. In 1970, profits had dwindled to only 3.5 percent. When Premier John Robarts realized this, he called upon a friend to take over the helm as CEO of the LCBO. He was also one of the nation's most respected leaders, a man who had not only been an eyewitness to the century's most significant events, but who had also played a role in shaping them — Major General George Kitching.

As a divisional commander during the Second World War, Kitching was known by thousands of Canadians, and he had a massive network in France and England. He was more than six feet tall, with movie-star good looks, and he was worldly in ways most of his generation was not. He had been born in China in an area ceded to the British and French, since his father was the manager of a company that sold pharmaceuticals, liquor and fizzy soft drinks to the Chinese. When the First World War broke out, his father volunteered for service, sending his wife and children to Canada. Soon young George was off to military college at Sandhurst in England, heading for a military career that lasted twenty-six years. He was in operations that included such key arenas as Sicily, Normandy and the Netherlands, where he played a key role in securing the surrender of the German forces.

When Major General Kitching retired in 1965, he was only fifty-five years old, with many productive years ahead of him. Two years after he left the military, HRH the Duke of Edinburgh appointed Kitching president of an award scheme in Canada aimed at helping young people attain goals in a prescribed period and measure themselves against standards set especially for them and their specific attributes. Kitching accepted the post with delight. He had always been around young people and regarded their training and education as fundamental to democratic citizenship. In 1968, he became involved in another project connected with youth known as United World Colleges, dedicated to bringing intelligent young people from different nations together to gain a better understanding of many of the world's problems. These projects enabled General Kitching to foster eager young people with fresh ideas, a sense of vision and the wherewithal to make courageous decisions.

Premier Robarts liked Kitching because he was quick in assessing people and he was decisive. "Get the facts," Kitching would say, "and make a decision. Don't waffle."

The premier briefed Kitching on the mammoth loss in revenue the board had experienced since the 1940s. Kitching asked, "What is the main purpose of the LCBO? Is it to raise money for the treasury or is it to satisfy the public?" Robarts replied, "Satisfy the public."

Kitching's perspective on beverage alcohol was different from most other men of his generation. He had been out of the country during the First World War and missed the alcohol-gone-amok times of Prohibition, as well as the belt-tightening period of the Depression. Consequently, he never really appreciated the rationale and legacy of control that had shaped the LCBO. He had a taste for Scotch and had broad experience with fine wines. With military decisiveness and a mandate to satisfy the public, Kitching made wine, beer and spirits more available across the province by increasing the number of stores from 290 to 500 during his six-year tenure at the LCBO. He started the Rare Wine and Spirits Store next to the St. Lawrence Market in downtown Toronto, the forerunner of Vintages, and hired wine specialists to sell retail. To have elegant men in green blazers

Major General George Kitching, CEO of the LCBO, 1970–1976

fussing about wine was very radical. General Kitching also doubled the number of imported wines by listing an additional 500 brands, up from 250. This act proved equally radical and set off a cascade of policies to compensate the angry grape growers and wine producers of Ontario.

Although Kitching was a hero to the hundreds of new wine consultants he had hired to expand the service, to the chair of the Grape Growers Marketing Board he was anathema. "Ontario hasn't been called the land of opportunity without just cause," said Ron Moyer to his fellow growers. "Ask any foreign wine importer." General Kitching would soon arouse their ire on a more contentious issue than imported foreign wines. If his read was correct, the new Ontario consumers liked wine — they simply didn't like the domestic wines available in the province at the time. Kitching felt the grape growers had a stranglehold on the wineries, since producers could make wine only from locally grown grapes. He saw two alternatives: if growers grew something different from the indigenous *labrusca*-base varieties, he could see hope for the consumer. The sherry- and port-style wines the industry was producing were not palatable "except to those on the verge of becoming alcoholics," commented a straight-shooting Kitching.

Second, if wineries couldn't get better quality grapes, then why not let them import the wine and blend it here with some domestic product?

The disastrous short crop of 1972 prompted the Canadian Wine Institute to call for permission to import grapes to blend into domestic product. The growers soon raised the price of their grapes, a move General Kitching called "stupid." To Kitching, it made no sense, since the government allowed 20,000 tons of California grapes each year to be imported duty-free by home winemakers in Toronto so that they could process grapes and make their own wine. They could have the grapes but the wineries could not. Kitching thought the wine drinkers of Ontario were being held hostage to a handful of grape growers, and that was dirty politics. Following the 1972 harvest, the growers conceded to allowing 18,000 tons of grapes as concentrate to be imported to make up the 80-percent shortfall.

Wine sales boomed, but in 1975 the wineries were short again, so the Wine Content Act was amended to permit the introduction of grapes grown outside Ontario, as well as imported wine. In 1972, the domestic content in each bottle of wine had to be 75 percent. By 1980, the required domestic content was reduced to 70 percent. The Wine Content Act would be amended several times over the subsequent years, dropping domestic content to as low as 10 percent in 1993 and 2003 and back up to 30 percent by 2008.

One day, three months after Donald had applied for a licence, Harris, the LCBO vice-president, happened to mention in passing amusement to General Kitching that "some young kid was in here asking for a wine licence." "Of course," confirmed the dutiful manager, "he was denied." Hearing this, General Kitching stunned Harris by asking who the chap was and what his proposal entailed.

"Get me his address," insisted Kitching. "I want to meet him to learn more." Kitching wrote a letter requesting that Ziraldo come in and discuss his idea. When Donald arrived, the general greeted him courteously, moved from behind his desk and suggested that they both sit on the couch where they could talk more easily. Despite the fact that his vice-president had recommended against granting the licence, after listening to Donald, Kitching knew the time was right to reconsider Donald's request.

When Kitching sampled Karl's wine, his view was "to get out of the way and let them do their thing." That was the key. Kitching became their champion, going to the ministry on their behalf to fight hard to try something new. Kitching could recognize the entrepreneurial spirit in Donald and Karl and believed these two young men had promise.

About the same time, in 1973, the licensing ice had been broken when Karl Podamer was granted a manufacturer's licence to produce sparkling wine. Podamer, a Hungarian with four decades of winemaking experience, was using the traditional Champagne method to produce his wine, but was using predominantly *labrusca*-based grapes in the base wine. The method required at least two years in the bottle before it was ready to be released for market, so a retail licence was yet to be granted.

In April 1974, Kitching granted Donald and Karl a one-year provisional licence to produce 450 gallons (1,700 litres, or 2,000 cases), which would be sold through the new Rare Wine and Spirits Store. If that went well, the LCBO would look into a permanent licence, not only to manufacture wine, as the Podamer licence stated, but also to retail wine.

In 1975, when they received their permanent licence, Kitching agreed they had to give the winery a better name than "The Winery." Kitching's presence had instilled such a sense of confidence in Donald that, when Kitching suggested a name, accepting it seemed but a small expression of Donald's debt of gratitude. Donald mentioned to Kitching that the Crown land on his newly acquired property had been originally granted to a veteran of the War of 1812, Regimental Commander Cooper of the Inniskillin Fusiliers. Kitching recognized the name as that of a very famous regiment in Ireland. It was a wonderful name.

The boutique Inniskillin Wines were the beginning of something new. John Tait and Claudius Fehr were two of the new blazer-attired wine consultants in the Rare Wine and Spirits Store. For them, having a new Ontario table wine of quality was exciting for the trade, and customers responded. Tait was so intrigued by the project that he went to Niagara-on-the-Lake to visit the makeshift winery that was going to set the world on fire. Ziraldo and Kaiser, with their devotion to making great wines from Ontario fruit, enthralled Tait. They were bright lights, and Tait, like other wine consultants, supported their efforts. The wines were in short supply, so they sold out before the subsequent vintage, which created a pent-up demand. A policy borne out of necessity proved shrewd.

When their permanent licence was granted to make and sell wine in 1975, twenty-six-year-old Donald commented, "It's probably one of the biggest things that's happened to me in my life. It's a dream come true." From that moment onward, although he worked in the vineyard, Donald's agricultural background would only inform his work. Karl Kaiser would make the wine and Donald Ziraldo would sell it. In the end, Karl Podamer's accomplishments, appearing to be just steps behind Inniskillin's, would be only a footnote. He would partner with a consortium of Niagara businessmen to open a winery in Beamsville, Ontario, called Montravin and Podamer Champagne Company, subsequently sold to Magnotta wines in 1993 as a retail store and crushing facility. Twenty-four days before Karl Podamer received his licence to do the same, Donald Ziraldo and Karl Kaiser would go down in history as the first Ontario winery since 1929 to be awarded a commercial licence to make and sell wine.

Kitching kept his word and mentored Donald long after leaving the LCBO. Donald, young and impressionable, held Kitching in high regard. His presence and sense of integrity would serve as a benchmark for Donald in all his future business dealings. But those dealings would constantly test his character. The stigma of the old-style domestic wine accompanied Ziraldo every step of the way. It didn't help when, in 1974, actor Christopher Plummer said about Ontario wines made from *labrusca* grapes, "My God, they're terrible. I had a glass on the train from Montreal and my arm nearly fell off." Although he was not referring to Inniskillin wines, the power of that generalization attached itself for many years to come to the so-called wine cognoscenti who wanted to be seen as in-the-know. The wine lists of Toronto's finer restaurants had little room for a domestic wine. Donald took this as a challenge: "If I can't sell it to the best restaurants in Toronto, what's the point?"

He had crossed one threshold when he got the winery licence and became a small player among eight huge corporations. Now he had to go head to head with them in the marketplace. He packed up a case of Maréchal Foch and set out to meet with the restaurateurs from Toronto's top establishments: Winston's, La Scala and the Windsor Arms.

His first stop was Winston's, where proprietor Johnny Arena threw him out. "What? Are you kidding me? I have the world's most famous wine list." Donald's next stop was to La Scala, where proprietor Charles Grieco sat him down in the corner chair, served him coffee, lectured him for a few hours on the perils of the trade and eventually bought Donald's wine. Next stop — Windsor Arms. *Go for broke,* thought Donald. By this time, he didn't know what to expect — would he get the boot or a cup of coffee? So he was cautious.

Frank Faigaux, the food and beverage director at the Windsor Arms, was notified that there was someone asking for him who didn't give his name. Faigaux could see through the two-way mirror in his office overlooking the Courtyard Café. It was around 4 p.m. and the room was empty. Donald was sitting at table twenty-three. Faigaux didn't know him, yet he was always available to talk to people, so he walked over to see what Donald wanted.

"Hi," he said. "My name is Frank."

"Here's my business card," said Donald. "I'm from Inniskillin."

"Yes, I've heard of Inniskillin," said Faigaux. "What can I do for you?"

"I have a speech to give in an hour. I'd like to make an appointment with you to try my wines," said Donald.

"You can see me now," said Faigaux. "What wines do you have? We can talk and talk, but until you pull the cork…"

Donald brought the wines he had in his car and they tasted them. Faigaux admitted that they were a far cry from what Ontario wines used to be; actually, he found them remarkable.

"Can I come and see you in Niagara next week?" asked Faigaux.

An astounded Donald made the arrangements.

When they met, Swiss-born Faigaux and Karl Kaiser spoke German together, Karl explaining that the idea was to limit production and keep the emphasis on high quality. He explained that the wines would not be pasteurized, nor would water be added. His wines would contain only 100 percent juice! Faigaux knew his wines. That afternoon he bought their

Donald Ziraldo, 2009

entire lot of Coderc, all seventy cases, and requested that those wines be exclusive to the Windsor Arms. The young producers were blown away. Inniskillin's Coderc would become an exclusive label for one of Toronto's signature hotels owned by Laurence Minden.

Ziraldo and Kaiser's success encouraged the larger wineries that had been experimenting with *vinifera* and French hybrids in their proprietary blends to also create an all-*vinifera* varietal wine. In 1975, Chateau Gai came out with a Maréchal Foch. This knocked the wind out of the Inniskillin partners' marketing plans for the moment. They were about to release the first varietal wine in Canada through the new licence with its expanded ability to sell to licensees and retail customers throughout the province. But Chateau Gai, owned by the powerful Labatt's brewing company, had beaten them to the punch when their sultry-sounding French-born winemaker, Paul Bosc, came out with a television commercial one month before the Inniskillin release. Bosc announced his new Maréchal Foch and teased, "Bedder tings to come."

Donald and Karl thought they were finished. What happened was quite the reverse. When customers came looking for the Chateau Gai Maréchal Foch that had quickly sold out because of the TV commercial, they bought the other domestic varietal wine, the Inniskillin Maréchal Foch. Years later, Donald commented, "I have always thanked Paul Bosc Sr. for that fantastic commercial, which really pushed varietal wines into the forefront in Canada."

The watershed year, 1976, aptly came mid-decade. The growers were upset with the increase in foreign product on the province's retail shelves, plus the wineries now had the ability to blend in foreign wines and still call the result, misleadingly, Product of Canada. Grape growers were mercilessly sandwiched in between, with their livelihoods seriously threatened. The LCBO was straddling a difficult dilemma with their double-edged mandate: how could they satisfy consumer demand for acceptable table wine, yet help to enhance and protect the domestic wine industry? In 1976, the provincial government introduced the Ontario Wine Assistance Program aimed at helping sell domestic products. The LCBO 1977 annual report stated:

> In the interest of protecting the Ontario grape growing industry, the Board entered into a program to provide assistance to the Ontario wineries. The program included the accelerated distribution of Ontario wines at our retail outlets; a decrease in the Board's mark-up of these products; and a moratorium on the delisting of Ontario wines.

General Kitching retired that same year.

It was clear that the market for domestic sherry- and port-styled wines had collapsed. The large companies had to create table wines to compete with imported brands such as Black Tower and Blue Nun, yet without the foul flavours inherent in *labrusca*-based wines. The Wine Content Act allowed the wineries to create blends that could compete. Chateau Gai came out with Alpenweiss, a blend of California grapes and local Seyval Blanc. However, the growers were left out in the cold, with still too much of the wrong kind of grapes to sell to unwilling buyers. The only answer was to do what the French had done a decade earlier when they wanted to rid their vineyards of French hybrids: renewal through creative destruction. To enable growers to replant the grapes that the industry could use, the government initiated a five-year, interest-free program to help growers change over from *labrusca* to French hybrid and *vinifera* vines. It became known as the pullout program, the first of two such initiatives.

A third event in 1976 created an even greater commotion. Steven Spurier, a U.K. wine merchant and writer living in Paris, held his famous "Paris Challenge," comparing California wines to classic French wines, upon which the film *Bottle Shock* was based. The judges were all French wine experts and the wines were tasted blind. The top wine selected, to the astonishment of the French, was from California. Michael Vaughn, wine writer for the *Globe and Mail*, held a much less notorious but no less explosive (for Canadians) tasting in England, where he invited fifteen of England's most prominent wine writers and critics. It was prompted by a BBC interview with Hugh Johnson, one of Britain's best-known wine authorities. The year before he had published his long-awaited *World Wine Atlas*, and had omitted entirely an entry on Canadian wine. "When quizzed about this on the BBC in 1972," Vaughn wrote, "Hugh let the bomb fly. Ontario wines were the worst he'd ever tasted. 'The foulness of taste is what I remember best — an artificially sweetened, soapy flavour. It's not in my atlas,' said Johnson."

The wines of 1976, however, bore little resemblance to those of 1972, explained Vaughn. It was in an attempt to discover how these new wine varieties stacked up internationally that Michael Vaughn held the tasting in England with several noted British wine writers attending, including Hugh Johnson. The distinguishing characteristic common to all the wines they tasted was that none of them had existed when Johnson did his original research for the atlas. The tasting was a success, reported Vaughn, "with several of the wines astonishing the panel with their quality." Hugh Johnson's favourite "without a doubt was the Inniskillin 1974 Maréchal Foch," with which the renowned critic Harry Waugh concurred.

Inniskillin's wines flew off the shelf once Vaughn's *Globe and Mail* piece hit the stands. In 1978, Donald and Karl were able to purchase the Brae Burn property in Niagara-on-the-Lake and build a modern winemaking facility and tasting centre. The CBC was so intrigued by the Inniskillin story that they produced a television show that aired on *Country Canada* on January 1, 1978, entitled "Ziraldo's Zap" — an homage to both the homemade wine that gave a knockout punch to Ziraldo's university football buddies and the prescient blow to the old wine industry that had been struck by Donald and Karl's project.

The fourteen-minute segment heralded the renaissance of the Canadian wine industry, driven by Ziraldo and Kaiser's belief about potential to produce high-quality wine from Canada's better-quality grapes. The harvest during filming was cold and rainy; it couldn't have been worse. One scene showed a farmer stuck in the mud with his behemoth harvesting machine straddling the rows of old *labrusca* vines. Whether it was his frustration with being filmed up to his ankles in muck, or perhaps out of a unconscious recognition that his type of farming was drawing to a close, he bellowed at the camera, "It's hell to be a farmer."

The grapes were unevenly ripe. A disappointed Kaiser complained, "If there were standards for sugar, these grapes wouldn't qualify." He knew the work that lay ahead to create those standards and he would take a lead in establishing them. Yet he found hope in the future. "There's one thing I do believe," said Kaiser, looking directly into the camera with unflinching conviction. "Good wines will always be appreciated all over the world, no matter where they are grown. I do think we can make very good wines in Canada."

* * *

The next chapter of their story began to unfold five years later, in the summer of 1983, when Karl and his neighbour Ewald Reif, a German-born grower who was in the process of establishing the vineyards that would eventually become Reif Estate winery, were sharing a bottle of wine at Inniskillin. Their conversation turned to an innovation no one in Niagara had yet tried. Why not turn Niagara's cool climate into a virtue and experiment with a style of winter wine native to their northern European homelands of Germany and Austria? Why not try to leave some grapes

Karl Kaiser, Inniskillin co-founder and winemaker, 1974–2006

on the vine until they froze, then press the vine-sweetened grapes, whose moisture would be left behind in crystals of ice. Since water froze at a higher temperature than sugar, the sweet juice would be pressed as liquid nectar. It seemed like a good idea to the ever curious and innovative Kaiser, and the winemakers at Hillebrand and Pelee Island thought they'd experiment as well. Karl left thirteen rows of Vidal on the vine at the winery entrance long after the traditional harvest. When the first freeze came on December 3, Karl was away at a wine conference in Rochester, New York. When he returned, the same rows of vines with grapes he had left desiccating in the winter sun, had disappeared. "What happened?" Kaiser asked his crew. "Did you guys pick it?" The unfortunate news was that a marauding band of starlings had dined on the entire crop the night before, after a half-metre of snow had fallen and covered the seeds and berries on which the birds normally fed. The winemakers at Hillebrand and Pelee Island were able to save some of their crops, but not enough for any commercial quantity.

The following year everyone netted the vines, which began the process that was to rekindle a style of wine that had virtually disappeared from the Northern Europe of its origins. Karl produced sixty-six cases, and in 1986 entered his 1984 *eiswein* (a term they would change to "icewine" when the VQA regulations were formalized) in an international wine competition, InterVin. It was the only Canadian wine to wine a gold medal. Karl and Donald were just starting to get a glimpse of what they had hit upon.

In 1987 Donald attended an international wine trade show held in Bordeaux called Vinexpo as a visitor. It had been mounted every two years since 1981 and in such a short time, had grown to 1,100 booths of wineries showing their wares to over fifty thousand attendees. He returned two years later, in 1989, but this time as an exhibitor, sharing a booth with a French producer. Representing the only Canadian winery there, he brought some of Karl's Pinot Noir, Chardonnay and Eiswein. Journalist Tony Aspler chronicled the event in the *Toronto Star*. "One memory . . . I will cherish," wrote Aspler, "is the sight of a Fronsac [French] producer arguing with a German vintner at Inniskillin's booth over the quality of Ziraldo's Pinot Noir 1984 (LCBO $9.50). 'Who wants to buy Canadian wine?' demanded the latter. 'The wine is excellent,' replied the Frenchman. 'It's as good as our wine.' Ziraldo just sat there smiling." The Eiswein was made from Vidal Blanc, a hybrid developed in the thirties by French breeder Jean Louis Vidal. A noted acquaintance of Vidal's from the University of Bordeaux, Professor Jacques Pussais, tasted the Inniskillin sweet wine and said, "Vidal would roll over in his grave with enthusiasm."

Donald recognized by then that, just by being there, he was making a statement. Two years later, in 1991, he returned, with his own booth, but this time, since the icewine had been such a hit, all he brought was Karl's 1989 icewine. The '89 had a delicate elegance enhanced by a touch of the same noble rot (Botrytis) that enhances the finest Sauternes. To everyone's complete amazement, Karl's wine won the Grand Prix d'Honneur for the best wine in the show, beating four thousand other international entries. It was an award heard around the world, but the news did not spread by accident. Donald, together with his talented public-relations director at Inniskillin, Debi Pratt, and publicist, Jane Holland, had photographs ready and a press release prepared. The announcement was immediately sent to the international media, restaurateurs and sommeliers.

An entourage of Japanese investors was also attending the show. Originally there to buy real estate in Bordeaux, as they had in Rockefeller Center and Pebble Beach, California, the Japanese invaded Donald's booth en masse in their quest to seek out the best in class and only the finest luxuries that money could buy. After the show, Donald took a plane to Tokyo, following up with tour operators and travel agents to assure that Japanese tourists would find their way to his winery on their pilgrimages to Niagara Falls and bring back the luxurious gift of icewine from Canada. At home, Debi Pratt was busy getting point-of-sale materials, brochures and touring signs translated into Japanese.

With the generous help of Ezio di Emmanuel, a Niagara Falls native who was Trade Officer for the Canadian Consulate in Tokyo, Donald developed wine-tasting events at the embassy, inviting Japanese celebrities and sommeliers. From there he worked the market in Hong Kong, Singapore, then China.

But marketing was not his only concern. Icewine needed a broader distribution platform. When Don Triggs, then president and CEO of Cartier (formerly Chateau Gai winery), approached Donald in 1992 to merge their companies, Donald welcomed the opportunity to expand his reach. Within the next few years, the newly formed Cartier–Inniskillin merged with T.G. Bright under the new ownership of Onex Corporation executive Gerry Schwartz. The new company was soon rebranded under the corporate name of Vincor, with Inniskillin Icewine as the cornerstone for their international marketing strategy. In 1996 Roger Provost, a marketing genius from Courvoisier, was hired as the executive vice-president of international sales and, for the next ten years, Ziraldo and Provost became sidekicks, teaching the wine world about a new category of luxury dessert wine it had never considered before.

Initially, when the combined marketing teams from Cartier–Inniskillin–Bright's had presented their sales forecasts at a meeting, Schwartz rejected out of hand the narrow scope of their projected targets. To Schwartz they were skittishly undershooting the market. He wasn't prepared to accept their proposed marketing plan, particularly with its lack of focus on ice-wine, which had already proven to be enormously profitable, selling for up to $110 a half bottle in international stores. Plus their plan had barely touched the U.S. market, which to Schwartz's mind had huge poten-tial. In addition, Donald was known by the best in the world. "Donald was an icon," said Schwartz. "The only Canadian winemaker with an international reputation."

The next step was to open the Asia Pacific market through Duty Free stores, which were sources of high consumer spending. Then they "invaded" the U.S. market as part of a strategy, they called "Ice Storm," a reference to mobilizing their sales force as the U.S. had recently mobilized its military in response to the Iraqi invasion of Kuwait in "Desert Storm." The Vincor board of directors committed a significant capital investment in the cam-paign by hiring five full-time sales reps in New York City, Miami, Chicago, Los Angeles and San Francisco, giving them the sole responsibility of get-ting up every morning to sell a single product — Inniskillin icewine.

These were the years in which the flamboyant side of Ziraldo took centre stage. He was a handsome bachelor with a taste for sleek cars, beautiful women, stylish clothes, Art Deco and extreme skiing. Evidence of his celeb-rity was constant. There were cover stories showing him smiling on the Great Wall of China while introducing his wine into the Chinese market. He travelled in the same circles as such taste-makers as Piero Antinori, Robert Mondavi, Robert Drouhin, Miguel Torres, Count Alexander de Lur Saluces and Angelo Gaja. He gave tastings for the wealthiest landowners in Singapore. And all the while he was getting Inniskillin icewine onto the wine lists of the best hotels and restaurants in the world.

Inniskillin-sponsored events showcased the best marketing marriages associated with icewine, such as international pastry competitions in Las Vegas. The company even invited three hundred sommeliers who were in Montreal for a competition to come to Niagara for a few days of tastings and tours in wine country and around Niagara Falls.

For every one contact, five new spinoffs would result. On one occasion while in France, Ziraldo and Roger Provost were wooing the executives from Cathay Pacific airlines over dinner at a five-star restaurant in Cannes. When they arrived, standing by the front door was a six-foot-wide display of Inniskillin icewines. A surprised Ziraldo took it in his stride, assuming

Roger had arranged it. After they were seated, three sommeliers came to their table and said, "Good day, Mr. Ziraldo," impressing both Donald and his guests. Dinner included a different icewine for every course, with the sommeliers snapping into seamless service. After the meal, Provost claimed that he knew nothing about the display.

The explanation was not long in coming. One of the sommeliers approached the table and said, "Mr. Ziraldo, when we saw your name on the reservation list, we wanted to honour Inniskillin. We were among the sommeliers you hosted in Niagara. You showed us such a good time, we wanted to return the favour. We understood your guests were potential customers, so we created the display."

That kind of reciprocity followed Ziraldo wherever he went, but at the same time he worked very hard at establishing and nurturing his network. If he had an idea about a marketing foray, he would leave no stone unturned until it worked. He dogged Georg Riedel, tenth-generation Austrian crystal designer, for four years until Riedel agreed to develop a crystal glass specifically designed for serving icewine. Then, with his usual flare, Donald gathered sixteen international wine writers to sample icewine from different stemware that Riedl presented. They were to decide which shape best presented the wine. With the results from that initial tasting, conducted by Riedel and Kaiser, Riedel spent the next nine months working with Donald to create the final design as part of his Vinum Extreme series. An extreme wine in an *Extreme* glass — a marketer's dream.

The benefits of developing this new product didn't stop there. Inniskillin provided the Riedel Icewine stem to restaurants as part of a premium "by the glass" program. This helped to get icewine into the mouths of consumers, because selling an entire bottle of icewine, then a relatively unknown dessert wine, was not easy, even for a seasoned sommelier.

In addition, Inniskillin would do tastings around the globe in cooperation with Riedel, utilizing the newly designed glass. One tour with George Riedel included Michael Mondavi and Ziraldo both serving their wines in the corresponding Reidel stem to three hundred guests at the Four Seasons in Toronto and then at the Casino in Montreal: Mondavi showed off his Cabernet Sauvignon and Ziraldo his Icewine. Guests at the event paid $300 per person just to experience how the taste of these splendid wines changed depending on the shape of the glass. Guests left with a selection of Reidel stemware and a memory of a evening with three divos of the wine world.

Ziraldo had a knack for picking up clues in the marketplace and maximizing to the limit the public relations he could garner from related events. At Vinexpo one year, Inniskillin's booth was adjacent to the French national booth. In the opinion of the French, the Canadian booth was "overcrowded," and they reproached Ziraldo for serving samples of icewine — because he was "enticing" people. Donald shook his head in amazement. "But everyone in the whole show is serving wine," he replied. The real problem was that most attendees had never tasted icewine, and the French knew that, once they did, they would be hooked forever.

Donald Ziraldo, the high flying, peripatetic wine marketer, had become a celebrity. But although it was a lifestyle he found easy to accommodate, he never lost sight of his roots and his deeper obligation to advance the wine industry in Canada. He realized that, for any wine region to be great, it needed an educational and research component to advance knowledge and prepare skilled young people in winemaking and grape-growing. That is one reason why, in 1997, he co-chaired with John Howard, then proprietor of Vineland Estates winery in Niagara, the fund-raising campaign to establish the Cool Climate Oenology and Viticulture Institute (CCOVI) at Brock University in St. Catharines. The institute would conduct research, as well as provide undergraduate and graduate degrees in oenology and viticulture. Within a few years he would do the same for Niagara Culinary Institute, a technical program in culinary arts and wine education at Niagara College.

While Ziraldo was globetrotting, his steady but shyer partner, Karl Kaiser, was at home, eschewing the limelight for the more comfortable surroundings of his lab and barrels. He dedicated himself to creating premium wine in order to meet the world's now high expectations.

Hugh Johnson, the same British writer who in 1972 said that Ontario wines were the worst he'd ever tasted, wrote in the preface of Ziraldo and Kaiser's book, *Icewine: Extreme Winemaking* (2007), "How often does a whole new category join the world's wine list? Niagara has moved icewine from a fringe benefit for ambitious vintners, occasionally achieved, to an international luxury item as dependable as it is luxurious." In a 2008 case study prepared by professors Geoffrey Jones and Jillian Hirawasa and entitled "Inniskillin and the Globalization of Icewine," the Harvard authors stated: "Icewine created a new segment in the dessert wine category of alcoholic beverages. After winning numerous awards and being showcased in prominent wine publications, it grew in popularity in wine-drinking circles. The success of this dessert wine could easily be attributed to the Inniskillin success story."

Ziraldo and Kaiser were often described as the "odd couple" of Canadian wine. As Tony Aspler wrote, "Ziraldo [was] the quintessential salesman, lover of sport cars, extrovert, with Italian blood of Friuli racing in his veins, and Austrian Karl Kaiser, [was] patient, professorial, a priest manqué, totally dedicated to the cellar and the lab."

As when they started out, Ziraldo and Kaiser still held a bedrock belief that things could change radically. They had needed General Kitching to find them, to listen and to champion their cause and, in doing so, to tip the course of events that launched a new and much improved wine industry. Ziraldo needed Karl Kaiser, whose vision wasn't bound by the same habitual mental models that characterized grape-growing in Ontario. Too many had accepted reality as it was presented to them. Kaiser saw with fresh eyes. Their bold idea to ask for a licence might have failed because it conflicted with deeply held images of how growing grapes and making wine in Niagara worked. Kaiser, Ziraldo and General Kitching could see what others were only starting to glimpse. But once the first possibilities began to come into focus, more and more followed. Ziraldo and Kaiser could have buried their heads and focused their energies on their own business and let the development of the industry take its own course, but over the course of the next thirty years neither man did.

Karl Kaiser and Donald Ziraldo continued doing what they did best until 2006 — making wine — establishing Inniskillin as the world's greatest producer of icewine. Their desire to elevate the wine industry continued and for that and for their entrepreneurship and lifetime achievements they received numerous awards over the years, among them the Order of Ontario (1993), an award they received together. Donald received the Order of Canada (1998), and in 1999 he was voted one of the top twenty-five CEOs of the century by *National Post* magazine. Karl won hundreds of awards for his wines and winemaking, and although his other passion was beautifully crafted Pinot Noirs, he became widely acclaimed as the father of Canadian icewine. Donald was passionate about many things, but felt the strongest about two accomplishments. The first was his pioneering efforts in developing the the Vintners Quality Alliance (VQA), a move that would accomplish more than any one effort to elevate the status and sales of wine made from 100% Ontario-grown grapes. The second was the international prestige he brought almost single-handedly to establishing Canada as the premier producer of icewine in the world.

Even after he formally retired from the wine industry in 2006, Ziraldo kept advancing the interests of the grape-growing and horticulture communities. He lobbied to secure the Green Belt legislation to preserve agricultural lands in Ontario, and he worked to unite research centres in Ontario by resurrecting the hundred-year-old Vineland research station, and becoming the first chair of what came to be known as Vineland Research and Innovation Centre. By 2009, destiny tugged at him once again, when a colleague who had a surplus of icewine asked whether Ziraldo was interested in helping him sell it. So interested was Ziraldo that he decided to sell it — under his own label, Ziraldo Estates. He removed a sixty-year-old cherry orchard on the old Inniskillin property and, in the spring of 2009, planted an experimental Riesling vineyard in cooperation with Cool Climate Oenology and Viticulture Institute (CCOVI) and Vineland Research and Innovation Centre, formerly HRIO. He also bought a vineyard of his own on the Niagara Parkway close to his first farm, and boldly began again, but this time making only icewine. His colleagues in the industry, plus politicians and bureaucrats, luminaries and wine lovers, will always consider him to be the visionary patriarch of the Canadian wine industry. When locals received the news of his new winery project, they welcomed him as they would a trusted friend and favourite son. Everyone knew there was simply no other person quite like him, and it was comforting to have him back home again.

4 LEN PENNACHETTI'S HIGH-SCHOOL REPORT

"Come to the edge of the cliff," he said.
"We're afraid," they said.
"Come to the edge of the cliff," he said.
"We're afraid," they said.
"Come to the edge of the cliff," he said.
They came.
He pushed.
They flew.

—*Guillaume Appollinaire*

The 1980 vintage was, by all accounts, a glorious one. A mild winter followed by a late spring, a not-too-humid summer and a languorous fall made this vintage even better than the two before, which were both very good. This string of splendid harvests gave hope to the small cadre of growers who had planted the new "preferred varieties." Their gamble looked as if it was going to pay off. They had seen the emerging reality in consumer tastes and were right to act in harmony with it. But there were still too many cynics who were waiting to witness their failure.

Outside of Bright's experimental farms, Bill Lenko was the first to plant Chardonnay on his Beamsville farm in 1959, adding more acreage every year throughout the 1960s. So, encouraged by his good luck, in 1974

Lenko planted Merlot. Paul Bosc, winemaker at Chateau Gai, had been experimenting with *viniferas* since 1962 in a back lot near the railroad track. By 1978, when he planted his own *vinifera* vineyard in Niagara-on-the-Lake, he was confident he could make a go of it.

John Marynissen, a peach farmer near Inniskillin and an award-winning amateur winemaker, took advantage of a five-year, interest-free loan in 1976 to plant Merlot, Chardonnay, Riesling and Gamay, which he sold to his friend Karl Kaiser at Inniskillin. Then, in a stunningly bold move in 1978, bolstered by his success, Marynissen became the first in Canada to plant Cabernet Sauvignon, the Bordeaux variety that demanded a long, dry growing season — and the patience of a wine-loving farmer — to mature. He treated the vines as if they were tender raspberries, carefully burying each plant's cane annually for security. It was a lot of work, but "no use growing them the old way," said John, "it just didn't work."

For these three men, a vision of providing better-quality grapes didn't need to be perfectly formed. It just needed to be good enough to get started. The important thing was that each had developed a capacity to avoid imposing old frameworks on new realities. There might have been about twenty other growers like them out of the nine hundred in Ontario, including a few who were resurrecting vineyards on Pelee Island and those establishing new ones on the north shores of Lake Erie in Essex and Kent counties. Growing the new varieties, for the majority of growers, meant a risk they were unwilling to take. Some saw no need to change. They had a comfortable market for their Concords and Niagaras. Farmers, conservative by nature, had also learned that wineries could be capricious. One year they could say, "Plant X," and the next year they could declare a surplus of X. When that happened, the best a grower could get was a deflated price for his grapes as he watched them being trucked away to Otto Rieder's distillery to make brandy.

To develop a new vineyard took financial reserves to sustain the three-year period before the vines bore fruit, plus it took the know-how to grow them, neither of which most growers had. It was easy to accept the prevailing wisdom local extension scientists offered — sooner or later, weather patterns would return to the bleak and hazardous winters of the past, and any investment would prove in vain. Farming was uncertain enough. The experts told them that growing even French hybrids was risky; growing *viniferas* was ridiculous.

Len Pennachetti and his father thought differently and chose to join the small "cell of contrarians" (in Len's words) who had decided the experts were wrong. Had they known that the new decade would bring a seismic convulsion that would threaten to annihilate the entire wine industry, they might not have been quite as adventurous. Len's year in law school might not have been as painful had he known that, with what he learned there, he would soon help shape that dramatically different future for the industry.

Len Pennachetti's grandfather had come from The Marches, a stunning mountainous Italian province beside the Adriatic Sea. His grandfather, and his grandfather's love of family, food and wine, had always captivated Len, who was near the middle in a family of six siblings. Like most Italian immigrants, Len's grandfather had a backyard garden, plus peaches and pears, but what he wanted most of all was a vineyard. When an old, abandoned *labrusca* farm became available in St. Catharines, in the shadow of the Jordan & Ste-Michelle winery's new location across from Ridley College, he bought it as a retirement project, then dedicated himself to bringing it back to life.

The first year, the summer of 1967, it was a pruning jungle. Len was thirteen years old — too young to work in his father's cement-block company in Hamilton and too old to hang around the house all day. Despite being more interested in playing basketball than tending vines, he was sent out every day with a lunch packed by his mother to help his grandfather in the vineyard. To Len it was more like being sentenced to the life of an indentured servant; however, with a transistor radio around his neck and pruning shears in his hands, the teen spent his days not particularly happily but productively. Every summer after that, he worked among the vines. Those were also the years he learned the practical side of farming — something he eventually grew to love.

Len's family lived in a subdivision along the base of the escarpment on Woodside Drive in St. Catharines, a residential neighbourhood abutting a primordial woods that UNESCO would soon declare a protected world biosphere. This proximity was formative. Len always felt that it was a special place, but not until high school did he learn why. It was in his geography class in 1970, where his teacher, Al Bodo, brought to life the rocks and formations, flowers, plants and wildlife that co-existed adjacent to the urban life that comprised the backdrop of Len's childhood. Bodo was working on his dissertation for a doctoral degree on growing *vinifera* grapes in the Niagara Peninsula. Those in geography class who listened received the benefit of his unusual research.

A new site-selection map had been developed at Vineland Station, outlining the zones where *vinifera* might best survive. Before this, where grapes grew was a matter of one's legacy, budget or luck. Some growers had inherited a Crown property from their ancestors and continued to farm it with the best crop the land could sustain. Others were hobby farmers with small plots on land that suited their time and purses. Others were immigrants from places such as the United Kingdom, Holland, the Ukraine or Hungary, who were no strangers to hard work but had limited experience with grapes. Few before the Pennachettis had given much thought to matching the location of the farm to the type of grape that might best grow. Concords and Niagaras grew anywhere — above the escarpment, below. It had not been part of the equation to match the grape variety to an appropriate site, until now.

The material in his geography class so intrigued him that Len dedicated his class report to researching the very best place in Niagara to grow the new varieties, taking into consideration the slope of the land, air drainage, soil type and zone. So serious was he about his project that he asked his father, who, at heart, was an entrepreneur and an adventurer, why they couldn't buy the right land and grow the new varieties. No stranger to the thrill of a calculated risk, his father was intrigued. Len made a compelling case — after all, they didn't have a cottage in the Muskokas, couldn't the family enjoy the pleasures of a hobby farm?

Along with Len's research, he and his dad soon consulted everyone they knew: Bright's fieldman John Ghetti, fieldman Lloyd Carmichael from Jordan's winery, winery owner Chris Pataracchia (also from The Marches, which was reason enough to pull out endless bottles of his wine to "discuss" the potential enterprise) and Jack Corbett, a manager at Jordan's who lived in their neighbourhood. They talked to them all and asked their advice. No one held back. All were collegial and very forthcoming.

Once Len and his father had a few potential sites nailed down, his father rented a plane to scout the properties from the air. It was extravagant, but so impressive to his teenage son. When they saw the Cave Spring farm, it clinched the deal. It was a special place, with an almost paradigmatic location on the site-selection map — a bull's eye in the most favoured Zone D.

They bought their first twelve acres (five hectares) in 1972, the same year Len entered Carleton University to study history, and an additional thirty acres (twelve hectares) the following year. Here Len planted French hybrids for nearby Jordan's from plants he bought from Ziraldo's nursery — Len on the furrow plow behind the tractor, with his mom and her friend Mrs. Critelli shoving vines up the row. By the time Len had completed his BA and entered law school at the University of Ottawa, his father had ordered their first *vinifera* plants — Riesling and Chardonnay.

It's hard to imagine the Canadian wine world in 1978. There were no wines from New Zealand exported to Canada, and with the exception of port, Australian wines were non-existent. A few Riojas came in from Spain, basket-covered Chianti from Tuscany, and industrial wines from Bardolino and Valpolicella lined the liquor store shelves. California was bulk wines in jugs, and wines from South America were not even on the radar screen. German wines were sweet and unctuous, and even France had a slim lineup of barely palatable Bordeaux. All this was to change within the next three decades, a forecast that the uncanny Pennachettis sensed.

Len's year in law school was lamentable — law was not for him. In the summer of 1978, the Pennachettis planted their new vines on the Cave Spring home farm, where Len had the solitude of the country to decide where his life would next turn. That fall he switched his academic aspirations to a Ph.D. program in social and political thought at York University, where he also landed a job teaching. But fortune was to look the other way. Within a few months, his father's business failed, an event that was a severe blow to him and their close-knit family, and one that would eventually take its toll on his father's health.

Jordan & Ste-Michelle winery in the 1970s and 1980s was one of the most prosperous operations in Ontario. It had a venerable past, originating in 1921 as the Jordan Wine Company, a reorganized version of Canadian Grape Products, which operated out of an old apple evaporator plant in the little hamlet of Jordan, Ontario. In 1948, its assets were sold to Distillers Corporation-Seagrams Ltd. and the Toronto-based Torno family, who owned Danforth Wines. The new company was called Jordan–Danforth Wines until 1953, when it bought the assets of Chris Patarrachia's St. Catharines Winery, whose licence dated back to 1922. In 1971,

Seagram's Bronfman family sold Jordan to Carling O'Keefe. In 1976, with the purchase of Ste-Michelle Cellars in British Columbia, the company hyphenated its name once again.

Jordan & Ste-Michelle was happy to buy Len's grapes. Lloyd Carmichael, Jordan's fieldman, had been advising Len and his father for years. Although Jordan's had hired the talented Dieter Guttler, a South African of German background, to guide their *vinifera* program, Carmichael had worked with Paul Bosc in the 1960s tending his *vinifera* vines, so he had some knowledge of what might or might not work in Ontario. Still, no one really knew how to cultivate *vinifera* under Niagara's growing conditions.

Lloyd used to get calls from Len Pennachetti at least twice a week in early days. He remembered him as a "whiny, skinny guy." He'd ask, "The leaves are turning yellow, what do I do?" Carmichael knew that was the way Len needed to learn. It was hard for Jordan's to find growers to take on *vinifera* projects, so he looked after Len as well as he could. Len, however, didn't understand the protocol. Because Donald Ziraldo had been so helpful when Len and his father were starting their farm, when Ziraldo asked Len for a tonne of his ripe and beautiful 1980 grapes, he gladly obliged.

Lloyd Carmichael was furious. He had been counting on them for Jordan's. But Mother Nature evened the score. Len's vineyard got clobbered during a Christmas freeze the following winter. "The Christmas Massacre," Len called it, in which he lost six acres (nearly two and a half hectares) of precious Chardonnay. Interest rates had reached double digits, one of the worst recessions since the Great Depression had begun, and a chastened Len Pennachetti discovered that the farm business was not "pencilling out." It was not a happy time. Since the failure of his father's business, theirs was no longer a hobby farm. Len had to find a way to make it work.

When the Ontario Grape Growers Marketing Board released the negotiated prices growers would get for their grapes for 1982, Len was outraged. Where *labrusca* varieties had increased by up to 9 percent, *vinifera* varieties increased by only 7 percent. In a letter to the chair of the board, Len accused the board of selling out the few *vinifera* growers. He called for the board to have a *vinifera* grower on the next price-bargaining committee. If that couldn't happen, he saw the need for a separate set of negotiations with the Wine Council. There was no incentive to grow better-quality grapes. In fact, there was a disincentive. He accused the board of trading

Len Pennachetti planting the Cave Spring vineyard, 1978.

off the interests of the majority of growers with the better grape varieties that were increasingly becoming more in demand. To inflame the chair further, Len stated: "Your new minimum prices are at once a perversion of the marketplace and a scandal on the marketing board."

What infuriated the board was Pennachetti's audacity to go public with his protest. Pennachetti felt that the *labrusca* growers had been dragging their feet, relying on the marketing board to keep prices for the less desirable grapes artificially high compared to prices paid on the world market. For a tonne of Chardonnay he would have received only $900. Len further irritated Jordan's by selling his grapes to a winery in Pennsylvania for US$1,200 a ton. Even the Jordan & Ste-Michelle winery was now looking at Pennachetti as a dissident. Undaunted, the young political-science professor held his ground and bitterly maintained his position to anyone who would listen, explaining how the entire government-run system was interfering and "Bolshevik."

In 1982, the large wineries held 55 percent of wine sales at the LCBO. That is, until the government allowed an increase of imported wines from

30 percent to 70 percent. Local wineries' profits plummeted. But there were other forces fomenting that would contribute even more to decreasing domestic sales of the larger operations. Within six years, sales would drop to an all-time low market share of 39.5 percent. Three wineries would never recover. Some policymakers were even starting to think the unthinkable: did Ontario really need a local wine industry at all?

* * *

Alex Karumanchiri was a chemist in the quality-control lab at the LCBO when his boss, chief chemist Percy Clarke, asked him to develop a method for testing Diethyl Procarbonate (DEPC), a product used in winemaking, to see if a known carcinogen, ethyl carbamate, was produced in wine. Alex tested fifty products and discovered that ethyl carbamate was in some products, but DEPC was not the sole source of the contamination. When he gave his report to Clarke, Clarke asked Karumanchiri to get confirmation from an outside lab, which took about a year to locate. By spring of 1982, Alex Karumanchiri received confirmation from the other lab that, yes, they too had found positive results.

The ethyl carbamate was formed when an additive used to increase the action of yeast was exposed to alcohol in the presence of heat, a process used particularly in the production of ports and sherries. Alex decided to test a hundred more samples and found the same results, which he reported to Clarke from time to time, suggesting to him that the matter should be reported immediately to the federal authorities. He believed that there was a violation of the Federal Food and Drug Regulations. But Clarke did nothing.

Karumanchiri, worried about the potential health consequences and his ethical responsibilities, finally decided to go over Clarke's head and report his findings to Clarke's superior, the assistant general manager, Jack Couillard. Couillard was sympathetic to what publicity regarding the contamination might do to the wineries' business. Although ethyl carbamate was known to cause cancer in rats, no authority in the world had yet established safe levels for humans. The science was evolving. Couillard and Karumanchiri took the findings to the chair, William John Bosworth, who followed up by calling Bright's president, Ed Arnold. Arnold then told his technical people to stop using the offending additive. With the wines they already had in storage, they found ways to dilute the amount of ethyl carbamate with non-tainted wine.

The taint was found in the products of other wineries, yet no other winery was notified. Couillard and Bosworth wanted to deal with the problem one winery at a time, so they asked Karumanchiri to keep the discovery confidential, which he did. Percy Clarke retired the following year, and Edgar Parker moved up to become chief chemist. When Karumanchiri discovered that Clarke hadn't briefed him on the ethyl carbamate issue, he revealed his findings. Parker was stunned and immediately devised a plan on how to handle the problem, which included advising all the wineries to stop using the offending product. He met with his boss, Couillard, who said no to Parker's plan, stating that "It could become a political football and the products would be flushed through the system in one or two years at the most." Parker was requested to monitor the problem but to keep strict secrecy. As employees of the Crown, if he and Karumanchiri had violated that directive, they could have been subject to criminal charges.

By June 1983, products from Barnes Wines tested very high. Even though the upper limit hadn't been set, it should have been in the neighbourhood of 10 ppb. Their wines tested between 269 and 429 ppb, with one showing concentrations of 4,190 ppb. The problem was now more widespread and serious. Couillard considered sending a letter to all wineries, but decided against it, believing that confidentiality couldn't be maintained. The LCBO would continue to deal with individual wineries as problems occurred. Parker called Andrés, Barnes, Bright's, Chateau Gai, Jordan and London to tell them not to use urea as a yeast additive. Despite the fact that Jordan's hadn't used the product since 1979, there were still high levels of ethyl carbamate found in many of their wines.

News of contamination of certain Italian wines had reached Monte Kwinter, the minister of consumer and commercial relations, who was responsible for the LCBO. Small amounts of another compound, diethylene glycol, had been discovered, and the products were quickly taken off the shelves. This same contaminant would soon bring the Austrian wine industry to its knees. Alert to the havoc and hazards of the two scandals, Jack Ackroyd, the new CEO replacing Bosworth, sent a memo to his executive directors requiring them to notify him immediately if they knew of any additives found in any product that could affect the health or safety of consumers. "You have 24 hours to notify me," commanded Ackroyd.

This gave Karumanchiri and Parker the opportunity, without recrimination, to officially report the case Karumanchiri had been told to keep secret during the last five years.

When Ackroyd found out, he went directly to the minister, who called a royal commission the next day, November 20, 1985. The Honourable Mr. Justice John H. Osler, a Supreme Court of Ontario commissioner, was asked to preside. After four months and forty-three witnesses, he concluded that the LCBO lab had demonstrated a high standard of excellence, but through a failure in communication at the senior levels and a lack of appreciation for the function of the lab as an important component of quality control, a much larger problem had developed. There was unnecessary loss of taxpayer money, wineries' loss of revenue from products (which were immediately delisted), and resentment from those wineries that were kept in the dark and who unknowingly produced potentially contaminated products. He also believed only very large concentrations of ethyl carbamate had to be ingested over long periods of time to be harmful. The contamination itself was no longer the issue; as the *Ottawa Citizen* wrote, the "corruption of purpose" was. To Osler, the coverup represented an ethical conflict "between the duty to protect public health and safety and the duty not to damage the business of producers operating in good faith." It was a difficult one to resolve, he stated, but "it must invariably be resolved in favour of protecting the public health."

Most of the LCBO managers who had felt it wiser to maintain secrecy had either retired or were let go. Alex Karumanchiri continued to work in the lab until his retirement in 1999. During that time, he witnessed a sea change in the way the LCBO operated, in particular in the restructuring of the chain of command. The head of the lab could now go directly to the CEO of the LCBO if his superiors ignored his recommendations, as Clarke and Couillard had ignored his. Increased respect for the role of the lab was engendered with the construction of a new and fully equipped modern facility, which would gain a reputation for being one of the most effective in the world. Although wineries such as Barnes, Chateau Gai and Jordan's had already been losing market share, this event broke the back of their reserves to sustain business, triggering a brief period of consolidation. Like one larger fish swallowing another, Bright's bought Jordan's in 1986; Chateau Gai bought Barnes in 1988; Chateau Gai's management team bought out the company in 1989 and renamed it Cartier. As a result of free trade and economies of scale, Inniskillin shocked the industry by merging with Cartier in 1991, and within two years merged with Bright's, which was predomiantly owned by this time by business mogul Gerry Schwartz. This conglomerate became Vincor International, the ninth-largest winery in North America.

*　*　*

In 1985, the same year the minister of consumer and commercial relations had called the royal commission to examine the "Testing and Marketing of Liquor in Canada," the minister of agriculture and food, obviously also concerned about the industry, had called a task force, headed by Dr. J.W. Tanner, a University of Guelph professor, to examine the long-term viability of the grape and wine industry. The members of the task force represented the small, medium and large wineries, the LCBO, and the growers. The minister also wanted the task force to "develop ways in which producers, processors and government [could] work together to enhance the performance and prospect of the industry." To reverse the flow of Niagara Falls would have been a more reasonable mandate.

Their findings were both naive and prescient. Canada had already proposed to the increasingly protectionist United States that tariffs be removed so trade between the two countries could be enhanced. The Tanner Task Force prefaced their recommendations by saying, "The Report is based on the assumption that unrestricted free trade will not transpire. In the event that it does, it would negate the value of the Report in that, under total free trade, the industry would be placed in dramatic jeopardy." The die had already been cast by that time. Their assumption was that free trade would occur like one blunt scythe cutting across the countryside, indiscriminately slicing through anything in its path. Had steps not been taken to address this possibility, their worst fears might have been realized.

Their recommendations were prescient in that many of their core points would eventually comprise the basis for a reformed industry, reforms that were ironically detonated by the free trade agreement itself. To the task force, the quality of Ontario wine was the most important factor to ensuring long-term viability. That was contingent on better grapes. These intrepid souls were the first to publicly call for the extirpation of *labrusca* grapes in table wine.

In 1986, the provincial government changed its markup system to favour

Ontario wines, and that resulted in a markup differential of 65 percent — 1-percent markup on domestic wines, versus a 66-percent markup on imports. The move caused the Europeans to later charge Canada with a violation of the General Agreement on Tariffs and Trade (GATT), and gave ample leverage to the Americans during the Canada–United States free trade talks.

About this same period, a third government-sponsored wine-industry initiative was established when the secretariat of the cabinet alerted the deputy minister of consumer and commercial affairs, Valerie Gibbons, that the Wine Content Act governing the wine industry was going to be terminated and needed to be renegotiated. Gibbons, a strong leader and not one to postpone a mandate, took the initiative to bring together representatives from the wineries, growers and the LCBO to participate in multi-party strategic-planning meetings. Over the course of the next year, they met to discuss ways to come together with a common vision. The most difficult part was the time it took to build trust among the parties. They all felt the others were out to get them. The winery representatives felt they were unable to make wine with the grapes the growers provided. *Labrusca* grapes in everybody's view were good only to make grape jelly. The Wine Content Act put limits on how much sugar, water and imported wine the wineries could add to dilute the flavors of *labrusca*. The growers thought their grapes were fine. The LCBO was accused of not marketing the wines well enough and putting Ontario wines on shelves where people couldn't see them.

Harmony was not easy to come by, but when the two Irish-descended leaders of Canada and the United States, Brian Mulroney and Ronald Reagan, got together at the Shamrock Summit in Quebec to sing "When Irish Eyes Are Smiling," the sour chord it struck would reverberate like a death knell throughout the wine industry. Theirs was a friendly gesture of co-operation intended to celebrate their agreement-in-principle to begin the free trade talks, yet it set off unparalleled paroxysms of uncertainty and fear in the industry. With the 65-percent markup differential coming down, it was anybody's guess what was going to happen to domestic wine. When Mulroney conceded to Reagan, "You drink our beer and we'll drink your wine," the wine industry felt sucker-punched, breathless and utterly abandoned by their own government. They had two choices — either be crippled by the threat or redouble their efforts to survive.

Liberal premier of Ontario, David Peterson, knew that the federal government was willing to trade away the entire wine industry. He didn't want to be outfoxed by Americans. He wanted to make sure that the industry could live with whatever deal was struck. To protect the industry's interests, he placed deputy ministers from across the government in charge of different sectors. Since Valerie Gibbons had been involved in industry discussions on the Wine Content Act, he asked her if she could now make a deal with the industry to bring them together in a more helpful accord; otherwise, the industry could be imperiled. He asked her to accomplish this monumental task over the course of a weekend. Nothing focuses the mind like a hanging.

Within two and a half days they were able to come to an agreement that the *labrusca* grapes were not going to be the foundation for a thriving industry. They would have to be pulled out and new grapes of better varieties planted. It was an immense sacrifice on behalf of the growers — and one they didn't take lightly. During the weekend they also sketched out a compensation program for each stakeholder, as well as a position the government could take to the trade negotiation table.

Into this climate of uncertainty Len Pennachetti and his nascent *vinifera* vineyard were thrust. That same year, 1985, his father died suddenly. If Len wasn't sure which career path to follow before this, academia or agriculture, he knew now. He came home from York University, where he was teaching, to settle his father's estate. Since the bank had closed his father's concrete business in 1978, much of his assets were still pledged, which now caused substantial distress for the family. There was no way to disentangle the assets because of the dire straits the main company had been in. There were land assets, however, that Len and his older brother, John, a Toronto developer, could catalogue and then decide what to do with.

Len and John found a way to develop some of the land on their own. High school geography once again came back to Len because of what he had learned about planning. He felt passionately about saving the fruit lands. The whole idea of not letting all of Niagara's agricultural resources get completely bulldozed was primary to him. That motivation, to work in a field where his values could have an impact on the future of agricultural land in Niagara, was reason enough for him to now get into the wine business full-time.

When Dr. Thomas Muckle, a pathologist and avid wine buff from Hamilton, suggested that he and Len set up a winery, Len welcomed the idea. Muckle brought to the developing partnership Quebec-born Carole Buteau as consulting winemaker and Cyriel Duitschever, a professor at Guelph. For the day-to-day work, Len asked his lifelong friend and fellow doctoral candidate Angelo Pavan to be the cellar master. The "cellar" in which they made their first wines was space kindly provided by the winemaker at Hillebrand, Peter Gamble. When that first wine was released, wine critic Peter Ward from the *Ottawa Citizen* wrote: "The chardonnay had such power, subtlety and balance, it was initially surprising that it could be produced from such a young winery."

As demand for their wines grew, they needed more room, so they leased space in the abandoned Jordan & Ste-Michelle winery. Len's original notion was to have a winery beside their vineyard in Beamsville, but when the Jordan facility came up for sale, Helen Young, Len's wife, who was practising law at the time, told Len to see the possibilities inherent in buying the entire 80,000-square-foot (7432-square-metre) complex, where inns and specialty shops selling antiques, art, fashion, food and garden accessories could thrive. By 1990, Len had managed to put enough money together through conventional financing to purchase the entire facility. Tom Muckle would soon go on to start another winery of his own (Thirty Bench), and Angelo Pavan, who had by now traded his doctoral studies in philosophy at Guelph University for studies in chemistry at Brock, became Len's full-time winemaker and business partner.

Len gradually developed what he referred to as "a pathological desire for risk" — like a poker player, he began to welcome the thrill of staring down the odds and coming out successful. Unlike some entrepreneurs of the late 1980s, who, like buccaneers, kept leveraging the pot to more and more success until everything was riding on one interest, he wisely invested only a portion. Now in his early thirties, he was discovering his aptitude for strategic thinking, searching for fundamentals, seeing both the big picture as well as what might lie beneath the surface. The theorists he had studied in graduate school, Ricoeur, Weber, Freud and Nietzsche, all wrote about the substructures that existed in the world. The world wasn't necessarily what it appeared to be; real meaning was to be found beneath the surface. For Freud it was the subconscious, for Marx and Nietzsche it was the economic substructure. Consequently, Len had learned to be suspicious of appearances.

When he got into the wine business, he looked below the surface to the soil and then to nurtured vines, better-quality grapes and the right location. He looked to the juice that made the wine; it had to be just juice, not diluted by water. Not all producers thought that way. They could legally "stretch" the juice from a tonne of *labrusca* grapes by adding water in unconscionable amounts. At one time, it was the only way to make the *labrusca* table wines palatable. Times had changed, but they could also blend in up to 70-percent bulk wine from California or Chile and still call it a Product of Canada. How was the consumer to tell the difference in quality between them?

As well as the larger wineries, there were now thirteen small estate wineries, most of whom were making wines from *vinifera* and French hybrids. Besides Len's Cave Spring Cellars, there were Charal, Château des Charmes, Colio, Hillebrand, Inniskillin, Montravin (later purchased by Magnotta), Pelee Island, Reif, Stoney Ridge Cellars, Vineland Estates and Willowbank. Since the early 1980s, Donald Ziraldo had been campaigning for the establishment of an alliance of estate wineries to educate the consumer on their wines and to establish quality standards that conformed to those established in the best wine regions of the world. Those standards would comprise the basis for an appellation system in Canada.

In the early days, a subcommittee of the Wine Council would meet after regular council meetings to hammer out the details. Membership in the organization was going to be based on winery application. Donald's first white paper outlined the purposes of a "Niagara Quality Alliance." The Board was established, with Donald Ziraldo as chair, Len Pennachetti as vice-president and Peter Gamble as executive-director. Then it became the "Niagara Vintners Quality Alliance," which included the larger, traditional wineries along with the estate wineries. Then, with Peter Gamble of Hillebrand's urging, it shifted to a wine-based quality standard. The name Vintners Quality Alliance (VQA) remained to suggest it was a ground-up set of rules that came from the producers themselves and was not government imposed. Rather than *wineries* being members, the way the Wine Council was organized, the *wine* would be a VQA member — if it qualified. It was an intentionally inclusive game in which all wineries could play, but not necessarily all wines.

If quality was to be assured, they found easy agreement in disallowing *labrusca*-based wines. But there were several other wrinkles that had to be ironed out. The first was where to draw the line on quality? Could a wine made of such lesser French hybrids as de Chaunac or Seyval qualify for the VQA just by taking the water and the imported wine out? Could French hybrids be allowed? If so, which ones? How would a 100-percent *vinifera* wine be differentiated from a French hybrid? Even though the large wineries felt the organization would never amount to anything, they wanted to be sure that their blended wines, which made up 99 percent of Ontario wines at the time, and which were now unacceptable for membership, would not be denigrated.

As a winery owner, Len Pennachetti was now a full-fledged member of the Wine Council and was invited to join the VQA discussions. He soon realized that the meeting notes had to become codified into regulations comparable to any in the world. Donald Ziraldo turned over the articulation of those details to Len, who applied what he learned in his year at law school to create a document that, with minor changes, would eventually become provincial law (1999). A number of others played key roles in the development of those regulations. Paul Bosc was the conscience of the group. Whenever one of the big wineries started to push for a much broader concept to include lesser grape varieties, Bosc would respond with an expletive every fourth word in highly elevated volumes. Being French, he knew what appellation laws were all about. Having been a winemaker at Chateau Gai, a major player, and now with his own winery, he understood both sides of the quality equation, so people listened.

Peter Gamble was adamant about setting standards higher than those allowed for imports. He insisted that an independent tasting panel be set up by the LCBO to determine the subjective side of quality. Len and Peter spent many hours over the phone working out the details of how the regulations should be framed. Gamble was teaching a wine-appreciation course at Brock University at the time and was also very familiar with international appellation laws.

The framers of the rules and regulations realized that standards were only as good as the transparency and independence of their enforcement. For those, Donald Ziraldo and Len Pennachetti turned to the LCBO. Working in conjunction with Leonard Franssen from the quality-control area, over the course of the next two years they agreed on four ways that the LCBO could be of service. The first was the establishment of an independent LCBO-run sensory tasting panel to determine whether submitted wines qualified for a VQA designation. The second service was one of audit. Since winery audits were already being conducted, the auditors added a series of VQA checks to see how well claims of volumes, grape types and declarations of estate or vineyard designations reconciled with what was in the ground, what was harvested and what was finally bottled.

In addition, the LCBO lab agreed to conduct tests additional to their mandatory analyses to determine the presence of methyl anthranilate, the defining compound found in *labrusca* varieties. The last service comprised of packaging reviews to make sure all labels and packaging conformed with VQA requirements.

The agreement was finalized in June 1990. The wineries were all very proud of their results and eager to voluntarily comply. The only part that disappointed visionary Donald Ziraldo was that the Grape Growers Marketing Board offically would not participate. He never figured out why. He was able to convince Donna Lailey, then a grower who sold grapes to Inniskillin, to sit on the VQA board as a growers' representative.

The renegotiated Wine Content Act had come into effect on September 1, 1988, banning the use of *labruscas* from table wines. It also reduced the amount of water allowed to "stretch" wines. From the quality standpoint, both measures were a good thing. To enable wineries to have sufficient volume over the adjustment period, the act more than doubled the amount of imported wine they could use in their blended products from 30-percent import to 70 percent. To protect the growers, the wineries committed to buying 25,000 tonnes of Ontario grapes each year for twelve years, starting with the 1988 harvest. The Wine Content Act would be the basis for continuing contention for many, many years to come.

Like threads unravelling and being simultaneously respooled, then gradually rewoven into a new tableau, a transformed wine industry was starting to emerge. But the threads were very fragile compared to the ropes pulled by the determined Americans and Europeans. The Americans wanted free access to the Ontario market. With Reagan, a Californian, as president, the U.S. trade negotiating team was unrelenting. When the European Union got wind of the American talks, they couldn't afford to be left out, so they charged Canada with a trade violation under GATT. As wine journalist Tony Aspler wrote in *Canadian Business*: "The Canadian wine industry is caught between the hammer of free trade and the anvil of the General Agreement on Tariffs and Trade (GATT)."

Because of the 66-percent markup on European wines, the European Union threatened to retaliate by boycotting seed potatoes from Prince Edward Island, blueberries from Nova Scotia and leather from Quebec. Fortunately, the feisty and courageous chair of the Grape Growers Marketing Board, Brian Nash, was sitting in the room when the GATT talks began. He was there, along with the head of the Wine Council, Jack Corbett, and the head of the Canadian Wine Institute, Jan Wescott, to protect their mutual interests. The Canadian negotiator opened by saying, "We will give you the Canadian brandy industry." As auspicious as the occasion was, Nash didn't hesitate to say loudly enough for the whole room to hear, "No fucking way!"

"Who are you?" said the negotiator.

"We've got to talk," said Nash.

To the feds, Niagara's wine industry wasn't worth saving. A thumb on a map easily covered Niagara, as one negotiator was quick to point out. But the farmer in Nash, one whose family had been farming in Niagara for six generations, dug in his heels and persisted to make sure the interests of the industry were fully conveyed.

In the end, the industry conceded to the elimination of a protective markup structure, but not without a hefty compensation program from the federal government that paid growers to pull out *labruscas*. The Ontario government paid wineries to promote the industry through the Ontario Wine Assitance Program. The LCBO markup adjustments (the 1-percent markup on Ontario wines went to 60 percent, and the markup on imports went from 66 percent to 60 percent) netted the Ontario government coffers $240 million and assured price supports.

None of the compensations would have occurred if Liberal Premier David Peterson hadn't put his government's full support behind the industry's survival. By the time the provincial government needed wine standards to bring to the negotiations, Len Pennachetti and Donald Ziraldo had codified VQA regulations. The government recognized these as a significant contribution toward industry reform and requested that they be utilized

Leonard Pennachetti, CEO, Cave Spring Cellars

during the free-trade negotiations — particularly with the Europeans. In turn, this recognition gave validation to the VQA. A framework agreement was signed with the United States and the details worked out later. Pennachetti joined the discussions at the end and brought what one provincial official expressed as a "wonderful sort of contagious enthusiasm." "This can be done," he'd say, "We're going to run with this." As with Donald Ziraldo's vision, commented another provincial bureaucrat, "they made believers out of all of us."

Had free trade come in as it was first suggested, the vintage of 1988 might have been Len's last. Years later, chief Canadian negotiator Simon Reisman admitted that giving away the wine industry had been a prerequisite to free-trade talks. The VQA wines of Ontario were just on the brink of success, demonstrating their ability to compete on the world market. To have their wings clipped at such an early stage in their meta-morphosis would have been a pity. Within the next seven years, more than 19,700 acres (8,000 hectares) of *labrusca* and hybrid vines would be pulled in one of the most dramatic agricultural revolutions in the province's history. The new industry would never go back to anything resembling its former life. The dashing Len Pennachetti had now joined Donald Ziraldo in representing the new breed of wine producer, helping to lead the industry through the next important make-or-break stage of its development.

Free trade would prove to be the most traumatic event to happen to the industry since Prohibition. How the adjustment would be made would determine whether the pieces could be reassembled into a premium wine industry. Al Bodo, Len's high-school geography teacher, went on to complete his doctoral dissertation and was very proud that Len, the tall basketball jock in the last row, had actually heard what he had to say.

Len would move on to transform the snoozing hamlet of Jordan into a sophisticated centre of local arts, antiques, shops and tasting rooms, which carefully respected the village's local character and architecture. In 1993, he and his wife, Helen, opened the first full-service upscale winery restaurant in Ontario, and one known for its focus on regional foods. To the original Jordan winery's stark frontage they added a terrace from one end to the other, with wrought-iron railings and intermittent entries for easier access, then lavishly landscaped it with splashes of flowers and greenery. Across the road in the former two-and-a-half-storey sugar warehouse, once used for ports, they built an inn with twenty-four stunning rooms, then added an elegant spa next door in an old home built in 1840. In the hands of less-capable individuals, Jordan could have become a haven for kitsch — wine country souvenirs made in China — but it did not. At the end of the road, on old Highway 8 (Regional 81), they renovated the bar and bedrooms of the Jordan House, the oldest roadhouse in Canada, once the only "wet" spot between Hamilton and St. Catharines. They retained its local feel, pub grub and domestic beers. It never lost a beat as a meeting place for locals and travellers.

Over the course of twenty-five years, these projects were intended to give a broader context to their wines, giving people a reason to come to a secluded part of Niagara. Mean-spirited locals occasionally accused them of forsaking their role as winemakers to become developers, but their organizing principle was always wine. Neither Len nor Helen had any formal training for their pursuits as winery owners, decorators, employers, restaurateurs, innkeepers, landlords or publicans, yet they were willing to learn each business from scratch. They turned out to be autodidacts — self-taught individuals with the conviction that to do things well was its own reward. They never lost sight of that. Neither did Len ever lose his intellectual predilection to challenge the accepted wisdom and occasionally go to the edge of the cliff, where he discovered, like the white hawk that graced his labels, when the purpose was right, he could fly.

5 PAUL BOSC'S JOURNEY

"In the depth of winter, I learned that within me lay an invincible summer."

—Albert Camus

The television commercials were only a minute long, but in 1975 they represented a sea change in the advertising of beverage alcohol in Canada. Viewers watched Paul Bosc, the alluring French winemaker from Chateau Gai in Niagara Falls, as he sauntered between manicured rows of grapevines speaking about a new dry red table wine he had made. Dressed in mid-1970s chic — a white turtleneck with tweed jacket — and sporting long sideburns Bosc spoke with compelling confidence as he announced that his Maréchal Foch, the French hybrid from Burgundy, planted in Niagara in 1965, was now available in quantity. "Eeet's a new dry red wine with a fresh aroma," he murmured, his French accent confirming the wine's provenance, "zat I know you weel enjoy."

There were three ads released that season, each slightly different, but his tag line on all three promised "even more good things to come," thus proclaiming that the transformation of the Ontario wine industry had formally begun. So seductive and convincing was Bosc that customers lined up, buying out ten thousand cases within the year.

Up until that time, advertising wine in Ontario had been severely restricted. Print ads were limited in size, content and location in newspapers and magazines. Billboards and outdoor signs were not allowed at all. Television and radio ads were strictly forbidden. By the early 1970s, a dramatic loosening up started to occur. A July 19, 1971, communiqué from the Canadian Radio and Television Commission (CRTC) outlined the new regulations. "The main criterion for approval of scripts is the adherence to good taste" — taste determined, of course, by the CRTC's regulators. More specifically, an ad could not encourage general consumption or attempt to influence non-drinkers to drink. Nor could alcohol be associated with youth or status symbols or used as a necessity for the enjoyment of life or as an escape from life's problems.

By the time the Chateau Gai commercials ran their course, Paul Bosc had become a popular personality. Three years later, in 1978, he resigned as head winemaker at Chateau Gai to go out on his own. After fifteen years of security and accomplishment, he now faced what others viewed as a life of foolish uncertainty. Did he have "jelly-for-brains," as one colleague admonished, to do something as risky as becoming an independent grower and winemaker of *vinifera*-based wines?

As risky as it may have seemed, nothing Paul did was without plan or calculation. It was part of who he was. He had experienced a traumatic and turbulent life only sixteen years before his decision to leave Chateau Gai. He would not risk the possibility of another loss or dislocation. Because he made that move, he was to become a pioneering model of "grower as winemaker," leading the way in vineyard innovation, agri-tourism and estate wines. His contributions to the advancement of the Ontario wine industry would eventually result in several distinctions, including the Order of Canada in 2005.

* * *

Paul Bosc was born in 1935 in the Mediterranean seaside town of Marengo, Algeria. His family on his mother's side had been living there since Algeria had become a territory of France in 1840. Prior to moving to Algeria, Paul's great-great-grandfather had been an orderly for a hospital in Alsace run by nuns. When they were asked to create a hospital in the new colony, the young orderly moved along with them. Eventually he was awarded a piece of land from the French government, a plow, two mules and a gun.

On that land he planted a vineyard and within a few years established a winery, which prospered, a tradition that would continue in the family for four generations. As a child, Paul helped his grandfather maintain their vineyards. It was this legacy that prompted Paul to attend agricultural school in Algeria, where viticulture and winemaking played an important part. To further refine his specialization in winemaking, he attended the University of Dijon in Burgundy.

When he finished school, he got a job as a consulting winemaker in Algeria, advising growers on how they might improve the quality of their wines. The notion of an "estate" winery, where the wine in the bottle was made from grapes grown on the same property, was the convention. Surplus grapes might be sold to the local co-op, but basically anyone who grew grapes also made wine. Paul soon became highly sought-after as farmers learned that his advice, when taken, vastly improved their wines.

In 1955, Paul went into the army, the same year tensions between the Algerians and the French, which had been fomenting for years, came to a head. French Algeria, although considered a part of France, had been colonized by thousands of other European immigrants from Spain, Italy and Malta, whose second generation became known as *pieds noirs*. The indigenous Algerians, who remained the majority, were dissatisfied with their lack of status and autonomy in what had once been their own country. The armed conflict was a result of the inequities they felt they suffered.

Paul was made to serve in the army for nearly three years, a year and a half longer than in pre-war days. Because he had been shipped to Egypt in 1956 on active duty during the Suez Canal crisis, at the end of his tour he was shipped to the south of France. He would have been happy to stay and make a home there. A timely letter from his mother, probably sensing her son's plans not to return, informed him of a fortuitous job opportunity at the local co-op. Serendipitously, he was released from the army shortly after. When Paul applied for the job as winemaker back home and got it, everyone was pleased. He then married his childhood sweetheart, Andrée, who was French-speaking but of Spanish ethnicity. However, the political events of 1962 would force him to leave after six years on the job.

France's President Charles de Gaulle was convinced that the drain of Algeria on the French economy contributed to the collapse of the French

Fourth Republic. He ended the war by granting Algeria complete independence, a move the more than one million *pieds noirs* opposed. Once the country was independent, the new Algerian government seized everything the *pieds noirs* owned. Paul Bosc, his wife, Andrée, and their one-year old son, Paul-André, lost everything. Their home in Marengo, their little seaside cottage, their family's winery, the co-op Paul worked for — everything was seized.

Even if they had wanted to remain, they couldn't stay in Algeria because of the violence and resentment that still existed. So, as citizens of France, they joined the exodus of the *pieds noirs* to the mainland, the mother country. When they arrived, their reception was less than cordial. The government hadn't expected the influx of more than one million people to spill into the cities. The French Algerian colonialists were greeted with hostility and defamation, which was encouraged by Charles de Gaulle. Paul and his young family felt like strangers in their own country, a sentiment portrayed by another *pied noir,* Albert Camus, in his novel *The Stranger.*

Within months, the Boscs decided to find another place in the world, one in which they could feel welcome and start a new life. They considered Spain, Italy, even Argentina or the United States, but Paul was now looking for stability more than anything else and Canada seemed like the best fit. He had a brother in Quebec City and a cousin in Montreal who could help him and his young family to get settled.

When they arrived, they had only a suitcase and $3,000 in life savings. The turmoil of their lives was about to end, yet it would forever affect the decisions Paul would subsequently make. The wolf would not only always be at the door, sometimes it would be in the room. Although Paul Bosc would lead change, his innovations were motivated by the need for security that financial gain could bring. Anything could happen to snatch good fortune away.

It took only two weeks before the highly qualified immigrant got a job with the liquor board in Quebec, the Société des alcools du Québec (SAQ), in the wine cellar of their bottling facility. His responsibility was to dump defective wine into a large barrel. As he dumped he kept noticing that a wine produced in Ontario (that a wine industry even existed in the province was a surprise to him) had a yeast problem that he knew he could correct. Since the company had a French-sounding name, Paul reckoned that his lack of English wouldn't be an issue, so he took the initiative to call their representative in Montreal and offered him a proposition: "Maybe your people down in Niagara might need an oenologist," said Paul and offered his diagnosis of their problem and a solution. The representative responded by saying the vice-president of the company would be in Montreal the next day. Did Paul want to come and talk with him?

Paul brought his diplomas from agriculture school and the University of Dijon and met with the vice-president, who, through a translator, invited Paul to fly to Toronto to speak with the president of Chateau Gai, Alexander Sampson, who was French-speaking as well.

Sampson asked exactly what Paul could do, listened, then offered him a job. Within a month of the SAQ releasing Paul, allowing him to leave and giving Sampson the go-ahead, Paul was in Ontario working for Chateau Gai. The only stipulation was that he had to work at one of their stores in Toronto while he learned to speak English. "We'll assess your progress in three or four months," said Sampson. Three months later, after daily lessons in English as a second language, Paul, Andrée and Paul-André moved to Niagara Falls, where Paul became Chateau Gai's production supervisor, then head of the lab. A few years later, he was director of research and development and, shortly after that, their chief oenologist.

Working at Chateau Gai, the third-largest wine company in Ontario next to T.G. Bright's and Jordan & Ste-Michelle, was a very good way to become familiar with the Ontario wine industry. It was a winery that, for Canada, had a long business lineage. It could be traced to 1857, when Achilles Roumegeous had opened a winery in Cooksville, Ontario, the same town where Johann Schiller, the "father of Canadian wine," had established his winery a few years before. Roumegeous stayed in business until 1890, when the Marsh family of Niagara Falls bought Roumegeous's assets and relocated their winery closer to wine country, calling it Stamford Park Wine Company.

Just after Prohibition ended in 1928, no doubt encouraged by the provincial government's urge to consolidate the wineries that had proliferated during Prohibition, a group of investors formed a company called Canadian Wineries Limited and acquired six existing properties: Peerless Wine Manufacturing (Toronto), The National Wine Company (Toronto), Dominion Wine Growers (Oakville), Lincoln Wines (St. Catharines),

The Thorold Wine Company (Thorold) and The Stamford Wine Company (Niagara Falls). In 1939, Canadian Wines Ltd. registered the "Chateau" trademark, and in 1940 they changed their company name to Chateau Gai, with Alexander Sampson as its president.

Paul worked well with Alexander Sampson, and, as long as Sampson was president, Chateau Gai was a very good experience for Paul. From a winemaking point of view, the portfolio of styles was broad. He oversaw the production of table wines, port- and sherry-styles, vermouth and sparkling wines — all made in time-honoured methods traditionally used in Europe. His lab was well-equipped and modern, which helped Paul to address the problems that the previous winemaking team couldn't seem to tackle.

* * *

His first test had come after only months on the job when he found himself back in Montreal, this time testifying before a judge on behalf of his new employers. Fifteen Champagne houses had sued Chateau Gai for appropriating the name "Champagne" on the label of their sparkling wine. The New World use of the term *Champagne*, similar to the liberal use of the terms *port, sherry, Chablis, Sauternes* or *Burgundy*, had lost their primary significance as geographical indicators of the places where the original wines were created, and had become a generic part of the North American wine-labelling vocabulary. Chateau Gai could show, as could many others, that they had been using the term for more than fifty years. Were the French justified in claiming exclusive use after so many years?

The French thought so. In 1933, France and Canada had signed a treaty that required each country to protect the appellations of origin of the other country if the name within the respective country didn't already have generic status, and if the name was registered by the other party. The term *Champagne* was registered in Canada under the Unfair Competition Act, which protected ordinary trademarks. Although other Ontario wineries were bottling sparkling wine they called Champagne, Chateau Gai was singled out as the target for the lawsuit. And it had all started with a marketing ploy that taunted the French into taking action.

Alexander Sampson, Chateau Gai president, was known as an innovator in Ontario wine circles at the time. In 1928, five years before the treaty between France and Canada, he had purchased the rights for Canada to use the "Méthode Charmat" to make sparkling wines, a process that enabled large quantities of wine to be made bubbly in special tanks. Whatever quality might have been sacrificed was compensated for by the savings in both time and money, and Canadian consumers bought lots of it.

Alexander Sampson was also a very aggressive marketer. Through a close family friend who was the manager of one of the largest department stores in Paris, he was able to put some bottles of Chateau Gai's Canadian Champagne in the window of this *grand magasin,* which attracted the attention of Parisian photographers and ignited significant publicity. The French producers in Reims didn't take the stunt lightly. They had tolerated the use of their term on Canadian wine labels for too many years. *Ça suffit!*

If they could have sued Chateau Gai for being bold, they might have. The grounds they chose was a claim that Chateau Gai had violated that treaty of 1933 between France and Canada that protected appellation-of-origin names. Chateau Gai asked that the lawsuit against them be cancelled on the grounds that the treaty had never been adequately ratified and that the word *Champagne* was not actually a trademark and therefore could not legally be protected in Canada.

As an oenologist for Chateau Gai, Paul was asked to testify for three days on behalf of his new company. Company officials asked him to say that they were making high-quality wine, therefore not damaging the reputation of French Champagne by inference. Paul defended himself well, but he could not bring himself to say, under oath, that the wine was as high in quality as Champagne.

"Don't try to make me say this," said Bosc to his superiors. They debated through the night on what quality meant, one side arguing that, as long as the process of making the wine wasn't compromised and the company didn't cut any corners in producing it, the way it tasted didn't mean anything, since taste was a personal matter. It might have been easier for Paul, the new hire, young and vulnerable to the possibility of losing his job, to comply, but he was still French. To him quality was, indeed, in the glass. When he went to his French winemaking texts, even they referred to the method of making the wine sparkle as the Champagne method. He creatively found a way to avoid testifying against his company and still stay true to his own principles.

The French-Canadian judge, in this early round of the litigations, understood it the way the French did, and ruled against Chateau Gai. A decade later, in 1974, the case would reach the Supreme Court of Canada, which decided, once again, against Chateau Gai, saying that the 1933 treaty was in force and that Champagne was entitled to legal protection under the treaty. In 1978, because of hefty pressure from the large Canadian wineries that had much to lose in rebranding their "Canadian Champagne," Canada withdrew from the treaty.

The Canadian federal government argued that the word *Champagne* had been used for nearly fifty years and no action had been taken against any Canadian vintner until 1964; but the real argument came when Canadian officials pointed to some French houses, who by this time had locations outside France and were calling their wines "Champagnes." To sue Canadian vintners for "passing off" was hypocritical.

Ten years later, in 1987, the case came to trial once again. The judgment by the Ontario Court of Appeal held that the use of the term Canadian Champagne in Ontario was not a violation of the Institut National des Appellations d'Origine (INAO). Canadian Champagne had acquired its own following over the years, and was not likely to be confused with the French product.

The use of geographical appellation-of-origin names would not be finally settled until 2003, when an *Order Amending the Trade Marks Act* was introduced to implement one of Canada's obligations under the Agreement between Canada and the European Community on Wine and Spirits regarding the use of the names Bordeaux, Chianti, Claret, Madeira, Malaga, Marsala, Médoc, Mosel and Moselle. These names could no longer be used on a Canadian label as of the date of the agreement in 2004. The names Bourgogne, Burgundy, Rhin, Rhine, Sauterne and Sauternes would be deleted by December 31, 2008. Chablis, Port, Porto, Sherry and Champagne would be removed from Canadian wine labels by December 31, 2013. Such terms applied only to wines that used a blend of imported wine and was never an issue with wines made from 100-percent locally grown wine certified under VQA regulations, which banned the use of the terms.

* * *

In the first few years at Chateau Gai, Paul was thrilled to be given the freedom to work as a problem-solver and innovator, always striving to improve the table-wine business. Even though Alexander Sampson was a bit of a tyrant and always encouraged Paul to go to church on Sunday, he left Paul

Paul Bosc, winemaker for Chateau Gai, 1968

alone to do his work. When Sampson died, Tom Comery took over as Chateau Gai president. Comery and Paul Bosc had a solid relationship. Comery continued in Sampson's fashion, consulting with Paul, respecting his judgment and compensating him well. Paul had gained significant experience in the processes of making their broad portfolio of styles. He had even discovered a technique that could almost eliminate the foxiness of the native *labrusca* varieties by concentrating the juice through a distillation process and then refraining from reintroducing the foxy esters. By the mid-1970s, aided by his assistant winemaker, Mira Ananicz, an extremely bright young Polish chemist, he developed the formula for Alpenweiss using this method. It became one of the best-selling Ontario table wines of the period.

Paul had known Mira was bright when he hired her in 1973, but he hadn't realized just how bright she was until he gave her a project to tackle, one that had been perplexing him and a scientist at the Horticultural Research Institute at Vineland, Dr. Tibor Fulecki. It had to do with a process involving continuous fermentation that could result in lactic acid, which could start the unwanted production of acetic acid, or vinegar.

When Mira scanned the formula they were using, which was based on the work of a noted French researcher, she found that it didn't make sense. She guessed that the formula must have been wrong in some way. Yet the French scientist was impeccable in his research. Something must have been lost in the translation from French to English. Mira then asked Paul to read from the original French, word by word. Together they found two mistakes in the translation. She then worked to create the corrected formula, which enabled Paul to proceed with his winemaking, a discovery for which Mira received a substantial raise and Paul's enduring respect.

Paul was not the type of person to go somewhere and say that he knew better than everyone else. If the scientists and growers in Niagara said that *vinifera* vines couldn't grow, Paul accepted that they must have a good reason to say so. But after a few years he grew increasingly dissatisfied with the raw material from which he was asked to produce fine wine. There were only so many techniques he could devise to mask the real problem that existed in all *labrusca*-based wines. Even though they were technically among the best products on the market, they simply didn't have the flavour he enjoyed drinking. Consumer tastes were slowly changing as well. He had to have better grapes.

Unlike Bright's, Chateau Gai didn't have an experimental farm. This frustrated his efforts to experiment with new varieties. On a family road trip to the Finger Lakes in 1965, he met Konstantin Frank, the first in the east to plant a successful commercial vineyard of *vinifera* vines. Paul had to experiment for himself. He bought some cuttings from France to see how they would grow. He soon grafted some vines, a practice he had learned in Algeria at agricultural school, doing it all by hand on a small room-sized plot in the back of the winery near the railroad tracks. He spent his lunch hours grafting his *vinifera* vines onto experimental rootstock to see how they might survive. Eventually, by the late 1960s, he had proof that vines such as Chardonnay, Riesling and Gamay could survive. He had proof that the conventional wisdom that it was impossible to grow them in Niagara could be seriously challenged.

Chateau Gai was, by now, a public company, with 50.03 percent of the shares owned by Wine Securities Ltd. of Toronto. John Labatt Limited had been in the process of diversifying its portfolio into the food and beverage industries for several years. They had already purchased Parkdale Wines in 1965, which they renamed Chateau Cartier. By purchasing the shares of Wine Securities Ltd. in 1973, they automatically became the major stockholders of Chateau Gai.

Under the Labatt ownership, both Chateau Gai and Chateau Cartier were centralized on the Chateau Gai site in Niagara Falls. Chateau Cartier continued as their marketing organization, also selling a line of products under the Cartier brand. On a Grimsby farm originally owned by Parkdale Wines, Labatt allowed Paul to expand his little experimental plot. Within a few months, he had replanted his original experimental vines, some of which dated back to 1962, onto the Grimsby site. It was also the Labatt money that financed the commercials that Paul hosted in 1975. All seemed well, but behind the scenes Paul and the new Labatt management were at odds. Whenever he would ask to change blends, they would say, "Let's wait and see what Bright's is going to do," a reply that had been a problem for Paul even before Labatt took over.

One day, so frustrated by his increasing lack of autonomy to innovate, he said to his superiors, "Hell, maybe I should go to Bright's and work for them!" He wasn't going to be pushed. Day by day his disenchantment with Labatt increased as he watched them implement new business housecleaning practices, such as giving only a five-year contract to long-time employees and then, two years later, buying back the contract and showing the person the door. Although his position as head oenologist was strong, he witnessed a malaise of incivility that was overtaking the company. When he looked around he realized that, of all his colleagues, he was the only one who had survived. Then came the day he decided to do what Donald Ziraldo had done two years before. Donald had cracked the system open. It was time for Paul to open a winery of his own.

By 1974, he had realized he wanted to experiment with more *vinifera* plantings on his own, and had bought a vineyard near Lockport, New York. The land was much cheaper than in Ontario and at the time the Canadian dollar was worth US$1.10. His family — wife Andrée, son Paul-André, now thirteen years old, and by now another son,

Pierre-Jean, who was nine years old — joined Paul in doing all the planting, pruning and harvesting on their own. Even though the twenty-mile (thirty-two-kilometre) trek across the border was not an onerous one, after working the soil for a few years, Paul realized that he preferred to pursue Niagara as a place to establish a vineyard and eventually a winery.

There were several properties he examined; a fifty-acre (twenty-hectare) block, unplanted, on York Road looked very attractive, and he almost bought it, but the $180,000 price tag was too high, so he turned it down. When the possibility arose to buy a more reasonable, already-planted vineyard of the same size, with a home, barn and farm equipment, he found two partners and bought it. Roger Gordon, a lawyer from St. Catharines, one of his partners, smoothed the way when it came to the administrative minutiae of applications to establish a winery. Gordon had everything filled in except the winery's name. "What are we going to call it?" Roger asked.

Roger insisted that, since Paul was French, the name should at least be more French-sounding — *Château* something. Paul remembered the time before his life was disrupted, a joyful time in Marengo where they had a little summer home by the sea, a charming little place they used to jokingly call Villa des Charmes. That's what they would call their new venture: Château des Charmes.

Much to his disappointment, when he started working the grapes, he realized that their charming venture was going to be a nightmare. Rather than throw good money after bad, Paul told his partners he was going to have to pull everything out and start over. One partner said no. Paul, never one to mince words or restrain the emotional fervour of his convictions, replied, "No? You work the goddamn land and you show me what you can do."

Paul bought out that partner, but the second one, Roger Gordon, stayed and would remain a silent partner through the years. The second year they had the vineyard, in 1977, they started from square one, this time putting in proper drainage tiles and plants with appropriate rootstocks. Paul's experience grafting vines in his little plot behind Chateau Gai served him well, and in a circuitous mix of good fortune, many of the vines for his new vineyard came from that original plot. As a parting gift, the managers at Chateau Gai allowed Paul to take his vines from the Grimsby experimental farm and replant them on his new Creek Road site.

Paul Bosc, examining sparkling wine, 1974

He resigned from Chateau Gai in 1978, staying on for six months while the new winemaker, Ernst Fischer, got acclimatized. After that, the family lived on his wife's salary as an elementary-school French teacher until the vineyard started producing. They moved from a comfortable home in the city of Niagara Falls to the small ranch-style cottage beside the farm. He built the winemaking facility in a concrete-block building on the property and made wine from purchased grapes, and he sold to restaurants. He had to keep the wolf at bay. He sold three thousand cases that first year and doubled that in the second. Visitors soon jammed the new boutique winery. As soon as his wife, Andrée, who became better known as Madame Bosc, the winery's chatelaine, came home from teaching, she would roll up her sleeves and start entertaining guests behind the tasting bar. Her jokes and radiant personality charmed everyone. Even the most austere connoisseur would melt in her company. "Wine is good for you," she would say. "Especially for sex!"

The model in the wine business up until that time had been based on a clear division of labour. Growers grew grapes and wineries processed the grapes into wine. The Bosc family tradition replicated that of most European wineries, where the two were not separate. In Ontario, having complete control of the grapes that went into one's wines was innovative.

By 1979, they had fifty acres (twenty hectares) planted, with a bare spot carved out in the centre for their eventual winery. No one in Canada had yet planted that many acres of *vinifera* vines at one time. Paul kept an experimental plot for plants he received from the renowned German researcher from Geisenheim, Dr. Helmut Becker. In addition, he planted other cool-climate varieties from Burgundy — Aligoté, Savagnin, Auxerrois, Gamay, Chardonnay, Riesling. Even though he wasn't convinced that the Bordeaux varieties of Cabernet Sauvignon, Cabernet Franc and Merlot could survive, he planted them as well. What he hadn't realized was that, even though these varieties required a longer growing season, Bordeaux was not all that warm a growing region. Bordeaux's season was longer, but Niagara's shorter season could have more heat units than Bordeaux in certain years. Paul had that yet ahead of him to discover.

Things moved fast for the Boscs. Clonal selection was starting to be known in France. With the co-operation of the president of the nursery association in France, a Burgundian, Paul was able to buy some clones that were not even known in France. He reasoned that, if they had been selected, they couldn't be that bad. He planted the entire farm with different clones and with different root stocks, then watched them grow. As he started to see differences, he kept in contact with the National Research Council. He was, by nature, very curious, and approached his work with careful precision. By 1982, he presented an idea for a project.

He reasoned that, for every one hundred thousand vines, there could be two or three mutations — some for the better, some for the worse. Instead of looking at individual vines, he wanted to look at individual canes and select new clones that way. A cane could carry three bunches — small bunches, big bunches. To Paul, that could make a different clone. Ezio Di Emanuele, a friend from Niagara Falls, was working for Minister of Agriculture Eugene Whelan, so Paul approached him with his idea. Di Emanuele knew Paul as a "little guy with a big vision" who had old-world values with new-world incentives. Paul's proposal clearly articulated how his idea could benefit the entire wine industry. The future of the Canadian wine industry rested on the selection of the clones the growers chose to plant — clones that worked best in Niagara's growing conditions. Whelan saw how the project could have long-term benefits, and granted Paul the $500,000 to conduct his experiments. With that grant Paul was able to hire a scientist, Dr. John Paroschy, formerly of Bright's, to guide his projects. He would identify winter injury to vines and select the hardiest, highest-quality and most productive clones or mutations. Twenty-five years later, this technique pioneered by Paul would become commonly used in France for clonal selection.

That project on clonal selection, the first of many research projects for which Paul would receive grants, resulted in the development of a new *vinifera* clone of Gamay that not only had more power and intensity in the wine it produced, but survived the winters well and produced good yields without sacrificing quality. Paul had noticed how one vine grew almost twice as tall as the vines around it. With cuttings he propagated from it, he planted more, and eventually was the first in Canada to develop a new clone called "Gamay Droit" (*droit* meaning "upright" in French), for which he would be granted International Plant Breeder's Rights in 1999.

Another project investigated the use of reverse osmosis, a method to improve the quality of grape juice by using a special membrane to reduce the percentage of natural water in the juice. This was followed by experiments that examined the effect of tile location relative to soil moisture and soil temperature, and another exploring new methods of canopy management. While other wineries were reinvesting in marketing, Paul's profits always went back into his land.

The economy in Canada was in a serious recession in 1982. Interest rates had risen to more than 21 percent, so high that the group of speculators who had purchased the York Road property Paul had originally had his eye on in 1976 could not make the payments. By this time, Paul had some savings. He called the bank and asked how much they wanted for the property. "If you have $89,000, it's yours, but we don't want a mortgage," the bankers replied. It was a buyers' market, so Paul's inclination was to try to bargain with the bank. "Just give them the $89,000," Andrée advised. Within two days the property was his. Only six years before, the asking price had been $180,000 for all fifty acres (twenty hectares). It was the deal of his life — up to that time. He bulldozed and reshaped it, planted more vines and began construction on a new home.

By the mid-1980s, Château des Charmes was becoming well known as producers of fine wine. Although not much of a joiner, Paul completely endorsed Donald Ziraldo's efforts to develop an appellation system for Ontario. Whenever the deliberations would slide into accepting mediocre grape varieties as part of the proposed regulations, Paul would raise his voice in defiance. He knew how the producers from the larger companies thought. He had been there. In order to compete, they felt they had to keep the price down, and they could only do that with lesser varieties. Now that he was a small, boutique producer, he knew that the future lay in the production of better-quality wine. No corners could be cut. Better-quality grapes could be grown here. Why settle for anything less?

His vineyards were so pristine and his commitment so courageous that, in 1988, the year of the free trade agreement and the accompanying looming threat of annihilation to the industry, he accepted the crown of Grape King. He was the first winemaker ever chosen Grape King, an honour Paul made use of to encourage producers to face the future with confidence. It wasn't going to be easy, but, "there's no doubt in my mind," he told his fellow growers and producers, "we can compete."

Just before his reign began, he noticed that the Bright's-owned property across the way from his York Road vineyard and new home was up for rezoning — changing from agricultural zoning to ten industrial lots. Bright's had been going through difficult times and was cashing in the 1,300 acres (526 hectares) of once experimental vineyards it had owned since the 1930s, very little still planted in grapes. On this York Road farm there were 100 acres (40 hectares), intact and about to be divided into ten smaller blocks. Despite the vagaries and threats of free trade, Paul had no intention of sitting passively by, so he decided to find the money to buy it himself.

Paul had read the signs. After more than a decade in the business, it was time to take the plunge and build the winery of his dreams. With the experience of their Creek Road winery, they knew wine tourism had great potential. His château would be bold — nestled beneath the Niagara Escarpment on the St. David's Bench, a castle of stone with a green copper roof, reminiscent of a Loire estate, but based on the nineteenth-century railway hotels of Canada, such as the Château Laurier. Like the Boscs themselves, it would be a blend of old-world tradition and new-world promise.

With the help of an Ontario loan for $1 million as part of the Ontario Wine Assistance Program (OWAP), he built a $6 million, 36,000-square-foot (3,344-square-metre) facility, the first in Ontario with such an extensive capital investment in a winery site designed to make wine, as well as to welcome visitors. The beautifully landscaped site would include a modern production facility, a hospitality centre with a theatre, a retail store and tasting rooms, and a wine bar. When "the Château" opened in May 1994, the wine industry breathed a sigh of relief. If Bosc could do it, so might they. Paul and his family would lead the way in winery tourism, establishing the benchmarks in Ontario for market-readiness.

Paul continues to be cutting edge. When his research on genetically modified grape varieties for winter hardiness slowed, he was the first to install twenty-five wind machines as another way to combat winter damage and frost. When temperatures reached the danger zone, the wind from the machines blew air across his vineyards, pulling warmer air from above down to ground level to save the crop. But before he invested in the machines, he hired a helicopter to do the same. Two degrees more of warmth could save the vines from damage. Though he was ridiculed at first for investing $625,000 into wind machines, Paul Bosc was vindicated when his innovative move paid off. When surrounding vineyards lost acres of vines because of frost damage in 2003, his 100 hectares (250 acres) of vines stayed frost-free and his annual $1 million worth of grapes survived.

Of all Paul's contributions to the wine industry, perhaps the most enduring has been the mentorship he has provided for others — either indirectly, as a model of an estate grower, or directly, almost as a preacher, if he had a willing and capable listener. Although he never suffered fools, for individuals who were willing to work and listen, he had all the time in the world. Len Pennachetti, the founder of Cave Spring Cellars, thinks of Paul as a mentor. "He brought old-world knowledge none of us knew," said Pennachetti, "and he was very good at sharing that knowledge. ... Paul was always pushing the bar higher for quality standards."

Paul's older son, Paul-André, has grown up in the industry, working closely with his father. Today he is the vice-president in charge of marketing and business administration and chair of the Canadian Vintners Association, the wine industry's national trade association. Paul Jr., as he is known in the industry, looks like his father's twin, right down to the mole on his left cheek. He is very aware of his father's contributions. "What he did," says Paul Jr., "was to accelerate the development of the industry." He is very intent on building on his father's legacy.

If Paul Sr. has had a reputation for being demanding and impatient, shy and uncomfortable in crowds, his wife, Andrée, has been the opposite. Madame Bosc captured the people's imagination and made them feel good. She ran the house. This freed Paul Sr. to focus on his research and his work. She gave him that opportunity. During the early years, when he wasn't drawing a salary, they lived off her teacher's salary. Paul could not have succeeded without her.

Pierre-Jean, their younger son, made wine with his dad for a few years, then realized his *métier* was outside the cellar in a business of his own, selling agricultural equipment. Paul Jr. now quite capably runs the day-to-day business operations and his wife, Michèle, is in charge of tourism marketing and staff training. Together they raise their young son, Alexandre. Paul Sr. and Madame Bosc are still very much involved. What's important to Paul Jr. now is how he will be judged in handling the transition from the first generation to the second. As the custodian of his father's dream, it is important to him that "the transition be handled with dignity." Consequently, he introduces major changes only after consultation with his father. For instance, at one time Château des Charmes was producing ninety

Paul Bosc, winemaker/owner, Château des Charmes, 2009

thousand cases annually, but fifty thousand cases of that total was in imported blends. Through Paul Jr.'s steady encouragement, they stopped that program completely in 2002. Now they produce seventy thousand cases a year and have capacity for more. With this added capability, in 2008 they entered a partnership with Canadian golfer Mike Weir to make wines for his label in the Château des Charmes facility.

Throughout his career, Paul Bosc learned that, even in the depths of winter, he and his family could survive, as they had done nearly fifty years before. With four farms and 270 acres (110 hectares) of producing vineyards, they are the only company of their size that is completely self-sufficient, and Paul did it by being, as fellow grower Steve Murdza put it, "the most uncompromising man in the industry today."

6 PAUL SPECK'S CHALLENGE

"When two go together one sees before the other and both are wiser in thought, word and deed."

—Homer, *The Iliad*

Vinifera vine importer Lloyd Schmidt pulled his truck into the drive of the old Pelham farm with an order for Paul Speck Sr. Across the road he could see him with his three sons: the youngest looked about twelve and the two older boys in their teens. The boys were wearing cut-off jeans and white T-shirts with beer logos. *City slickers*, thought Allan, Lloyd's twenty-two-year-old son, who was sitting next to him in the truck.

"Dad," said Allan, "they're working so hard and they're doing so much wrong. How will they ever survive?" Allan had been born and raised on his father's vineyard in British Columbia, where Lloyd had founded Sumac Ridge winery. He knew what planting, pruning, tending and harvesting was all about. He could see these teenagers had no clue.

"Dad," said Allan again. "Look, they're not driving the tractor straight, and the way they're holding that augur, the holes'll never be right." There is a certain grace and flow to operating farm equipment that farmers understand; it's easy to detect when a novice tries his hand. "What's going to happen to them?" he asked.

"Don't worry," said Lloyd. "They're buying the right grapes and they're asking me my advice, and they're asking all the right questions. They're going to be all right."

It was 1985 and the wine industry was about to enter a period that would be filled with equal parts chaos and promise. Within two years the free-trade talks triggered anxieties in the industry felt equally by wineries and growers. The wineries believed that they were about to be sold out by the federal government for a few pieces of the silver-lined American market. When growers realized that the trade bargaining might result in the pullout of their native *labrusca* vines, they felt gobsmacked. What was wrong with Concord or Niagara that a little technology in the cellar couldn't fix?

Yet, new adventurers were beginning to take the lead of Ziraldo, Pennachetti and Bosc, who, after nearly fifteen years of success in the marketplace, had articulated a vision that others could follow. Among those to open wineries were: Joe Pohorly (Newark, 1980), Enzo de Luca (Colio, 1980), Ewald Reif (Reif, 1983), Jim Warren (Stoney Ridge Cellars, 1985), Herbert Konzelmann (Konzelmann Estates, 1986), Len Pennachetti (Cave Spring Cellars, 1986), John De Sousa (De Sousa Wine Cellars, 1987) and Hermann Weis (Vineland Estates, 1987). It was a time for thinking the unimaginable and doing the unlikely. Their sights were on quality, but their scale was still small and change was incremental.

* * *

By 1988, however, the pace of change was accelerating. Free trade was speeding up the creative destruction of the old industry in confusing and destabilizing ways. One survey of the effects of free trade predicted that the industry would disappear in five years. Canadian wineries would be "washed aside by a tide of cheap California wine." Existing patterns were breaking apart and new alignments were being forged. What were needed were industry leaders who were capable of replacing the broken links with the past with engaging ways to mobilize the needs and aspirations of a new generation.

In spite of the doomsday scenarios that pronounced the end of the Ontario wine industry, Paul Speck Sr., a one-time priest, private-school educator and owner of The Annex Village Campus school in Toronto, decided that the time was right to open a winery of his own. Six years earlier he and his wife, Bobbi, had purchased land from his cousin in Niagara, who had put up for sale a small parcel that had been in the family since the late 1700s. Their great-great-great-grandfather, Nicolas Smith, had received a land grant as a tribute to his efforts as a member of Butler's Rangers, soldiers who fought for the British during the American Revolutionary War. In the 1840s, Nicolas's son, Henry, had inherited a portion of the land, on which he built a carriage house, an inn and a coach stop at a popular intersection in an area called Pelham on an old Mohawk Trail that led to York (Toronto). To differentiate himself from other Smiths in the area, he signed his name *Henry of Pelham*. It was Henry's sixty-five-acre (twenty-six-hectare) property that Speck bought to keep the family ties to the land intact.

At first he thought he'd lease it to farmers, but he soon discovered he couldn't make enough money on the land to cover his costs. He had grown up in Niagara, and like everybody else who grew up here, he had also made wine. Perhaps a better use of his land would be to plant grapes and sell them to local wineries. That was why, during the summer of 1985, he and his sons, Paul, Matthew and Daniel, were planting the new varieties, Riesling, Chardonnay and Gamay, plus a French hybrid called Baco Noir. His plan was eventually to use his grapes to make enough handcrafted wine to sell out of his cellar door — small volume, nothing crazy. Free trade and the threat of being outflanked in the marketplace by American wines was never an issue. Although he was not in favour of free trade, its potential impact on his project was a remote, macro-level issue that didn't concern him.

As the negotiators were signing the agreement in principle in 1988, he was outfitting the old barn on the property of his new winery, Henry of Pelham, with tanks and presses, a de-stemmer and barrels. That was the easy part. The harder part was making the wine, getting it into the bottle and selling it. It didn't take long for him to discover that running a private school in Toronto at the same time as an estate winery in Niagara wasn't quite as idyllic as he first imagined. His fledgling business needed someone there on a day-to-day basis to move it along.

His eldest son, Paul, was the likely choice. Middle son, Matthew, was still in university, and Daniel was in his early teens. When Paul graduated from St. John's College in Annapolis, Maryland, in 1989, his dad prevailed upon him — he who had no experience in running a business — to move to St. Catharines and organize the winery operation. He had been a philosophy major, a "lover of wisdom," who enjoyed thinking about thinking, the nature of knowledge, the justification of belief, the nature of reality and the conduct of life. There was not a course in finance, accounting or managing human resources among those he had taken. He knew even less about wine, but he was at the fearless age of twenty-one and nothing seemed impossible. He would go to Niagara and just "figure it out."

At first, his father accompanied him to a few Wine Council meetings so Paul could better acquaint himself with the industry and learn about the players and the key issues. He could see that the members liked his dad. He was flamboyant and affable. He was also sincere and stern, and this they liked the best. They trusted him because he operated on the premise that, if he didn't like what you were saying, he'd speak his mind rather than grumble and complain after a meeting. Paul Speck Jr. looked a lot like his dad, and the council members would soon learn that he, also like his dad, would speak up and work hard for what he thought was right.

It didn't take long for young Paul to see how the balance of power among the wineries was shifting. The government had spun an artificial protective environment like a cocoon around the wine industry, and winemakers had only to be half as good as foreign imports. In return for a 66-percent mark-up differential on American and European wines, the industry's Faustian bargain was to comply with a complex system of interventions and regulations that made real change for the larger wineries, no matter how incremental, next to impossible. Paul could see that although there was a lot of talent in their ranks, these big companies had grown lazy and unimaginative over the years. If free trade meant placing them on a more competitive footing, then perhaps it would be a good thing.

Even though those whom he perceived as the "dinosaurs" at Bright's and Andrés were still capable of breathing fire at meetings, Paul Jr. could also sense that they were running scared. Their market share was being slowly eroded by imports. Domestic "boutique" production was up by 12 percent. They had spent a generation making commodity wines, and didn't seem to understand the modern wine industry at all. Although they had dabbled in *vinifera*-based varietal wines, their core business model was in generic bulk wines. From what Paul Jr. could see, they had bought into the fear that California was going to obliterate everybody. Perhaps as far as they were concerned they had good reason. Their culture had been one of

The three brothers, first harvest. Paul, Daniel and Matthew Speck

imitation based on whatever French, German or Italian bulk wine was popular at the time. For every German Black Tower, there was an Andrés Hochtaller. For every French Piat d'Or, there was a Bright's Entre Lacs. For every Italian Carlo Rossi, there was a Chateau Gai Capistro. They seemed to be hiding the fact that their wines came from Niagara.

These bulk producers were also in a different league from the modest business Paul's father had in mind. Consequently, Paul Jr. took his lead from the newcomers with smaller aspirations, moving into their circles, slowly at first, gauging where and how he might best fit in to get his father's business at least on a par with theirs. Inniskillin was located in an old barn, albeit a stunning one, but it was still a barn. Château des Charmes was on Creek Road in a concrete-block building. Vineland Estates had moved the furniture out of the dining room of a 1840s farmhouse to create a tasting room. When Paul walked through these properties and found small, unsophisticated operations doing a reasonable business, he thought, *I can do this.*

He should have been worried or at least a little concerned. Free trade, and with it eventual parity with American wines — not just bulk wines, but American wines of quality — could have marked the end of the line for his family's project. Paul blissfully felt it was just a matter of finding a creative solution to marketing and distribution. Even though the stability of the old marketplace was being severely threatened, he and his new colleagues believed they understood the marketplace well enough to find equilibrium again, only this time with better-quality wines — wines they believed could compete with any import. Their optimism was enough for Paul to feel confident he could accomplish the job he was charged to tackle.

If some people in the industry were still in denial about the inevitable necessity to change, as Donald Ziraldo noted "free trade was a whack on the side of the head" that rattled them into facing reality. One can only imagine how hard it must have been to accept the inevitable shattering of old relationships and expectations. Many growers and producers simply surrendered. They couldn't see themselves operating. To stay viable in the marketplace, the province had by this time conceded that *labrusca* grapes could not continue to be the foundation for a thriving, competitive industry.

Two separate-but-parallel deliberations were occurring during this period that intersected during the free trade talks, with lasting consequences. Each represented the interests of the industry's main stakeholders: the large producers wanted modifications to the Wine Content Act to enable them to compete in the bulk-wine market; the small producers toiled with the framework for the VQA to differentiate their wines by challenging themselves to higher standards. As the industry grew, this dichotomy became more blurred, particularly when some small producers chose to make import blends and the larger producers started to produce *vinifera* wines.

The wine industry had been governed since 1972 by the provisions of the Wine Content Act, which regulated such issues as the amount of domestic wine that had to be blended into imported wine, or the amount of water or sugar that could be added to a *labrusca*-based wine to ameliorate its naturally foul flavours. As seen earlier, in 1987, just before the old Wine Content Act was about to sunset, the secretary of cabinet asked the deputy minister of consumer and commercial relations, the energetic Valerie Gibbons, to lead a group of multi-party stakeholders in a series of strategic planning meetings to discuss how the Act's contents should be modified. Her mandate was to forge a common vision after isolating the difficulties each stakeholder saw, eliciting outcomes they hoped for, and then deriving reasonable solutions everyone could live with. No small challenge.

They had been meeting bi-monthly for more than a year when Liberal Premier David Peterson phoned Gibbons one Friday afternoon to ask whether she could call an urgent meeting over the weekend with her committee. Trade talks were coming around to the wine industry. Could she come up with a reasonable package of recommendations that could serve as a basis for trade negotiations — by Monday? Peterson had been opposed to free trade. He thought the deal was a bad thing, one that would hang over the country like a black cloud for a long time to come. As far as Peterson was concerned, Ottawa was intruding into entrenched rights of provincial jurisdiction when it came to wine and liquor. If the free trade deal didn't comply with six of his points, he was prepared to veto it and perhaps even take the feds to court. Peterson was determined that the Americans would not outfox the Ontario wine industry.

By Sunday night, Gibbons and her committee came to an accord of general principles regarding quality and price, an accord that would not have happened without the year-long groundwork they had already laid. "We're not going to be perfect," reminded Gibbons, "but we are going to have two industries survive." Everyone agreed that the quality of wine had to be improved, which meant no *labrusca* content, and provincial and federal money had to be spent to beef up the industry as it went through the transition. The substance of the Wine Content Act would follow from the free trade decisions.

Donald Ziraldo had also received a call from a government official around the same time regarding the rules and regulations his VQA committee was finalizing. The official asked whether he could use VQA standards for the free trade negotiations. "We have to table some standards for quality," said the official, "and we don't have any. Can we use yours?" Ziraldo and his committee were elated. Before that call the VQA was strictly a group of producers volunteering to abide by a set of rules they had established to produce better wine. When the government took it on, the committee's work became informally legitimized. The next step was to have the VQA enacted as provincial law, a task that would soon be spearheaded by Paul Speck and Len Pennachetti, but it would take another decade to achieve.

As a result of the free trade agreement, the Americans were granted "national treatment," which meant their wines would receive the same treatment in the marketplace as Canadian wine. Differential charges on wine were to be phased out over a seven-year period from 1989 through 1995. Any other discriminatory pricing measure was eliminated immediately. Since some wineries had off-premise retail stores, the Americans wanted the privilege to have stores as well to sell their wines. To avoid this additional competition with the LCBO and the subsequent Pandora's box it would open, as of October 4, 1987, any new private wine outlets other than on-premise winery retail operations were to be eliminated. Existing wineries could maintain the off-premise licences they already had, which amounted to about 350 additional stores divided among the large operators. New wineries would not be afforded the same privilege. The inequities of this part of the agreement would cause severe bifurcations in the industry for the next two decades.

If domestic wine was going to go head to head with California wine, and, by this time, through GATT negotiations with the European Union, European wines as well, then the LCBO wanted some guarantee that domestic wines were saleable at the increased prices at which they would now have to list them. It became official. They would not sell wines made from *labrusca* grapes or their hybrids. Several issues now had to be resolved: How could *labrusca* growers survive if they no longer had a buyer for their crops? How would they be compensated for the losses they incurred if they pulled out their old vines and bought and planted new ones? How would the wineries survive during the interim?

The transition to better-quality grapes was traumatic and long. Gibbons and her committee had forecasted these issues and offered recommendations on how each might be addressed. When Peterson received her report, he checked with the Provincial Treasurer. Did the province have the wherewithal to comply with the approximate figures Gibbons had outlined? Within a few months, Peterson had earmarked $145 million to insure a prosperous domestic wine industry. Ontario would not become just bottlers of industrial-size American wine. The Grape and Wine Assistance Program, better known as the "pullout program," would assure that.

The whole negotiation process had been a two-year ordeal that forced everyone to think differently. Implementing the assistance program was in the hands of the Grape Growers Marketing Board from their offices on the South Service Road in St. Catharines. From there, a small committee oversaw the removal of approximately 8,600 acres (3,480 hectares) of vines that were judged to have no future demand based on application criteria formulated jointly by grower representatives and the government. Through this committee, local farmers were also assisted by a reimbursement of $1,100 an acre of pulled-out vines, allowing them to buy new machinery to improve productivity. The growers were granted $100 million of the earmarked $145 million for the pullout. Unfortunately, those growers who had already planted *vinifera* at their own expense, such as Paul Speck, Len Pennachetti, Paul Bosc and Donald Ziraldo, plus their contracted *vinifera* growers like Stan Murdza, Ken Dyke or Bill Lenko, received no compensation.

No matter how much money was designated to accomplish it, for the *labrusca* growers it was still a time of dread and indecision. The first to leave farming entirely were many of the part-timers — those who were working at General Motors in the winter and only when the plant shut down in the summer for retooling would turn their attention to the farm.

Many other growers worked off bank loans, which the banks were starting to call in. "We just don't know what's going to happen to you in the adjustment program," the bank officers rationalized. Brian Nash, the chair of the Grape Growers Marketing Board and chief negotiator on behalf of the growers during the trade talks, spent much of his time returning bank managers' calls to assure them that everything was going to be okay.

Of those growers who decided to take the money and sell their farms for a more stable life, some did so with an air of defiance, as if thumbing their noses at those who chose to remain. It wasn't uncommon to see luxury cars driving through country lanes and concessions with taunting words such as PULL OUT on their licence plates.

Some growers blamed their chair Brian Nash for not stopping the train. Granted, at first the farmer in him wasn't prepared for the guile of international negotiations and posturing. At free trade negotiation meetings he had been bushwhacked, undermined and arm-wrestled. At some point in the negotiations there was no naïveté left in him. But even though he was slightly jaded by the time the talks were over, he had stood up to the federal negotiators and steered a steady, aggressive course to negotiate a deal in which he believed, and which history now confirms served his growers' and the industry's best interests. The train had left the station, but he could make the inevitable journey less painful and the destination more hospitable.

Even if a few felt differently, Nash, a *labrusca* grower himself whose farm had dated back to Queen Victoria and a Crown grant, recognized the time had come to change. The contents of the Grape and Wine Adjustment Program would cover the costs of the massive transition that lay ahead. Nash played a prominent role in the talks, representing his eleven-hundred-member growers' organization. The wineries didn't have the same political infrastructure. Of the $145-million budget, the winery part of the adjustment program consisted of $45 million in forgivable performance loans. Several wineries received grants to upgrade their wineries, and in some cases to build new ones.

The next issue to be resolved was how the wineries would survive during the transition. To help them stay in business, the Wine Content Act was renegotiated. The pressure for increased access to cheaper, international grape supplies came almost entirely from the three big producers — Bright's, Andrés and Chateau Gai. They were the companies who faced direct competition from California bulk wines such as Gallo.

As seen earlier, up until 1972, all domestic wines had been made from 100-percent domestic grapes. When wineries were left with a short crop of only 39,500 tons of grapes that year, and only a very small portion of it in *viniferas*, they asked for permission to top up their domestic wine with imported wine. At that time, cheap wines from Europe and the Soviet bloc were flooding the market, and the domestic wineries were having difficulty competing. The Canadian Wine Institute produced studies that showed, given their present trajectory, that by 1977 they would need 92,000 tons of grapes. To meet this anticipated need, they asked the government to allow them "to provide for the limited inclusion of grapes grown outside Ontario in Ontario wine." This change allowed them to import the equivalent of 10 percent of their domestic purchases and blend up to 25-percent imported product in any one bottle of wine.

In 1980, when another grape shortage occurred, the act was amended to allow wineries to raise the percentage of imported wine per bottle to 30 percent. This time the amount wasn't connected to the percent of domestic grapes they purchased.

In 1989, the percentages of domestic to imported wine were reversed. Because of the pullout of domestic grapes, wineries were allowed to produce a bottle of wine with Product of Canada indication on the label with

70 percent of it made from imported grapes or wine, and only 30-percent domestic. This, the government felt, would get the wineries over the free-trade hump until the act was scheduled to be renegotiated in 2000. The Wine Content Act, however, would divide the industry for the next several years because of its inherent inequities.

Only existing wineries at the time of free trade could use imported wine as a blend in a domestic product. Although the larger wineries, by necessity, felt they had to, some of the smaller wineries, such as Inniskillin, Château des Charmes and Hillebrand, also took advantage of the policy. But for others, like Henry of Pelham, Vineland Estates and Cave Spring Cellars, it had not been part of their business plans to use imported product in any of their brands. The purpose of the VQA regulations they had been working on for the past seven years was to differentiate their wines from the import-blended wines. It was just a matter of clear labelling and differentiated category placement at the LCBO. It was seemingly an easy task, but it took several years of wrangling to accomplish.

Then came the vintage of 1993 and severe crop losses due to winter kill. The act was once again amended seven years before it was expected to sunset, to allow a minimum of only 10 percent of Ontario-grown product. A year later, in 1994, the act was changed back once again, not to its pre-1993 amount of 30 percent but to a lowered minimum of 25 percent of Ontario-grown fruit. There were those who argued that this intervention in the natural flow of the market forced a false foundation for a non-sustainable industry. When strawberry farmers had a short crop, they couldn't package imported strawberries from Mexico to top them up.

Wineries were also encouraged by the government to consolidate in order to have enough volume to sell to the Americans. In retrospect, this was a fanciful notion when one considers the intricacies of doing business with fifty different states, each with differing requirements and laws. Sufficient volume was the least of their worries. Nevertheless, a flurry of consolidations took place over the same period. This is when Chateau Gai became Cartier in 1989, then in 1992 the venerable Inniskillin merged with Cartier forming Cartier–Inniskillin, and about a year later Cartier–Inniskillin was acquired by T.G. Bright and renamed Vincor.

The strong were getting stronger, but so were the smaller operators. After Paul Speck Sr. began Henry of Pelham, Stonechurch was founded in 1989, then Marynissen Estates and Hernder's in 1990. In 1991, retired amateur winemaker Eddie Gurinskas opened Lakeview Cellars, and on a farm in Maple, Ontario, Bill Redelmeir opened Southbrook. This was the same year that Inniskillin won the most prestigious prize at Vin Expo — the Grand Prix d'Honneur for its 1989 icewine — the best wine out of a field of thousands of international entries. It was an award that Inniskillin received, but every producer in Ontario shared and celebrated. If one of their own could make the big time, so too could they. Grape grower Gary Pillitteri opened Pillitteri Estates in 1993, the same year Vincor erupted onto the marketplace. Confidence in the future of the industry soared.

* * *

It was also a heady time for Paul Speck Jr. Five years into his new career, he was still learning the business. He learned how to keep financial records from his accountant, who suggested that pieces of paper with figures crossed out might not be the best way to manage the finances. He set up a simple system in a format Paul could use. Even though Paul knew he didn't know a lot about the business, he soon realized that his young colleagues didn't know a whole lot about it either. Everything was in the beginning stages. A new era was being formed and, for a young philosophy major with classical ideas still swirling around in his head, it was an exhilarating time.

Paul Jr. hadn't expected to enjoy the business. His first career choice had been to become a race-car driver but that was not going to happen. International law was his next choice. With the free trade agreement just about to be implemented, he thought he might go back to New York City and join a firm taking cases on U.S. and Canadian trade disputes. Anyone sitting next to him at early Wine Council meetings might have noticed LSAT study notes slipped between Wine Council handouts as he grabbed every moment to prepare for his law-school qualifying exams. Len Pennachetti and Paul had become good friends by this time, finding they shared much on which to build a common bond. Besides both having slightly skewed but hearty senses of humour, they shared a western humanist moral compass based on their liberal-arts backgrounds. Paul had grown up in the Annex neighbourhood of Toronto where Len had spent his formative university years. Len had a year of pre-law, so when he discovered Paul was contemplating the profession, he told him he was out of his mind. "Hire a lawyer," cautioned Pennachetti.

They both had read the "Great Books" and often talked about the possibilities of the wine industry using reasoning from the great thinkers. When they talked about governance, they would invoke Aristotle or Plato. When they worked to broker consensus among their colleagues regarding the VQA regulations, the details of which they both had spent "ridiculous amounts of time bickering about," they talked about *The Federalist Papers* and the arguments Hamilton, Madison and Hay formed to persuade the American electorate to ratify the new U.S. constitution.

By now, Paul's brother Matthew had joined him, taking charge of the vineyards while Paul was still knocking on licensee and LCBO doors for better distribution. All the while he kept searching for other channels through which to sell his wine. He found one. Prior to the free trade agreement, additional retail licences (endorsements) could only be granted by buying a winery that held the licence. In a brief unofficial window between the signing in principle of the free trade agreement in 1987 and the ratification in 1993, almost as if to give the smaller operators a leg-up, the government looked the other way when wineries applied for additional off-premise licences. All a winery had to do was show it had a lease agreement for an additional retail site and the licence was granted. Hillebrand, for instance, had accumulated nearly fifty of these endorsements in the span of just a few months. Paul Speck Jr. and Len Pennachetti had each gathered five leases of their own, some in gourmet shops, others in key grocery stores or complementary establishments in upscale neighbourhoods. They expected that soon they would have the money to outfit them and create additional outlets.

In March 1993, their hopes were dashed. It was St. Patrick's Day and a cold snap had arrived overnight, so frigid that several hundreds of acres of grapes in Niagara were lost. That day Paul and Len had a previously arranged an appointment with Andy Brandt, the CEO of the LCBO. They had asked to meet with him in Toronto regarding their request for additional licences. They hadn't anticipated the night's killing temperatures that would set in motion their first major business setback since opening. Reluctantly they drove to Toronto. When they arrived, Brandt confirmed that the LCBO was no longer endorsing additional retail licences. They would have until October to open their additional stores; otherwise, he would have to deny their requests. Len was in the throes of opening the first winery restaurant in Ontario, On the Twenty, so his attention and funds were limited. It was unrealistic for Paul to gather the money it would take to get five stores up and running in time. The retail window of opportunity had slammed shut.

On the trip back to Niagara it hit them: they had got killed in the vineyard and now they were getting killed in the marketplace. Len, in typical Pennachetti fashion, called it their "St. Patrick's Day Massacre." They laughed — what else could they do — but something much worse was about to happen to Paul.

They were just starting to turn the corner. Paul Sr. was getting a sense that there was a future in Niagara. Until then their fortunes had been up and down. Within three months, however, Paul Speck Sr., who suffered from heart trouble, was dead. Paul Jr., at twenty-six, inherited a project that had several bills and a sizeable mortgage. Len's father had also died suddenly when Len was barely thirty years old, leaving him to manage a business in chaos. Paul was now charged with the same task. He had to find a way to make it pay. Many of the new entrants into the wine business were coming from successful careers that they could rely on financially to get through the rough times. Others were being supported by wealthy silent partners. Not so the Speck brothers.

Paul Speck Sr. had purchased the original land cheaply enough, but it was still heavily mortgaged. There were bills from Matthew's education at St. John's College. Could they afford for their youngest brother, Daniel, the same life-changing education that they had experienced? Paul drove down to his old campus in Annapolis, Maryland, and met with school officials, who let him and his mother finance the whole thing. The Canadian dollar hovered at sixty-two cents U.S., so it cost nearly double what his and Matthew's education had. The timing wasn't ideal, but Paul knew the value of a liberal-arts education.

Four years later, Daniel emerged with the same philosophy background as his brothers and ready to take his place beside them. Because Matthew enjoyed the outdoors, he had taken over the management of the vineyards. Paul was the administrator. This left sales and marketing for Daniel, which didn't particularly interest him — until he got on the road. He was affable and organized, and was an immediate success. Like Paul and Matthew, with no preconceived notions on how things should be done, he was learning the business from the ground up.

They realized that to stay solvent all three had to get up in the morning with a little more energy and work a little longer. They were undercapital-ized and in debt, so to make things work, they had to be creative. None of the brothers had studied finance, viticulture or even marketing, but their philosophy background had taught them how to think and how to learn. Like their father before them, they knew how to seek advice and to ask the right questions.

They were also clear on their priorities. Locals asked why they didn't do more with tourism, and the reason was simple — the site didn't deliver. They couldn't afford the renovations required to make their place market-ready for wine tourists. They were still spending their time in Toronto, building up their brand through the LCBO and licensee distribution. They could afford to be a hidden gem for a while.

*   *   *

Several things sustained them, not the least of which was their increasing awareness that they were part of a generation that was leading an industry through fundamental change. Others felt it as well. In 1987, Allan Schmidt had been hired by Vineland Estates owner Hermann Weis to be his new winery's winemaker and general manager. At twenty-four, and billed by the media as "Canada's Youngest Winemaker," he was planning to stay only five years, then go back to British Columbia. Before long, however, he realized that there were people here creating breakaway paths. That was when he fell in love with the Niagara of the future. He wasn't going home. This was going to be a fun ride, and he wanted to be part of it.

Sandra Marynissen and her sister also wanted to be part of the future. As growers around them were selling their farms, they pleaded with their dad, grape grower and amateur winemaker John Marynissen, to open a winery. John had been one of the pioneer growers who, a decade earlier, was among the first to plant *vinifera*. From his best vines he was making stellar wines, with his daughters as his biggest fans. The pullout of the *labruscas* to replant with *vinifera* merely confirmed what they had already known.

Sandra and her dad got the courage to open their winery from the groundwork prepared by people such as Donald Ziraldo, Len Pennachetti, Paul Bosc and now Paul Speck and Allan Schmidt. It felt like a privilege to join this group. The Marynissens believed they were joining a collec-tion of highly principled men and women who were working together for a great cause, one that the Marynissens had believed in for years.

Sandra remembered the early days as great times — smaller producers getting together and greeting each other with open arms. It was almost like entering a brotherhood.

Their cause — to make excellent wines and to change people's minds — united them. They were routinely dismissed at Wine Council meetings by the older, traditional players. If they accepted that serious wine could be grown here, they didn't believe there was any money in it. When Paul and his colleagues, with their broken-down barns and no capital, said, "We're going to make a twelve-dollar bottle of Chardonnay and not a European knock-off like Entre Lacs or Hochtaler," the representatives from the larger wineries shook their heads. They treated the newcomers like overly ambitious children. "We know this business. We've tried it. What you want to do can't be done."

Wine Council meetings were seldom uncivil, but the ideological lines that divided the two sides were clear and often unyielding. The smaller wineries banded together to gather strength to make goals and stick to them, to remind themselves of their mutual commitment to integrity and to reinforce their rightful claims to shared power. They drew strength from one another; they needed to be tough, but they also had to be right. On the other hand, it was clear to Paul and a small group that they had to work together with the bigger players. The government had given them money for distribution and marketing. From that they also had to carve out money for the VQA — a program designed to distinguish the old-style wines and the import-blended wines from the new.

They struggled to find a balance — to promote the VQA without denigrating the import blends, a struggle often not popular with those producers who believed all wine made in Ontario should be made with 100-percent Ontario grapes. When the industry ads — "We're ready when you are" — finally came out after the free trade agreement and consumers responded by fuelling overwhelming sales, working together became a little easier. Then one Ontario winery brought a serious lawsuit against the VQA board of directors. The lawsuit forced the entire membership, large and small, to work even more closely with one another. Spending hours together, they met every month as a board, laying aside their differences to protect the industry for what they believed was a principle worth defending. The lawsuit took millions of dollars to defend, requiring everyone to write cheques for thousands of dollars over a ten-year period as their portion of the defence. Although questions about the outcome remain, the settlement seemed to satisfy all parties. And the VQA designation was intact.

The VQA and expensive Canadian wines were essential to the new wine-makers. And Paul Speck Jr. knew it. He could subtract and multiply, and although he didn't know anything about the wine business when he began, he was a good student. He watched, listened and imitated, and as he did, one thing became clear to him. As he studied the system he realized that there were dozens of different taxes, and taxes on taxes, some of them on percentages. But there was one simple flat tax of $13.50 on each case of wine, the same amount whether he was selling wine for $20 a bottle or $2 — except with a $20 bottle, there was more money for the winery.

Pricing an Ontario wine above a $10 to $12 price point had been unheard of. The larger companies believed that such a marketing gambit would fall flat. It just wasn't done. When the mathematical epiphany dawned on Paul, he began to push the Henry of Pelham wines to the premium category. Glamour and romance drove the business for some, but Paul Speck built their business model on pure mathematics. He knew that they had to work to get volume up. His winemaker, Ron Geisbrecht, was a graduate of Guelph University and had worked in the lab at Bright's. The wines he made for Henry of Pelham were excellent, wines that Paul could sell at a premium.

But Paul was wrestling with a paradox. When they were promoting VQA wines, they were really referring only to *vinifera*-based wines. On the one hand, everyone in his group, including Paul, was saying Chardonnay, Cabernet Sauvignon and other *vinifera* varieties were the future, yet he had ten acres (four hectares) of the lowly French hybrid Baco Noir. These were among the second-rate grapes being pulled out. Under VQA regulations, they, along with eight other hybrids (Chambourcin, Chancellor, Couderc, Muscat, Maréchal Foch, Seyvel Blanc, Vidal, Villard Noir), were acceptable as varietal table wines (plus fifteen other hybrids that may be blended up to 15 percent but not labelled as varietals). But, according to the VQA rules Paul had helped to refine, hybrids such as Baco Noir could only use the provincial appellation designation of "Ontario" and nothing more specific — and therefore nothing more prestigious. Would Baco Noir be the anomaly in their premium-based portfolio?

They wanted at least to try to use what they already had in the ground.

Winemaker Ron Geisbrecht treated their Baco as he might a more noble Pinot Noir — by aging it in oak and making a medium-bodied, soft-tannin red wine, an expensive practice not usually awarded to a hybrid. Paul knew he was swimming upstream with this product. When he first went to the LCBO with his Baco, they were de-listing all their Baco Noirs, with the goal of eventually being completely rid of the category. Paul didn't give up. He liked the wine, so, for a lark, he entered it in the Toronto Wine and Food Show, which was in its infancy. To everyone's surprise, it received a silver medal. Paul later learned that it had really won a gold, but the judges were so embarrassed they downgraded it to a silver.

Within a few years, the Henry of Pelham Baco Noir became the best-selling wine in their portfolio. The episode taught Paul that often it's not what the critics say, nor is it always what you're supposed to do. What matters most is whatever people like. When he finally sold the wine to Vintages, it flew through the system and became the first Ontario wine that the LCBO had to limit to six bottles per customer.

By 1996, Canadian wines were at parity with American and European wines. As the Grape and Wine Adjustment Program and its largesse was winding down, the tables had turned. It was becoming increasingly clear that the playing field on which Ontario wineries were competing was neither level nor fair. Most of the jurisdictions from which the LCBO was sourcing wines for the Ontario market were regions that enjoyed many different kinds of subsidies, subsidies that were precluded for Canadian companies under the free trade agreement. Ontario producers had to somehow secure better margins. One strategy was to change the laws regarding direct delivery to restaurants. Paul had concentrated on getting Henry of Pelham wines into the best restaurants in Ontario, and he would get riled every time he had to shell over to the LCBO its usual 58-percent markup. Paying the government what amounted to a tax for a service the wineries performed was outrageous.

Paul worked closely with Allan Schmidt from Vineland Estates. Allan's brother Brian, by this time, had come to take over the winemaking side of the business, since Allan was spending 30 percent of his time on industry-related business. At Wine Council meetings, Allan was always the "numbers guy." They'd say, "Al, you do a spreadsheet on that." When Allan was in British Columbia, wineries had had the right to deliver wines directly to restaurants, saving the 30-percent service markup of their provincial liquor board. In Ontario, the LCBO kept that 30 percent, even though they performed no service. Allan worked very closely with the LCBO's Rowland Dunning to convince the board that sales to restaurants were different from those sold to the LCBO. Six years and hundreds of spreadsheets later, they devised a plan to sell wine to restaurants on behalf of the LCBO, using the LCBO's GST number and keeping a commission that equalled the 30-percent markup. Allan, on behalf of the team, had scored a touchdown. With strategic lobbying of the new Wine Council president, Linda Franklin, in 1996, the wineries won the right to deliver directly to restaurants and keep the markup as profit.

Paul, like Allan Schmidt, Len Pennachetti and Donald Ziraldo, knew that the burgeoning industry was too young to do battle as individual wineries. There was much more at stake than their individual interests. In 2000, and for the next five years, Paul Speck Jr. served as the chair of the Wine Council, the first person from a smaller winery to do so since its inception in the 1940s. Many people at first thought that Paul was a token appointment — it appeared to be a magnanimous concession on the part of the large wineries — but many expected that he'd actually just be the large wineries' mouthpiece. When he negotiated consensus, many would still say, "It's what the big guys wanted." Just such a real compromise was negotiated by Paul when the Wine Council received money to market wines. The large wineries said it should be used for their import blended wines, since those wines represented 80 percent of all the domestic wines sold in Ontario.

Paul's strategy, which could have been to come out of the gate saying "no g-damn way. Don't you see that would be suicide," was to find a happy medium all could abide by. The LCBO consented to promote both categories: one promotion would be an Ontario promotion, with private money spent, another selling period would focus solely on VQA products, paid for by the VQA marketing dollars. By this time, Vincor owned Inniskillin and Jackson-Triggs, and Andrés owned Hillebrand, so both these large companies had vested interests in also promoting VQA wines.

During his tenure, Paul, with the help of John Peller, president of Andrés, was able to achieve a strategic plan for the industry, called "Poised for Greatness." He did it the way they had moved the industry forward before — in a collaborative manner. Since another channel for distribution was the winery itself, and approximately 75 percent of the sale was kept at the winery or at off-premise winery retail stores, as opposed to only 42 percent when sold through the LCBO, the strategy was to concentrate on wine tourism. If they couldn't have another channel to bring their wines to the consumer, they would find better ways to bring the consumer to them.

But there were problems. Several properties had portfolios that weren't diversified enough, or their brand images lacked perceived quality or sufficient romance to compete with foreign brands, and many of the properties weren't sufficiently market-ready. Together with growers, the wineries (now forty) and the government, Paul guided the proceedings as they set out to put a numerical stake in the ground, to get the plan approved by the members and the LCBO. Their goal was to identify what wine and culinary tourism activities existed, which held promise for growth, and where gaps existed. These were areas they might then recommend for expansion. They set 2020 as the date when they wanted "to be recognized as one of the best wine-producing regions in the world and achieve $1.5 billion in sales," up from the 2006 level of $436 million.

The launch date to publicize their vision was originally scheduled for September 11, 2001, but was postponed to the following spring. That inauspicious beginning also ushered in the first major agricultural incident the industry had experienced since free trade. Even the short crop of 1993 was not in the same magnitude. Then one event after the other would test the new chair's mettle.

Nobody paid attention as a horde of orange-and-black ladybugs infested Niagara in October 2001, clinging to the sides of buildings, crunching underfoot, swarming in great pumpkin-hued clouds of wings. All ladybugs, up until then, were considered the farmer's friend, but these multicoloured Asian lady beetles (MALB), as the species were later identified, silently stole the 2001 vintage and millions of dollars of revenue, because of the taint they caused in finished wine. They arrived on an air current from the west, chasing an aphid infestation so heavy that the cover on the Toronto Sky Dome arena had to be closed in order to continue a Blue Jays game. On the lady beetles' way, they stopped to nibble on the aphids that had settled in local soybean fields in Niagara. When the aphids were depleted, they moved to nearby vineyards. As the harvest came in, they were still clinging to clusters that, when dumped into crushers and fermentation tanks, alerted

The three brothers, first harvest. Paul, Daniel and Matthew Speck

their defence mechanisms, and, like a skunk at the first sign of danger, they emitted a fright compound called methoxypyrzene.

Slowly, as the 2001 vintage started to be released, tasters discovered an off-note in certain wines that ranged from a strong herbaceousness similar to the green-pepper notes in a cheap New Zealand Sauvignon Blanc to a disgusting flavour of rancid peanuts. Once wineries learned that there was no health hazard, the Wine Council's response at first was to say little until researchers could figure out the cause and test ways to possibly address the wines that were still in tank or barrel. Winemakers themselves discovered that they had different thresholds to identify the taint and, if they could detect it, they quickly adapted to it and could no longer detect it. The taint also developed more intensity in the bottle. Once a strategy was developed, consumers would then be alerted and they would be reimbursed for all tainted wines they returned. Some wineries took their tainted wines off the shelf. Others waited, since some of their customers either didn't notice the taint or actually liked the flavour.

An irate media viewed this as a cover-up, with wineries cavalierly trying to dupe unsuspecting consumers into buying the tainted product without prior warning. The whole episode caught the industry off guard, and it had to be handled judiciousnessly, a process Paul Speck, as chair of the Wine Council, was charged to manage. Producers watched with anguish as they had no alternative but to dump their wines. Research at Brock University would subsequently offer measures to manage the little beasties, but that would take time.

By now, Paul was accustomed to trial by fire. In 2003, the industry was hit, as it had been a decade before, by frigid winter temperatures that killed thousands of vines. Many entire vineyards were lost, not just that year's crop. Paul had to negotiate the second unpopular short crop change in the Wine Content Act, the first being in 1993. Nobody was carrying enough inventory to weather yet another loss of product.

* * *

By the end of his tenure as chair, Paul was only thirty-eight years old. He had worked to develop the conditions that could enable three brothers to carve out a successful family business, now producing sixty thousand cases of wine a year on a farm where, over the course of fifteen years, together with their mother and partner, Bobbi Speck, they had assembled 275 acres (100 hectares) of grapes. If they had a problem, they sought innovative ways to address it. If they couldn't sell Baco Noir, they aged it in oak to accent its *vinifera* background. Winterkill? They invested money in wind machines. Paul's talent had been, and continued to be, his ability to unite his brothers to achieve better momentum and a fulfilling outcome.

He did the same as chair of the Wine Council — bringing his colleagues together to pull as one for the good of the whole. As chair, Paul Speck Jr. had a knack for balancing both the temperate and the direct through humour. Some of his colleagues had a hypothetical timer at meetings, taking bets on how long it would take for Paul to say the f-word. When he did, they'd hit the imaginary timer and holler out the winning time. He never said it to anyone personally, but used it in a respectful way to get people laughing and to break the tension at pivotal moments.

By the time Paul was forty, Henry of Pelham was considered to be established. He was acutely aware that, even as young as he and his brothers were, there were twenty-one-year-old sommeliers who had been infants when the brothers began. Along with him and his family's winery, the industry was maturing, and already he felt the bittersweetness of a new era. The early days when they were small, young and single-minded would never return. There was a creative glee that permeated everyone's collaboration in those days. It was as if a deck of random names was tossed in the air, and what the gods sent down was a group of like-minded people who got along well and who enjoyed one another's company. They were individuals who worked together for a better collective deal rather than just their immediate commercial interests. Paul was able to rise to the challenge of his times, enable others to replace the broken links with the past and create new and meaningful ones. Paul's talent as a consensus-seeker was the oil in the hinge that opened the door to this seminal time — a once-in-a-lifetime period in the course of the new industry's evolution.

7 DON TRIGGS AND THE RISE OF VINCOR

"Life is either a daring adventure or nothing."

—Helen Keller

B
ob Luba had kept in touch with the career of his former marketing manager Don Triggs ever since Triggs had worked for him in the 1970s at John Labatt, Ltd. Luba was then senior vice-president of packaged foods, which included the company's wineries, grouped under a holding company called Ridout. In 1971 Triggs was hired by Peter Widdrington, Labatt's president, to build the Cartier wine and beverage division of Ridout's numerous wine brands, and he soon became the vice-president of its U.S. holding, La Mont wines, the largest winemaking facility in the United States. The Canadian property, Chateau Gai, had also been part of the Ridout group.

"Do you remember Allan Jackson?" asked Luba, "the VP of operations at Chateau Gai?"

"Of course," replied Triggs. "Labatt hired him in 1977 to oversee wine-making for the company."

"Labatt's is looking to sell their wine holdings, and Allan came to speak to me about a management buyout. I told him they would need a person experienced in managing buyout and acquisition situations. Any interest?"

Luba had left Labatt in 1983 to head Crown Life Insurance and then the Royal Bank Management Investment Inc. By 1989, he was a partner in an investment firm that specialized in mid-market investments. Triggs, after ten years with Labatt, had also moved on to run the North American division of Fisons PLC, a global U.K.-based firm that sold pharmaceuticals, scientific equipment and horticultural products. This day, seven years later, Luba was calling Triggs about a possible investment opportunity.

Triggs had managed his division at Fisons through several mergers and acquisitions as they consolidated the company to be more competitive in international markets. He knew the territory well, but he also knew that the entire wine division of Labatt had been regarded as the black sheep among the company's larger diversified divisions when he was running it in the late 1970s. On the other hand, when Labatt bought Chateau Gai in 1973, they soon followed with the purchase of Casabello in British Columbia and Stonecroft Cellars in Alberta, which amounted to a lot of real estate to consider.

"Well, what do you think?" said Luba.

"I think it's intriguing," said Triggs, "but I've just accepted the job as chairman and CEO of Fisons' horticultural division for the world, with responsibility for divisions in the United Kingdom, France, Belgium, India, Canada and the United States. Elaine and I and the girls are moving to Ipswich in the fall."

"Why don't you come down and just look at the numbers?" suggested Luba in a nothing-ventured, nothing-gained tone.

Don Triggs was educated in agriculture, with a major in honours economics at the University of Manitoba, but his real brilliance was in strategy, marketing, finance and team leadership, talents he honed and expanded at the Ivey School of Business, where he earned an MBA in 1968. It was at Ivey that he also learned what it meant to think strategically — to anticipate where the train could head rather than simply meeting it when it arrived. His ability to visualize and project trends and tastes had consistently amazed his colleagues. If anyone could size up the potential of the Labatt deal, Triggs could.

Labatt's was a conglomerate of several disparate enterprises that included

Catelli pasta, Olgilvie flour, Sealtest dairy, Laura Secord chocolates, the Toronto Blue Jays, The Sports Network and a New York City-based rock music talent agency. By 1989, only 30 percent of their revenue came from brewing. But now the clock was ticking on the viability of their future. Most of their businesses had been protected by tariffs, which were now being taken away by the free trade agreement. Stock prices were depressed and Labatt was under pressure to divest.

The winery managers from across Canada knew something was going to happen, because the interests of beer and the interests of wine were not aligned under the agreement. As far as the feds were concerned, the wine business was an easy "give up." Because the brewery business was nine times larger than the wine industry, they managed to win an exemption from the free trade agreement. The wine industry was unable to do so. If Labatt was to remain globally competitive, they had to return to their core business, brewing, and expand their distribution and production capacity outside the United States. For that they needed money; so the divestitures began.

In February 1989, the general managers met at the Chateau Gai winery in Niagara Falls. As they sat around the table, it became apparent that their moods were as grey as the day. No one felt confident about the future. All they knew for sure was the inevitability of imminent change.

"We should look at doing a buyout," suggested one manager, an idea that the others regarded as sheer madness.

"No, I'm serious," he said emphatically.

It was true that there had been an increase in the past ten years in the number and type of leveraged buyout financing sources available. He persisted until they conceded to run some scenarios of current sales and profitability. They moved the meeting to the office of the company's financial analyst, Peter Patchet, who ran some spreadsheets that projected the possibilities. The figures looked as if a buyout could be very interesting.

Allan Jackson explained their bold idea to the president of Chateau Gai, who responded as any right-minded executive might during a time of such chaotic and upside-down change as their company was experiencing. He refused to support them, which temporarily made them reconsider their resolve. But upside-down change required upside-down thinking, so before they gave up their idea entirely they sought professional advice from a trusted investment analyst, their old boss Bob Luba.

Allan Jackson and Peter Patchet made an appointment to see Luba. On the way up in the elevator to Luba's office, Allan's mood about the project vacillated from total uncertainty to measured confidence. "He's either going to go into hysterics of laughter and think we're nuts," said Allan, "or think maybe there's something here."

Luba could see it was a dicey proposition. The managers didn't have a lot of money, and free trade was a real question mark in his mind. Free trade was the reason Labatt was selling. With the protective tariff on American wine taken off the table, there would be no preferential treatment for Canadian wine. On the other hand, Allan's figures painted a different landscape that showed a path to a renewed, even a transformed, industry. There was beer in the Labatt glass that they saw as half-empty. Allan Jackson and his colleagues had wine in theirs, which they just knew was half-full. Luba felt, perhaps, if they could refocus their energies on generating cash flow rather than market share, they could create a reasonable business over time. Yet a lending institution would look for someone in the group with broader management experience, one who understood finance and international markets and had the finesse required to stick-handle a restructured company based on cash flow and not market share. That's when he called Don Triggs, a man he knew possessed the wherewithal to lead a management buyout. He also knew Triggs had an irrepressible and unrequited entrepreneurial gene in his makeup.

Triggs weighed Luba's proposition to go down to Niagara and take a look at the numbers. He knew that the move to Ipswich, England, could be upsetting for his family. His wife would have to interrupt her studies as a chartered accountant and their three daughters were at those maximum-inflexibility ages of thirteen, fifteen and seventeen. Perhaps he should at least explore the Labatt deal. Triggs went to his boss at Fisons and said, "I have an opportunity to buy into the wine business and I've always had a desire to have my own business. I feel like this is a ship passing in the night." Knowing full well he might lose one of his star employees, his boss said, "Go ahead. Check it out."

For three months, instead of going to Vancouver to be with his family at the end of his ten-day multi-country round of meetings, Triggs headed for Toronto to do due diligence on the deal. He was very tough and determined to do it thoroughly — like a bulldog with a bone, once he thought an idea might be on the right track, he wouldn't let go. As the son of a grain and cattle farmer in rural Manitoba, he had learned the meaning of hard work and possessed the energy it required to do it well. He was also extremely competitive, a characteristic he developed as an identical twin, who, like most twins, grew up constantly testing who was faster, smarter, taller, stronger. If a wine business could provide a base to be the best, he would find a way to accomplish the buyout.

While Triggs was checking financial forecasts and interest coverage ratios and verifying the facts and assumptions contained in the offering circular, Luba was locating potential investment companies and coaching Allan Jackson in ways he might generate cash flow to demonstrate their capacity to repay the loan. Triggs, Jackson and Luba's strategy was four-fold: reduce working capital, squeeze other assets, generate new sales and streamline all processes, including a reduction of around 10 percent in the payroll.

Triggs believed that it was a stretch, but could see hitting the goal of a 50-percent increase in profit over two years, an increase that they would need to keep their financing in place. This was a critical decision. Don did not have his job at stake should they lose out on the deal. His present job was challenging, and he had just been promoted and was the first non-British executive to be invited to sit on the main board of directors of Fisons PLC. Not only was he considering leaving an attractive career at Fisons, but he was also considering investing to become the largest single shareholder if the buyout was successful. When he chatted with some of his best friends and advisers, it was all they could do to avoid breaking out in laughter.

But Triggs saw some positive opportunities that suggested it could be done. The Free Trade Agreement was bolstered by a federal government fund to assist in the grubbing out of *labrusca* varieties and included incentives that encouraged the planting of the preferred *vinifera* varieties. The FTA also agreed to allow the importation of blended wine. This would allow wineries to convert to more acceptable flavour profiles in the near term while they waited on the newly planted vineyards to bear fruit. Triggs also saw a lot of fat on the company's balance sheet and also in the operating budgets. In some ways the company had also developed some bad habits under the protective wing of Labatt. The executive team was unanimous in their belief that leaving the Labatt nest would be, overall, a net positive. One example was its receivables, which were inflated to over three months.

Following the purchase, those receivables would be reduced to less than thirty days and at one point reached fifteen days outstanding. This reduction in receivables was the single most important event in reducing the company's debt to more manageable levels. Triggs personally monitored the cash flow on a daily basis and would not allow money to be spent if the funds were not in the bank to cover the expenditure.

Triggs gave much thought as to how the team could be brought together to manage the transition. It would be led by four senior partners: Allan Jackson as senior vice-president responsible for winery operations; John Hall as vice-president and general manager of Ontario sales and marketing; Peter Grainger as vice-president and general manager of Atlantic Canada; and Triggs as the president and CEO. Triggs knew that he needed a world-class team if he was going to be successful in building a world-class business

Meanwhile, Jackson found ways to do a better job at collecting receivables while stretching payables as long as possible. He found ways to tighten up the supply chain by being in touch with his managers at the properties and asking them daily how many cases they had in inventory and what was the value. If a manager was going to package anything, he needed to get Jackson's approval. If they had an order for two thousand cases of L'Ambience and Jackson had fifteen hundred on hand, he'd give the okay to run half a shift of a thousand cases and keep the remainder for their retail stores. The more of a month's inventory they were carrying, the greater the loan, and the higher the interest, so Jackson paid close attention to the amount of finished goods they had compared to what they could sell.

Jackson conceived of several other ways to generate revenue. One was a project he created with David Nichol, the marketing whiz from President's Choice, to brew iced tea in the winery's unused tanks and bottle it. Another project solved the problem of the devalued wine he had inside many of his other tanks. As a result of free trade, the *labrusca*-based wine was now worth one-quarter of the price he had originally paid. With good advice from a tax lawyer, Jackson made a visit to Revenue Canada to convince them to forgive the taxes on those wines for five years. This saved the company millions of dollars at a critical time. It was cost-savings and cash-flow-generating measures like these that persuaded a German bank, the Dresdner, to back the buyout in principle, but for how much money, Luba could not yet say.

It didn't take long for Luba to see the potential that the deal presented and become a partner, taking equity out in shares rather than charging for his services. His next move was to speak about their bid to the CFO at Labatt, Bob Vaux, a man Luba had hired for Labatt a decade before.

"We'd like to buy the business and put in a bid," said Luba. "If we put in a bid, are you prepared to accept it?"

Vaux replied, "We've got a process and we want to see who else is interested and what their price might be."

"I can understand that," replied Luba, "but it's your own employees who want to bid. Would you give us the right to match the bid?"

"Yes," said the CFO. "Yes, we will."

On a Thursday afternoon several weeks later, Luba heard that Labatt had accepted a bid from Joe Peller, president of Andrés Wines, without informing Luba. Although formal papers hadn't been signed, Peller was announcing the handshake deal to his people who were on a retreat in Florida. Luba immediately called Vaux.

"I understand there is this rumour. Is it correct?" asked Luba.

"Yes," replied Vaux.

"You can't do that," said Luba.

"Well, we've done it," countered Vaux.

"You can't do it. You gave me your word," asserted Luba.

"We've done it," fired Vaux. "You guys don't have the money and I've got a bird in the hand who is the logical buyer."

The gloves were off and the masks removed.

"You simply can't do this," contended Luba. "You gave me your word. The employees deserve this." Determined, Luba pulled rank and ended the conversation: "I want to see you first thing Monday morning."

Vaux was now facing an ethical dilemma. Should he break his word to his employees or to his prospective buyer? In what ways might one promise trump the other?

The partners needed financial leverage, true, but now they needed more than financing. They needed moral suasion. When Allen Jackson got word of Luba's conversation with Vaux, he flew back from a meeting in British Columbia and spent the weekend in Niagara gathering the only support he knew could sway Vaux — pressure from the union to whom he promised no job losses or salary modifications. Monday morning Jackson handed Luba a stack of letters from the employees.

"Before we start Bob, have a look at this," said Luba when he met Vaux.

"Shit," said Vaux. "What's your price?"

Luba replied, "Same as Andrés."

"But you don't know what it is," contended Vaux.

"I told you we would match the price!" retaliated Luba. "If it makes sense to Andrés, it will make sense for us, plus!"

Relenting, Vaux replied, "I'll give you ten days to come back with a bid and your financing in place."

Luba now had a figure with which he approached the Dresdner Bank. Although their terms were better than the Canadian lender he was also exploring, their processes of doing business were ponderously slow and methodical. Vaux was now calling every day, embarrassed because Andrés had gone away disappointed and angry. He didn't want to be held responsible for losing the deal. The ten-day deadline came and went. It would take three weeks before Luba could get all the financing in place. The four partners had raised $1.5 million by mortgaging their homes, selling their cottages, boats and second cars. Sixteen other employees chipped in as well. The Dresdner Bank came through and lent them the rest — $26.5 million.

July 5, 1989, only five months after Jackson's initial conversation with Luba, the deal was struck and a new company was created, which they called Cartier Wines, the name of the former wine marketing division of Ridout. In a few strokes of a pen the business was converted from one in a financially healthy condition with little debt to one with a massive debt and two major competitors biting at their heels.

If the Dresdner Bank provided the financial leverage to lift the partners from being employees to proprietors, Luba was the fulcrum, the influential pivot around which the success of the deal hinged. Luba understood that management-leveraged buyouts contain a certain conflict of interest. Before buyout, there could be incentive for managers to mismanage the company, thereby depressing stock prices and then, once the company is sold to them, profit by implementing more sound practices. Luba had avoided that conflict by telling Vaux that the managers would match any bid that was acceptable to Labatt. Of course, it didn't hurt that Luba's previous stellar employment record with Labatt underpinned their trust.

Don Triggs resigned from Fisons the same day the deal was signed, working up to that time with Jackson and Luba by daily phone conversations.

Now in town, they worked with military discipline to drive cash flow. They were all well aware of the things that could go wrong. They could have overreached their financial ability to pay and defaulted on their loan. There could have been irreconcilable differences among the partners as to how to respond appropriately to their need to generate cash flow. Talented individuals could have defected. With very little operating slack, any unanticipated strain on their finances could have had disastrous consequences, and, for all these reasons, it almost did.

While the business had to operate to meet very demanding cash-flow targets, Triggs also marshalled his troops to fine-tune a long-term vision for the business. It was clear in Triggs's mind that, with the free-trade impact of lower markups and retail prices on imported wines, the company would need to become more cost efficient. One possible way to do this would be to grow rapidly, possibly by acquisition. Triggs also saw the segment for premium wine growing, and spent many hours working to convince some of the other senior partners and managers, who were more comfortable with the winecooler and blended-*vin-ordinaire* segments, to move to a more premium platform. Triggs saw these two strategies, "Scale and Premium," as critical to the future of the business and set about combining these strategies with a focus on excellence.

These initial strategic sessions also crystallized some values that became the foundation of the company's culture, and they were implemented rigorously throughout the business. He emphasized a performance culture, rather than one of entitlement, in which compensation was tightly tied to results. Each manager negotiated targets for his and her area, targets that were always set in the context of "best in the world," not just "best in the wine industry." The operating costs and results of a salesman or plant manager were compared with the performance of top companies in the world. "Management by Objectives" was one of the key strategies that allowed them to expand so quickly. It allowed the company to monitor manager performance at key checkpoints while staying out of the way and letting managers drive for their objectives.

As a new entity they had to go through the delicate transition from being a partnership of equals to being a corporation with a legal structure regulated by provincial law. Being owners didn't entitle them to make decisions independently of the others without consultation. As it happened,

Don Triggs, president of Vincor, 1993–2006

one of the partners had a strategy to garner additional cash flow, which the bankers and other partners couldn't support. Because Luba had included a shareholders' agreement that outlined the measures that would be taken if a person left the corporation, any vitriol would be avoided. The leaving manager would offer his shares to the remaining partners, and, because the partners were of limited means, they could pay him over a period of time.

The partner's departure couldn't have happened at a worse time. Even Don Triggs, the constant optimist, asked himself, *What am I doing?* This period of heavy debt would be one that Triggs and the other partners would live through, but one they vowed they would never get into again. In the end it turned out well. John Hall, the departing partner, took his shares and invested in Reider Distillery, which he later renamed Kittling Ridge, and built a very successful wine and spirits operation producing one of the finest whiskeys in Canada. The remaining partners survived their financial crunch and were able to pay down the debt by half within two years, which enabled a new bank to listen when Triggs approached it with his first proposition for an acquisition.

Triggs always saw the future in premium wines. Being a pragmatist, he figured there were two ways of developing that vision: by developing their own brands and vineyards or by acquiring or merging with the best premium wineries that they could afford to buy. An acquisition or merger would get them out of the gate sooner. They had a national sales force and a substantial retail chain in Ontario that could give a premium winery the chance to grow faster, which in turn would add more synergy and better return in a shorter span of time. Inniskillin had been operating for seventeen years as a successful premium winery with an accomplished reputation. Part of Inniskillin's success was the fact that Donald Ziraldo was everywhere and people related to him. He was sharp, appealing, fashionable and smart — the chic embodiment of his brand. He had established a strong export network that garnered international media attention from Napa to Verona, with the best agents in the world representing Inniskillin.

His marketing strategy was the same as it was the first time he hit the road in 1974 — he continued to go to high-end restaurants, high-end retail stores and the best sommeliers to get them excited about a new region they could promote. After Inniskillin had won the coveted Grand Prix d'Honneur for its Icewine at Vinexpo, the prestigious wine competition held biannually in Bordeaux, sales soared.

When Don Triggs approached Donald Ziraldo with his proposition, the timing was right. Ziraldo had spent six years devoting his energies to getting the industry consolidated behind the VQA, giving the smaller players a stable platform. It seemed like a good time to initiate change.

"Donald, you're the best there is," began Triggs. "Here is what we might do together." For the next twelve Sundays, Triggs and Ziraldo met over breakfast, sorting out the valuation of both their businesses to reach an agreement on what was acceptable to both. Ziraldo saw a merger as an opportunity to expand nationally and gain access to the independent retail stores owned by Vincor in Ontario. With Inniskillin, Don's new company, Cartier Wines, could get a foothold in the premium market faster. Ziraldo and Triggs struck the deal.

Within a few months Don Triggs orchestrated the purchase of Okanagan Vineyards in Oliver, B.C., and changed its name to Inniskillin Okanagan, thereby expanding the Inniskillin brand out west. It was a merger of minds and strategy, but in financial terms, it was a share exchange, with Inniskillin giving up ownership. Triggs respected Ziraldo and the business and reputation he had grown. He saw him as a visionary.

When Ziraldo announced the merger with Cartier Wines to a gathering of industry associates and friends, the intake of breath was audible. He had been their leader for so many years. He had become the personification of all they strived for; why would he abandon them now? Many people in the industry never got over Ziraldo's merger with Cartier. For most others, he was living proof of the viability of the vision he had forged for the industry for so many years. If a large company such as Cartier could invite him and his winery into their fold, perhaps the vision for the VQA could have more power in the marketplace. For one year, 1992–1993, the new business would be called Cartier-Inniskillin Vintners. During that time, the merged management team focused the integration on developing new world-class incentive programs and operating practices for what was to evolve into what Triggs proudly referred to as "the Vincor All-Star Team."

Cartier got the jewel in the crown of Canadian wineries, swiftly establishing them in the premium and ultra-premium wine category. Inniskillin gained a broader retail presence as part of the off-premise network of stores that Cartier had accumulated. However, perhaps Inniskillin's most significant enhancement was eventually gaining the marketing brilliance of Roger Provost, who in 1996 would become the executive vice-president for Vincor's international division and Donald's closest ally in the international sale of icewine.

Provost, a ten-year veteran with the luxury cognac Courvoisier, had been hired by Triggs to build the business internationally. As far as he was concerned, the last thing the world needed was another Chardonnay, especially if it came from Canada. Icewine, on the other hand, was something unique that could provide a sustainable competitive advantage with other players from around the world, so he chose to focus on Inniskillin's icewine. Once Canada was established as a winemaking region, its other wines could be introduced.

He called his marketing plan "Ice Storm," so named after the Gulf War ("Operation Desert Storm") that was still fresh in the minds of people all over the world. His objective was to invade the world with Inniskillin icewine, building both Inniskillin and the entire category of icewine — which was a wine quite unfamiliar to consumers at the time. His strategy was to position icewine as a luxury product, competing in the luxury segment of alcoholic beverages. He'd focus on duty-free stores in the Asia Pacific sector, where it flew off the shelves. In the United States, he hired sales representatives in six major cities and had them call on the top-100 *Wine Spectator* honour roll of restaurants to get listed. Over time they got four thousand establishments to sell it by the glass. Then they did the same thing in Europe, and even made a media splash as the first entry of icewine in China, with Ziraldo smiling broadly with a bottle of icewine in front of the Great Wall. Provost and Ziraldo worked well together. Provost saw Ziraldo as essential to the promotion as the key ambassador, and Ziraldo respected Provost's character and experience. The whole campaign elevated the stature of Inniskillin beyond Ziraldo's greatest hopes.

But all this happened after 1996. Between 1993 and 1996, the integration of Inniskillin within Cartier had the expected organizational collisions, as does any merger of two cultures, especially when it contains two strong leaders. With such a large company, Don Triggs had to manage many priorities. Although they had identified the need for some investment in the hospitality, retail and tour program at Inniskillin, it took over five years to arrive at an agreement for the budget on the project. In the initial years there was an expectation of an expenditure so large that a financial return would have been impossible; unfortunately, it took a long time to agree on a plan that made good marketing and financial sense.

The first vintage of Jackson-Triggs was launched in the fall of 1993, a brand erected from scratch to over five hundred thousand cases before the company erected a dedicated winery, which opened in mid-2001. That was ten years without an address to market the brand. Finally, Triggs felt they could not wait any longer or opportunity would pass them by. Jackson-Triggs was the second-largest VQA brand in Canada and required additional capacity, not just a new home. The financial return was the highest in the history of the company for internally generated projects. They scoured the world to bring the latest winemaking technology and hospitality services to the project. They wanted the winery to be a leader in all aspects of quality, design and marketing and promotion. Part of the strategic vision was to continue to drive the quality of Canadian wine higher and higher. Triggs and his wife, Elaine, even bought a vineyard of their own — called Delaine — dedicated to growing premium quality grapes.

The integration of Inniskillin into the Cartier culture was a blip on the radar compared to the integration that was soon to follow. They were just finishing the Inniskillin integration, aligning systems and staff, when they learned that Bright's might be up for sale. However they were not in a position to move until they had completed the integration. It would be another six to twelve months before they would be able to take on something new — especially something as large as Bright's.

Triggs realized that the two companies, Bright's and Cartier, had completely parallel footprints across the country. Cartier had a winery in British Columbia, two in Ontario and one in New Brunswick, while Bright's had wineries in British Columbia, Ontario, Quebec, and Nova Scotia. The economics of putting them together could be significant. When Triggs learned that entrepreneurial genius Gerry Schwartz, president of Onex Corporation, had a commitment with the Hatch family to sell their shares to him and no one else, Triggs immediately went to Schwartz and offered him $5 million to sell his lockup to Cartier-Inniskillin. Triggs proposed that Schwartz sell his shares to Cartier and facilitate Cartier's acquisition of Bright's. Schwartz looked at Triggs and said, "If it's worth that much to you, we'll talk after the deal is done."

The managers at Cartier–Inniskillin took this casual suggestion with a grain of salt. But, less than three months after Schwartz had bought Bright's in 1993, he phoned Triggs to see how they might put their businesses together, and invited Triggs and Donald Ziraldo to his home for lunch to discuss the possibilities. Two bottles of 1961 Lafite Rothchild later, the deal was informally struck. By the time lunch was over, Schwartz felt confident with the economic potential of a merger, and equally comfortable about the leadership talent that resided in both Don and Donald. All three men were about to change the competitive landscape of the wine industry in Canada.

There were significant operational synergies and cost reductions to access — easy on paper but complicated to enact. Schwartz had paid $50 million for Bright's and now he was offering to buy out Cartier-Inniskillin. The key shareholders at Cartier had accepted a deal to merge with Bright's, with the key Cartier shareholders receiving 80 percent of the purchase price for Cartier in cash and 20 percent being rolled over into stock in the new company, which would own both Bright's and Cartier. When the deal was done between Cartier shareholders, Schwartz made the bold move of asking Triggs to become CEO, Allan Jackson to become senior vice-president of operations, and Allan George to become CFO — and all to sign employment contracts to run the combined enterprise. In reality, this amounted to a reverse takeover. The smaller entity was to control the larger one.

In the sale of Cartier-Inniskillin Vintners, the partners got 80 percent of their money back from the 1989 leveraged buyout of Chateau Gai from Labatt's. Schwartz's newly combined company bought the Cartier–Inniskillin shares and the partners hung around as shareholders in the new company, maintaining a stake in the business. They paid back their original Dresdner Bank loan in full. The intention was to put the combined entity together and eventually go public. Prior to the sale, Bright's was private and Cartier-Inniskillin was private. Together they would realize economies of scale, sell off real estate and then go public with the new organization to generate more revenue for further growth. The consolidation deal, backed by Onex Corporation president and CEO Gerald Schwartz and the Ontario Teachers' Pension Plan, doubled annual sales to $125 million and marked the creation of the eighth-largest wine company in North America. A new company was forged: Bright-Cartier-Inniskillin Vintners.

For three months until the deal was closed, the managers at both Bright's and Cartier assumed they would each have a shot at running the operation, so they were all busily making plans for integration. Triggs and Jackson felt that they were in a good position, but they couldn't say for sure, as the deal to sell the company had been done before there were any discussions as to whom the future management would be. For Jackson it was the worst three months of his life. The corporate cultures at each organization were dramatically different. Bright's was more laissez-faire. If a salesman agreed to his sales targets, even if he didn't respect his expense allowance, and yet had solutions for the problems he faced, he was left alone. Cartier-Inniskillin was more disciplined — expense accounts were reined in, accounting systems were tightly monitored and inventories minimized.

Those differences were differences in business practices that could be relatively easily introduced. Far too many mergers failed, however, not because of differences in accounting or operational systems, but because of the mishandling of people. Triggs and Jackson were determined to avoid that. They were to follow a strategy that systematically drew from the best people each business possessed to create a company that was neither Bright's nor Cartier-Inniskillin. Triggs's goal was to draft an all-star team, the best from both companies. It became a whole new world of rationalizations that happened very quickly with accompanying high levels of discomfort and resistance to change. It was three years of very heavy lifting on all sides. The Bright's union seniority list, for instance, was the source of one of the most difficult issues they had to resolve. Bright's union thought that since their company bought Cartier-Inniskillin, the top people on their seniority list should be retained and what was left over in terms of personnel needs the Cartier-Inniskillin employees would top up. If the combined companies needed seventy people and there were fifty on the Bright's seniority list, fifty spots would go to Bright's and the remaining twenty would come from Cartier-Inniskillin.

This strategy, however, would not allow Triggs and Jackson to hire the best from both companies. Nor was Jackson going to abandon the union people from Chateau Gai who had rallied to support the earlier leveraged buyout. Without the union support there would have been no buyout. With the advice of three different labour lawyers, Jackson tried to explain the principle and necessity of dovetailing. In other words, each union's seniority list would be dovetailed with the other until a combined workforce was selected, fifty-fifty. Jackson was not a popular guy. There were times he jokingly asked his chief winemaker, Mira Ananciz, if she would go start his car.

They followed a similar strategy with non-union personnel. Sales managers from both sides were asked to put forward the names of their best employees from which the best of the best survived. To the employees at

Bright's, the new regime was introducing budgets, sales targets and other promotional objectives, which were monitored monthly. To the managers at Cartier-Inniskillin, they were merely reconciling the differences through sound business practices. Some individuals resigned, some were let go, others were promoted, but in the end the new company, renamed Vincor International, Ltd., came out with significant efficiencies of production and scale and a massive and dynamic sales force across the country.

In 1996 Vincor went public, which gave them the resources to develop an international business. The first step in becoming a public company came when they bought Dumont Vins et Spiriteaux in January of 1996. This doubled their market share in Quebec and became the sizzle that attracted investors. By June they were a public company. Domestically, Triggs had the promotion of premium wines on his mind, and was determined to build another winery, this time from scratch — one that came in just under the ultra-premium brands from Inniskillin but above the *vin ordinaire* and imported blended lines of the Chateau Gai and Bright's brands. He saw a huge segment of the market that he thought a new winery could fill.

In 1997, when Triggs brought the idea forward to his managers, there was animated debate, mostly negative. Triggs encouraged the exchange of ideas, often paraphrasing John Stuart Mill: "An idea that could not withstand vigorous debate would not survive." His managers spoke freely and vigorously against it. Visibly displeased, in a moment of exasperation he stood up and gave each manager a piece of paper saying, "Okay, you've heard the pros and cons of the project. You've seen the numbers. Vote yes or no and we'll go with a majority decision," and then he left the room.

When he returned, they counted the votes. The new project was a go. As one senior executive later explained, "Despite having a hard time getting people on board, as with most things, we all realized he probably saw the market better than we did, and all but a couple of us changed our vote. In the end, he was proved right."

They would name the new winery Jackson-Triggs to connote the personal pride that the proprietors took in their wine. Vincor launched the brand in 1993, making the wine out of their Niagara Falls facility for seven years. In 2001, they opened their new multimillion-dollar facility in Niagara-on-the-Lake amid sixteen acres (six hectares) of vines in vineyards. The Jackson-Triggs label went on to became Canada's number-one VQA selling brand, producing 250,000 cases annually, about half of which were produced at Jackson-Triggs Okanagan. The establishment of the Jackson-Triggs brand was a critical turning point in the company.

When Vincor went public on the Toronto Stock Exchange in 1996, it raised $40 million at $8 a share, then rapidly continued to expand its revenue base in a flurry of milestone acquisitions: London Winery, R.J. Grape (1997), Spagnols (1998), Le Clos Jordanne joint venture with Boisset (1999), Hawthorn Mountain, Sumac Ridge and a joint venture with Groupe Taillan (2000).

It was clear in early 1999 that Vincor was at a critical point in its evolution. The company had become very successful in Canada. It had developed a broad portfolio that covered all sectors of the market and was selling one out of every 4.5 bottles of wine consumed in Canada. Vincor's sales and profits had grown every year since it went public in 1996, and in fact since its inception in 1989, but financial markets were not happy. Because Vincor had amassed a very large share of the Canadian market, financial analysts were questioning how it was going to continue to grow at the pace of the past few years, especially since further acquisitions in Canada were becoming fewer and less practical. It upset Triggs when he heard that analysts who were in the middle of the dot-com binge were describing Vincor as part of the old-world economy, especially when many of the dot-comers had never made a nickel of profit. Senior management and the board undertook a strategic review of the global market and concluded that there was an opportunity to build a new-world wine company with a portfolio of new-world brands that could be marketed in the highest-gross-margin new-world markets. The company would focus on buying brands in the rapidly growing super-premium segment and in countries where the margin per case on super-premium wine was in the top five in the world. In addition, it would buy only companies that already had in place highly effective sales forces and marketing and distribution capabilities in their home markets. It was careful not to overpay by following strict financial guidelines to ensure the achievement of acceptable returns. Vincor's vision was to build a portfolio of brands which would complement its Canadian portfolio so that the sales forces in every country would be able to carry more clout and service to the individual retail or licensee buyer. The company could now use its U.S. sales force to sell its Canadian, Australian and New Zealand wines in the United States and its Canadian sales force to sell its Californian, Australian and New Zealand wines in Canada.

Vincor purchased R.H. Phillips in 2000, Hogue Cellars in 2001, Goundry in 2002, Kim Crawford in 2003, Amberly and Western Wine — a U.K. distribution company that included a South African brand, Kumala — in 2004. Hardly a year went by that they didn't mark with an acquisition.

He was convinced that the quality of their Canadian wines could be improved if Vincor could access the viticultural expertise of Burgundy and Bordeaux. Triggs and Jones went to France many times between 1998 and 2001 with the specific goal of finding a French partner would work on a fifty/fifty basis with Vincor. The brain trust at Vincor believed that Chardonnay, Riesling and Pinot Noir had the greatest potential in Ontario, and that the Bordeaux varieties (Cabernet Savignon, Merlot, Cabernet Franc, Malbec, Petit Verdot , Sauvignon Blanc and Semillon) had star quality in the Okanagan. The French partner would have total technical control over viticulture and winemaking, while Vincor would bring along its sales, marketing and financial expertise. Both partners would invest equally, and the companies would be run by a separate board, with directors nominated from both companies. Triggs and his team scoured the Niagara Peninsula and the south Okanagan for sites, which were then subjected to exhaustive study by the French partners, who also assisted in recruiting talented winemakers and relocating them to Niagara and Oliver. The Boisset family of Clos Vougeot became Vincor's fifty/fifty partner in Le Clos Jordanne of Niagara and the Antoine Merlaut family of the Taillon group — who owned five châteaux in Bordeaux, including Gruard Larose — became a fifty/fifty partner in Osoyoos–Larose of the south Okanagan.

Triggs and Jones also saw a huge quality and volume opportunity for Okanagan wines, but were stymied by the fact that most holdings suitable for vineyard development were ten acres or less, and often included numerous houses and other buildings, making the acquisition of vineyard land very slow and expensive. Vincor already had a relationship with the N K Mip Indian band of Oliver, where Vincor's winery had been built on land leased from the band. Two-thirds of the employees at the winery came from the N K Mip band. Triggs went to see Sam Baptiste, the former chief, and Clarence Louie, the current chief, about the possibility of leasing land from the band. The band had over a thousand acres of prime land on which it was currently grazing cattle and horses on sagebrush and which had prime vineyard potential.

After almost a year of negotiations, a deal was struck that resulted in over 850 acres of N K Mip–owned land being planted to vineyard within the next ten years. The plan called for Vincor to operate the vineyard on long-term leases, selling the fruit to Jackson-Triggs. It helped Jackson-Triggs win the title of Best Canadian Winery of the Year four times at the London International wines show.

The partnership evolved to include a joint venture, creating the N K Mip winery, with Vincor owning 49 percent and the band 51 percent and each working through an independent board of directors. The band saw increased employment at the winery and in the vineyard and received over $2 million per year from Vincor in wages and lease payments. For its part, Vincor had a steady supply of quality grapes that became the backbone of its series of award-winning premium wines.

Triggs, with his CFO, Richard Jones, sought to build a portfolio of products they could sell, and visited every property. For retailer or restaurateur, a portfolio of products with wines from all over the world was a more efficient sell. Triggs and Jones lived on planes in a campaign of research, targeting the segments of the market they wanted to be in and calling on prospects they thought might be willing to sell. Some threw them out and some were receptive; others were eager. Triggs and Jones walked away from deals until they found the right one.

Shares in Vincor kept rising annually until August 2005, when, after disappointing quarterly results, shares plunged 13 percent, making the company very vulnerable. The Kumala brand from the UK acquisition wasn't making the returns they had anticipated. Like a lion eyeing the weakest prey in the herd, Constellation Brands, the largest wine company in the world, fired off an unsolicited takeover bid to acquire Vincor for $31 a share, a cash offer worth $1.4 billion.

Don Triggs dropped the gauntlet by stating the bid was "opportunistic and inadequate," hoping their shareholders would not accept it, but he didn't ignore it. He confronted the problem directly by forming a special committee of the board to consider alternatives. Mark Hillson, chairman of the board and of the special committee of independent directors, soon issued a statement:

After careful consideration and analysis and receipt of the recommendation of the Special Committee, the Board of Directors unanimously recommends that Vincor's shareholders reject the Offer from Constellation to acquire all of the outstanding shares of Vincor International for a price of $31. We believe that this offer significantly undervalues the business operations of Vincor, a view supported by BMO Nesbitt Burns and Merrill Lynch ... the Board recommends that Vincor shareholders do not tender their shares to Constellation's inadequate offer.

Richard Sands, the CEO of Constellation Brands, sought to gain the advantage by coyly expressing his admiration for Triggs's accomplishments, then criticized Vincor's management for their mediocre performance outside Canada. "After all," claimed Sands, "Vincor isn't exactly a 'marquee brand' like Mondavi." In a final offensive, Sands then made the tactical mistake of suggesting to Triggs and Jones that Vincor might be worth up to $36 a share by virtue of its cost-saving synergies.

Vincor had not put the company up for sale, but it was now on the market. Triggs and the board had no option — it was a *fait accompli* that only the shareholders could resolve, but not without the directors making their recommendations as to whether the bid was acceptable or not. The managers and directors had to manage the press, while looking for other buyers in order to tease out the best price. Richard Jones, Vincor CFO, worked night and day building models and projections, creating presentations about the company for potential investors and getting the data room ready. Within twenty-four hours of the Constellation bid, the hedge fund buyers started buying shares with quick profit as their only interest, which resulted in Vincor losing almost half its loyal shareholders. Triggs and the directors had to convince the shareholders if they hung on it would eventually pay off — the quality in Okanagan Cellars, the strength of the Jackson-Triggs brand, the growth of the Kim Crawford brand in New Zealand, the momentum they had in the United States with Toasted Head — all those factors augured well for the future of the company.

In the course of the second meeting with Constellation, Sands said that they wanted to be friendly.

"We'll offer you $31 per share and if in due diligence we find its worth more, we'll up our bid." *What turnip truck to do you think we fell from?* thought the negotiating team from Vincor.

Constellation soon became hostile by issuing a letter to Vincor shareholders, stating that they, Constellation Brands, would offer $31 a share to buy the company. The lion was gaining on them. In a timely disclosure, Vincor retaliated by issuing a press release that questioned the $31 offering and reiterated Sands's earlier claim that Constellation might offer up to $36. The stock immediately went to $36, effectively killing the $31 bid. For Constellation it was an uphill battle after that. Triggs and Jones kept up their quarterly shareholder meetings and for the next few months met all the new shareholders and building shareholder loyalty — taking their lumps if they had bad results and taking their bows when the stocks showed positive results.

This was a critical time, with Triggs and Jones meeting shareholders in Toronto and New York every week and also calling all other shareholders on a weekly basis. Triggs was also concerned that the flurry of takeover activity might disorient and distract the management team. Triggs relied heavily on Frank Syer, the head of HR, to assist in organizing weekly communication sessions with the management teams in every country on a weekly basis. The managers were then responsible to take the communication out to all employees. They wanted the entire team to be totally informed. Most important, they did not want any key employee prematurely jumping ship out of anxiety over the future. The entire team stuck together in spite of many headhunters trying to seduce them away. As a consequence, shareholders were able to make an informed decision about holding or selling. Vincor's disclosure had caught Constellation flatfooted tactically and forced them to come back with another bid. This would give the managers the time they needed to improve their hand.

By Christmas, Constellation upped their bid to $33 a share. Could Triggs and his managers convince their investors to hold just a little longer? The $33 bid failed abysmally, with less than 25,000 out of 44 million shares tendering to the $33 bid. By March 15, 2006, a contrite Richard Sands called Triggs to begin talks again. Shortly after, in response to Sands's offer, Triggs announced that after taking advice from their advisers and board, the new bid represented "full and fair value" and it was "definitely in line with the expectations of our shareholders." At $36.50 a share, plus a 15-percent dividend, or $1.52 billion, it was roughly the same amount Constellation had paid for the "marquee brand" Mondavi in 2004 and BRL Hardy of Australia in 2003. On June 1, shareholders voted to sell, thus ending eight months of intense discussions. Observers of the acquisition were astounded. It was clear that Vincor's consistent strong financial performance over ten years and its sound long-term strategic position had clearly held the day when it came to valuing the company. For the managers and directors at Vincor it was like being in a high-stakes thriller — using outwitting manoeuvres, calibrating risks, standing firm on principles of worth. The *New York Times* wrote: "That any company, let alone the world's largest would want a Canadian winery at more than $1 billion surprises many people." For those shareholders who still owned the stock that they had purchased at $8 per share in 1996, the final return on the sale in 2006 averaged 16.99 percent, compounded every year for ten years. Triggs later confessed that he "took enormous satisfaction from the fact that the management team he had assembled was world class, that the company was strongly positioned for the future and that the shareholders had received an outstanding return." Not a bad day's work.

Don Triggs, the affable builder and champion strategist, quit the next day. Triggs felt no acrimony against Sands or his company. He felt that the culture, values and decentralized structure of Constellation Brands could be a fitting complement to Vincor. Their people were as passionate about the business as he and his colleagues were, but his independent spirit precluded implementing someone else's vision. CFO Richard Jones left within the year. Allan Jackson stayed on for two years to assist in the transition of operations. If it hadn't been for Allan's courage and initiative to pursue the idea of a management buyout, history would have taken a different turn. Bob Luba continued his own Toronto investment firm, Capital One. All of them exited with sufficient capital to relax and enjoy life.

And so, Don Triggs, the dirt farmer from Manitoba, the man whose unflinching business acumen and passion masterminded a young enterprise into becoming the fourth-largest wine company in North America and eighth-largest in the world, left the building. Bob Luba summarized the experience for them all: "There are only so many adventures in life and that was a truly great one."

8 PELLERS' CELLARS

"All the forces in the world are not so powerful as an idea whose time has come."

—Victor Hugo

A ndy Peller had an uncanny ability to challenge the entrepreneurial unknown with the optimism and excitement of a child in a playground — so many opportunities, so little time. He had owned a grocery store, a machine shop, a newspaper, a car dealership and a brewery, with only the machine shop and the brewery earning a profit. Despite the fact that up until this moment he had been kicked in the teeth several times, his resilience sustained him. His latest project was a winery in Port Moody, British Columbia. Midway through construction he realized that he was undercapitalized; his initial estimates had been insufficient. As a last resort he approached a bank for a $150,000 loan.

"Mr. Peller," said the bank manager, "I wouldn't give you a cent. You aren't going to get this business off the ground." It was 1961, and Andy's dream of bringing dry wines to the Canadian table was teetering.

"Oh well," replied Andy, "you don't have to give it to me. I just came to ask." Andy had faced rejections and disappointments in his life that were much worse than one man's opinion of him and his new venture.

As if a brusque refusal wasn't enough to diminish Andy, the unctuous banker added a final swipe: "You'd better forget about the whole thing and go home to Hamilton." Then he dismissed the fifty-eight-year-old Hungarian immigrant whose accent still bore the guttural inflections of his German mother tongue.

Andy was sizzling inside, but he wasn't discouraged; in fact, the episode re-energized him. Two banks later, he got his loan. Had he taken the first bank manager's advice and gone home to Hamilton, the story of Andrés Wines Ltd., later to become the eponymous Andrew Peller Ltd., Canada's largest Canadian-owned wine company, might have unfolded very differently, if at all.

Andrew (Andràs) Peller was born in 1903 in a German enclave in Hungary, the youngest of fourteen children, of whom only four lived. His father was a bricklayer, thin and sickly, who saw enterprise as unnecessary. "God will take care of everything," he'd say. Andy's mother, on the other hand, was an entrepreneurial dynamo, whose ingenuity helped to feed and clothe the family with the profits she made selling eggs, butter and candles on consignment. From his mother he inherited his irrepressible desire to address hard times with his own ingenuity and drive to succeed.

The First World War had left Andy and most other rural Hungarians depressed, poor and out of work. Jobs went first to returning soldiers, which created a pervasive restlessness. When he and his young wife, Lena, lost their first son to meningitis due to the unavailability of sound medical care, and then nearly lost their second, he knew he had to leave Hungary for a better life.

Friends had immigrated to Canada and extolled its beauty and the availability of jobs. When Andy learned that Canadian National Railway prepaid fare to Winnipeg from Budapest in return for a short commitment to work on a farm in Manitoba, he booked passage in March 1927, leaving pregnant Lena in Hungary until he could earn enough money to bring over his young family. By the end of May, Lena announced the birth of their third son, Andrew. More desperate now than ever to earn money, Andy took a train to southern Ontario, where he found a job working at a brewery in Kitchener that was in need of mechanics to loosen up the inactive equipment that had rusted during Prohibition.

He finally had a better-paying job when a dreadful letter from Lena arrived, telling him that their new son, Andrew, whom Andy had never seen, had died of pneumonia. They were devastated and wanted desperately to be together. By October 1927, Lena, Andy and their son, Joe, were united again.

A salesman visiting the Kitchener brewery mentioned that Cosgrave's Brewery in Toronto was looking for a mechanic; Andy quickly followed up. The prospects looked good, so he packed up Lena and three-year-old Joe, handed in his resignation and moved to Toronto. But the job didn't materialize, so Andy found a job in a machine shop, followed by another job as a mechanic and millwright, and Lena got work in a laundry. With worsening unemployment in the fall of 1929, Andy looked around for additional income. When a grocery store came up for sale, he borrowed $100 from a friend, put in $300 of his own and for a few weeks it seemed to work out. Then the stock market crashed.

The grocery business proved to be too tenuous — too much work for little return from cash-strapped customers. When they found an interested buyer, they sold. Just about that time, a man from Cosgrave's Brewery came looking for Andy. "We have a job for you and you can start right now." The move to Toronto had panned out after all. Andy would stay for the next thirteen years, first as Cosgrave's chief mechanic, then, after a year studying at a brewery institute in Chicago, as brewmaster. When anti-German sentiment became strong in wartime Toronto, he was fired on accusations that he was a German spy. Nothing he had ever experienced had prepared Andy for this humiliation. He was forty, his son Joe was in Grade 13 on his way to pre-med at the University of Toronto and Andy was without a job, blacklisted in an industry he had grown to love.

At a total loss, he soon sank into a deep depression, half-heartedly looking for work, until a business acquaintance intervened to try to snap him out of it. "Instead of looking for a job in someone else's plant," he suggested, "why don't you go into business for yourself." Okay, thought Andy, swallowing his pride at going from being a brewmaster to once again being a mechanic at half the pay, at least he could be his own boss. He found a welding shop on the market that consisted of one piece of equipment and one welder, who was competent when sober. He refurbished some second-hand lathes, installed them and opened for business. Wartime work in 1944 soon kept him so busy that he had to find a larger space. With borrowed money he rented a building and set up a machine shop and called it Peller Machine Industries, making precision bolts for tanks, shock-absorber parts, and sections for machine guns and handling a huge contract to make range-finders. He was able to hire a good salesman, more workers and a general manager. With money in his pocket, confidence in his heart, time on his hands and the prescience to anticipate that the machine business would be winding down as soon as the war was over, he started to think again about returning to the work he loved — the production of beer. A lucrative con-tract to produce neon signs made it possible for Andy to sell Peller Machine Industries to his general manager for $10,000. Andy was freed to devote all his time to his new project — a brewery on Burlington Street in the city of Hamilton, today Lakeport Brewery.

After raising $200,000 from investors, Peller's Brewery was incorporated on March 9, 1945, the first licence to build a new brewery in Canada since Prohibition and the first company to make a brewery into a showcase with tours and tastings. All the equipment he bought was second-hand, purchased from three defunct breweries in the United States. He had it shipped to Canada, then refurbished and installed it. By Christmas, he had on the market Peller's ale, lager and stout.

When E.P. Taylor, the beer magnate, approached Andy in 1953 to buy him out, the timing was right. Peller's Beer had grown significantly and needed to automate. The additional investment was causing friction with his board. Taylor paid more money for Peller's Beer than Andy had ever dreamed. He was now a wealthy man, with so much money he had to hire a firm to invest it for him.

That was short-lived. He was fifty years old and too young to retire. After a few weeks evaluating his life, he bought a newspaper, the *Hamilton News*, which lasted two years, until he closed it down. It wasn't his milieu. It was a tough lesson to learn, and sapped most of his newly acquired wealth.

Down but not out, in 1956 Andy had enough money left to invest in a General Motors car franchise, which also failed to captivate him. Two years later he sold that and broke even. What would he do next? Maybe the wine business. He had considered it for some time and couldn't understand why the culture of wine and food, so common to the European way of life, had not yet become part of Canadian life. He was convinced that, with the arrival of better times, all Canadians needed was better table wine, something other than the heavily fortified ports and sherries that then characterized the domestic wine industry.

He pestered the commissioner at the LCBO for a licence to open a winery in Ontario. Absolutely not, he was told. Ontario had six wineries, and that was six wineries too many as far as the commissioner was concerned. The only way he could open a winery was to buy an existing one, and there were none for sale. The obstacles in Ontario persisted, so he turned to British Columbia, where grapes also grew, the laws were more flexible and the government seemed more interested in creating jobs in the province. He flew to Victoria, never having been to British Columbia before, and met with the B.C. Attorney General, who told him that if he bought a vineyard and promised to use the grapes in the wine he made, a licence could be forthcoming. Andy couldn't get to the Okanagan Valley fast enough to buy some property and begin planting his vineyard.

Before long, the persuasive Andy had gathered some prominent Vancouver businessmen to be on his board. His son, Joe, was now practising medicine in Hamilton and also got some of his Ontario friends and colleagues to invest. Although Vancouver real-estate prices were high, thirty minutes east of Vancouver, in the town of Port Moody, land was cheap and the city fathers were receptive to new business.

The board of directors wanted to call their new venture something British Columbian, such as The Vancouver Wine Company or The British Columbia Winery, but that didn't appeal to Andy's imagination. He proposed Andrés, after his baptismal name of Andràs, because it sounded French. But more important, he figured, it started with an A, and since everything was listed alphabetically in provincial wine stores, it would be at the top of the list. What he didn't know at the time was that Ontario was the only province that listed alphabetically by producer.

Andy then travelled to California to hire a winemaker and locate machinery and vats he could ship to his new site. He cleaned and repaired them, as in the old days, and made them ready for installation. With the additional $150,000 borrowed from the bank, he and his new company could be ready for their first crush that autumn. That first season, all of the local grapes were already contracted out to other wineries, so he sourced grapes from California.

In April 1962, Andy took six varieties of wine to the B.C. Liquor Board for approval and listing. Weeks went by before he heard anything. Finally he asked his lawyer to call the Attorney General. He found out the B.C. liquor authority had decided to raise the price of Andy's wine by fifteen cents a bottle above the cost of other local wines, because he hadn't used domestic grapes.

"They can't do that," said Andy's lawyer. "It will put us out of business."

"They have done it," said the Attorney General.

Andy never hesitated when the lawyer broke the news.

"We'll take it," said Andy. "We're going to go under anyhow if we can't sell wine. We can't do any worse." His worst fears, however, never materialized. By August, the wines had flown off the shelves. Consumers assumed that, if it cost more, it must be better. "Thank God for human nature," said Andy.

People who had Andy's work ethic loved working for him. They admired his guts to plough forward like a bull without apologies for his lack of education or experience. If he had something to say, he said it without sugar coating, euphemisms or spin. You knew where you stood with Andy.

In early 1964, a grocery broker from Alberta appeared in Andy's Port Moody office suggesting to him that, instead of shipping across the mountains, it would be a good idea to build a winery in Alberta. This was the beginning of the oil-and-gas boom, and there was plenty of money to invest. By the end of the year, Anjo Winery, a contraction of the names of Andy and Joe, his son, would be up and running. Andy had raised $300,000 by selling shares, retaining 51 percent of the voting shares.

From Alberta to Nova Scotia, where Joe's brother-in-law, Lloyd McGuinness, a news broadcaster for CBC television in Nova Scotia, approached Andy with the idea of building a winery. McGuinness reassured Andy that he could round up a group of investors to build on a centralized site in Truro. In June 1964, the construction began on his third winery, Abbey Wines, using the same plans as the Calgary plant. During the summer and fall of 1964, Andy was involved in an endless round of cross-country travel and planning. Then his start-up businesses started to go sour. Building complications multiplied, costs were skyrocketing and staffing problems were exacerbated when his winemaker returned to California. Now sixty-two, he was starting to feel the strain, trying to do everything himself. He needed help he could count on.

Joe's medical practice in Hamilton kept him busy, as did his job as chief of medicine for Hamilton Civic Hospital and as chief of the radio isotope laboratory. To add to that, Joe was on the board of all three of his father's wineries. One night, when Andy was in town spending time with his wife, Lena, Joe stopped by their home in Ancaster, just outside Hamilton.

"How are things going, Dad?" said Joe, concerned that his father appeared to be under extreme stress. Joe was aware that all his father's enterprises were in debt, with angry directors nipping at Andy to sell.

"Here's the situation, Joe," said Andy. "I'm sixty-two years old and I just can't take the strain anymore. It's getting to me."

Then, in a moment Andy would later describe as a "step I otherwise would not have taken," he said to Joe, "It's all this robbing Peter to pay Paul and not having someone I can trust who won't do me in every time I turn around. You're the only one I can turn to. Would you consider coming in with me and taking over the Port Moody plant?"

Joe was a son first, a family man and a doctor, but never a business-man. He had his patients who depended upon him, let alone his wife and six children.

"You mean you want me to give up medicine?" said Joe.

Andy realized what he was asking his son to do, so he recanted.

"On second thought, I can't ask you to do it. But it's good just to be able to talk it out."

"I'll think about it," said Joe.

The building in Nova Scotia was finished, but none of it was paid for. They hadn't sold enough shares. Andy was spending more time in Nova Scotia, which angered the B.C. and Alberta directors, who worried about their investments. There was much discontent, and Andy's abrupt and dis-concertingly frank interactions with them didn't help to soften their bitter-ness. Then Lloyd McGuinness died suddenly, the one man on whom Andy had relied in Nova Scotia.

"I have to help my dad out," explained Joe to his hospital administrator. "I need a six-month leave."

Like any good doctor whose purpose in life was to rescue and heal, Joe felt he had to try to help his father, even if he knew nothing about wine and even less about running a business. To get more familiar with the wine business, he first spent two weeks in California meeting with oenologists and owners, and working around the laboratory building a network of contacts who turned out to be very helpful. While there, he hired a winemaker, Guy Baldwin, who had been with Christian Brothers for many years. Guy was in his mid-forties and was willing to leave California to make wine in Canada, a move his colleagues regarded as unbelievably wacky. Maybe it was Joe's charm or tact, but the winemaker came. Ed Arnold, a young former brewmaster Andy had hired (the same Ed Arnold who ten years later would become the president of Bright's), would assist Baldwin.

When Joe arrived at the Port Moody plant, he applied his skills as a diagnostician to the problems the business was facing. Where his father had been impatient and blunt, Joe was patient and diplomatic. Soon his six-month leave from medicine slipped into twelve months. Then another year passed and another, until he reluctantly gave up his practice and his leadership roles at the hospital. It was becoming apparent that he had little chance of returning to his life in medicine. The good news was the wine businesses were starting to turn around. Many attributed his success to his ability to inspire and motivate his people and then leave them alone to do their jobs. By 1969, although they were still heavily debt-ridden, the directors could see a turnaround that would soon lead to increased dividends. Joe's next priority was Ontario, the centre of the largest market for their wines.

The only way to sell wine in Ontario, besides being listed with the LCBO, was to own a winery, so Joe called on the Chief Commissioner of the LCBO, Mr. Harry G. Shepherd, a retired president of IBM.

"How can I get a winery in Ontario," asked Joe, hoping the attitude of the LCBO had changed since the time his father had asked the previous chair.

"We haven't issued a licence since Prohibition," said Shepherd, "but I know of a winery that might be up for sale. Give the owners at Beau Chatel a call."

Beau Chatel was the brief attempt of Imperial Tobacco to diversify into the wine business by buying the Welland Winery on the outskirts of Welland, Ontario. Andy had once looked at the property when it had come up for sale in 1965, but it was too small, the location had little appeal and, at the time, his mind was more on salvaging the businesses he had already begun in three other provinces. With tobacco interests underwriting the Welland

Winery project, Imperial was able to relocate it from its mid-peninsula location, rename it and build a brand-new facility in Grimsby, strategically situated alongside the Queen Elizabeth Highway. When George Ross took over as CEO of Imperial Tobacco, however, he had different ideas about the beverage-alcohol business, particularly when he read about the losses the subsidiary was experiencing. With LCBO Commissioner Shepherd's encouragement, Joe wasted no time flying to Montreal to meet with Ross at the Imperial Tobacco headquarters. Ross was just as eager to meet with Joe.

"We want to get out of this," said Ross. "You are the natural buyers."

"We'd like to submit a bid," said Joe, "but our problem is we haven't any money."

"Who do you bank with?" replied Ross.

"The Royal Bank," said Joe.

"I'll help you," assured Ross.

Ross contacted Roynat Capital, an investment firm then controlled by the Royal Bank, with the Bank of Montreal and the Bank of Commerce as minor partners. They put up enough money to buy Beau Chatel from Imperial Tobacco. Along with the opportunity to produce wine in the larger Ontario market, the Pellers were once again up to their necks in loans and debt. Roynat was to become a shareholder, and before long Beau Chatel proved to be one of the best investments Roynat ever made. Close to a decade had elapsed since his father's approach to the LCBO about a winery licence. Joe's accomplishment gratified Andy, but his gratification was soon to increase.

Prior to the sale of Beau Chatel, the owners stipulated that the Pellers could not visit the inside of the plant. If the staff became suspicious, the owners felt there was a chance they would quit before the sale was complete. Andy and Joe could see from driving around the outside that the company had spent a fortune on its development. Could the inside be any less? Perhaps, but it was a risk they were willing to take. When the sale was completed on November 17, 1969 (Andy's birthday), Andy and Joe drove immediately to take their first look at the inside of the plant. Andy was overwhelmed — magnificent state-of-the-art machines and glistening stainless-steel tanks lined the immaculate cellar. It was more than they had ever allowed themselves to imagine.

When they took legal possession on January 1, 1970, they announced to the employees that they would retain everyone, with the exception of one or two people, provided they changed their work habits to suit any new procedures the Pellers might introduce. The one person Andy Peller did fire was the general manager, who happened to be a man whom he had previously fired from Port Moody — an embarrassing situation for both men.

The Pellers would make the Ontario winery the head office. Winemaker Ed Arnold came to take care of the winemaking and was elevated to executive vice-president. Joe continued in his administrative role as CEO and president, and Andy, now sixty-seven, became the family presence in the business, taking daily trips around the plant to chat with the staff, whom he regarded as friends — his "boyz and girlz." Within the first year they managed to reverse the losses the former owner had experienced by introducing more stringent controls. But the best was yet to come.

Just before they bought Beau Chatel, table wines had gone into a slump. The biggest-selling wine, in a squat bottle resembling a soldier's cask, was a slightly sparkling Portuguese wine called Mateus, soon followed by different bubbling variations on the same theme. Cold Duck wines, which were a 12-percent-alcohol blend of still red and sparkling white, were selling well in the American marketplace. The name Cold Duck originated with a German winemaker in Michigan who named his blend after a ceremony that Europeans used to practise when the party wound down. Everyone would empty his or her glass into a common bowl and share the last drink. The mixture was called "the cold end," or, in German, *das caulde ende*. Not wanting to call his wine Cold End, he took the meaning of a similar German word, *ente*, which translates to "duck." The Cold Duck story might be apocryphal, but Gallo and everyone else ran with it — and so did sales.

Another category of bubbling wine was called *crackling*, which the Italians called *frizzante* and the French call *pétillant* — slightly effervescent. Andrés had two similar wines: one they called Crackling Rosé and the other Chanté. Both sold very well, not hindered by the fact that, around this time, Neil Diamond had a hit with his song "Cracklin' Rosie," the title of which referred to a bottle of wine as a store-bought woman. When they got complaints that the wine didn't have enough bubbles, Joe asked winemaker Ed Arnold to "bubble it up" with more carbon dioxide. Then Joe got a call from Ottawa.

"We just checked your CO_2 levels and you're way over the top," said the official. "You're going to have to pay Champagne tax on that."

Joe flew to Ottawa and explained that they had made an error and would stop doing it right away. But sales were so good. How could they still capture the new wave of consumer preference for bubbles, yet not pay the hefty tax?

Sales were ultimately on the minds of the guys from Andrés when they gathered together in a bar in British Columbia after work one evening. Joe Peller, Ed Arnold and John Boychuk, their head of marketing, complained about high taxes, markups and the Prohibition mentality that still pervaded people's attitudes about wine. As they continued talking over glasses of wine, the conversation changed to marketing.

"We've got to do something, guys, to get our sparkling line moving," said John. "It's a growing segment."

"The Cold Duck in Michigan is doing well," said Ed Arnold. "Made from Concords."

"There's no money in that," said John. "It's the $2.50 Champagne tax per gallon that gets us."

"What if we made a 'baby' wine similar to the Brits' Baby Cham, which is sparkling wine at a lower alcohol level and only twenty-five cents per gallon?" said Joe.

"Ed, can you make it?" inquired John.

"Sure," replied Ed. "We could bring the juice in from Ontario."

There are many versions of this scenario, each laying claim to taking credit for originating the idea. Don Ferguson, a flamboyant sales manager for Andrés in British Columbia, said it was his creation and his idea. Andrew Wolf, Joe Peller's cousin, who had worked for the company for two years in the early 1960s, then opened a winery of his own, said it was his. Success has a thousand fathers.

Despite the fact that scores of wineries were making a Cold Duck version of their own, no one made the same profits in Canada that were to come close to Andrés. No one. The real difference was the marketing genius that lay behind their product. By 1973, two years after its launch, one out of every twenty-four bottles of wine sold in Canada was Andrés Baby Duck. *Saturday Night* magazine writer Winston Collins later explained the phenomenon by suggesting Baby Duck was the necessary transition wine for the baby-boom generation, who were moving from pop to low-alcohol, poplike wine. It may also have been the perfect transition to table wines for the sherry and port drinkers who found dry table wines too austere.

The real genius behind its success was probably Evan Crandall, the account director at F.H. Hayhurst, the Toronto advertising agency Boychuk hired to create an advertising campaign. When it was first launched, Baby Duck was one of Andrés's sixteen labels they called their "cellar dwellers," but when Baby Duck began to take off, Hayhurst suggested presenting it separately. The first classic Baby Duck print ad was absolutely inspired: "Quack open a Baby Duck." In 1974, Crandall talked Andrés into advertising on television. Reluctant to shell out millions of advertising dollars, Joe had to be persuaded it would be a good investment. If only he had known just how good it would be, he might have been less hesitant.

The television ad opened up with a shot of a duck egg from which issued a muffled *cheep-cheep* sound. A little beak poked at the shell until it cracked open, and out flapped a soft and fuzzy yellow duckling. The voiceover said, "What happens when you introduce a robust sparkling red wine to a delicate sparkling white? Andrés Baby Duck is born." Viewers then heard the sound of a cork popping as the duck cheeped, wine flowed and the voiceover said, "Andrés Baby Duck is Canada's largest selling wine." The print ads varied slightly, ending with "Waddle they think of next!"

Capturing just the right shot of the cute little duckling's first moments out of the shell for the label of Baby Duck was difficult. Their first failed attempts began with a dozen ducklings, which, when brought into the studio, either stood still or flapped their little wings all over the place. Crandall wanted the photographer to catch a duckling as it was coming out of its shell. The problem was how to hold that image long enough for the photographer to snap. To solve it, they took a broken, empty shell and glued it back together, after placing an already-hatched baby duckling inside with its foot taped to the shell. When the little guy pushed his way out and flapped his wings in his first exuberant flight, he could only flutter in place — for just the time it took the photographer to click. Crandall made sure the Humane Society was on hand for both the print and television shoots to avoid any claims of duckling abuse; however, one sympathizes with the duckling's inevitable angst. Perhaps he was recognized as a celebrity among his peers. This image of emergence would be the metaphor for a new generation.

The increasing success of Baby Duck became an effective means of promoting the Andrés name. "Yessir, that's our Baby," soon defined Andrés, a branding that was so firmly seared into the company's corporate identity that it would take three decades and a change of company name to overcome. But for now, the success of Baby Duck ushered in a windfall in wine sales, which soon prompted imitation.

Other "Baby" wines proliferated, with names more suggestive of Noah's Ark than a wine shop, writes wine writer Tony Aspler: Little White Duck, Luv-a-Duck, Baby Bear, Baby Deer, Pink Flamingo, Gimli Goose and Pussy Cat. Fuddle-Duck, another brand, capitalized on Prime Minister Pierre Trudeau's famous explanation of the expletive he was overheard uttering in the House of Commons: "I said 'fuddle-duddle.'"

Andrés was starting to make a profit, but the bank debt persisted. Joe knew little about finance, so he hired a first-class financial man, Newman Smith, who advised him to go public. Joe was reluctant, because he feared the loss of family control of the company started by his dad, yet he yielded to Newman's advice.

When the company first went public in 1971, the shares were listed at the three-dollar mark. By the end of the week, the price rose to eight dollars a share. Baby Duck had become very popular. By the end of two years, the shares were trading at forty dollars, so they split the shares. The Peller family's interest at that time was about 25 percent. Yet the loan with the Roynat was still nagging Joe. An investment adviser from Midland Doherty suggested that Joe consider a debt issue in the form of bonds to pay off the bank debt. It worked.

The interest rate was much higher than the bank's, so the bonds were all sold. For the first time since Joe had been called in by his dad, the Pellers were out of debt. Joe had mortgaged his house, as had Andy; both were able to pay off the mortgages. But they had given up control of the business in exchange. Their adviser then suggested splitting the shares again into voting and non-voting shares, paying the non-voting shares a higher dividend. That sounded good, to Joe, so he went for it. The net result was that virtually everybody took non-voting shares at a 15-percent increase over voting shares. The family interest in the business went up to 40 percent. At the end of two years, the shares had reached forty dollars again. They split again and the same thing happened. Now the family had 55 percent of the voting shares and control of the company once again. Within five years they were in a league they had never anticipated. From a relatively small family business, Andrès had grown to a corporate entity of importance on the stock market. In many respects, it functioned like a private company with the long-term perspective of family shareholders in control of the voting shares. On the other hand, it complied with the governance requirements of a publicly traded company.

In 1973 John Boychuck, now vice-president of marketing, hired marketing whiz Dave Ringler, who believed that what mattered most was to discover what customers wanted to drink, at prices they wanted to pay, in accessible and innovative formats. In 1975, he led the introduction of the one-gallon (four-litre) bag-in-box concept to Canada with Cellar Casks, which sold more than 400,000 gallons (1.5 million litres) annually for years.

As the Baby Duck star was starting to fade, it was up to Ringler to lead the development of brands that could become new standard-bearers. He spearheaded two new labels, Hochtaler, a German-style blend, to compete against Schloss Laderheim and Blue Nun, and Domaine D'Or, a French-style wine to compete against Kressman. Domaine D'Or would later make as much profit for the company as did Baby Duck. Ringler's mantra was to give the customer what he or she wanted and not to move faster than the consumer was ready to go. Despite the emergence of Ontario dry VQA varietal wines, consumer studies revealed that, although drinkers said they preferred dry wines, they were actually buying slightly sweeter wines. As Baby Duck was paddling into the sunset, Joe Peller was pleased that they had new brands to take its place. As a result of consumer preference, and Andrès' weak table-wine image, their entry into the varietal VQA segment would have to wait.

For a short stint, between 1977 and 1981, Joe thought the company needed new blood, so he appointed Peter Green as president. After a failed marketing campaign designed to promote Baby Duck in Britain, Green stepped down, and Joe was once again at the helm. Although a few disgruntled former employees felt Joe had picked their brains and let them go, more people, both inside and outside of the business, came to revere Joe, even if they might have disagreed with him. At the core he was a compelling person of humility and compassion. Where Andy was trusting, Joe was trustworthy. Andy had an insatiable need for independence, Joe for teamwork. Andy was at his best in adversity, Joe avoided it. What the father and son shared, however, was a total commitment to each other, to their family and to the family of employees they had assembled; the business was an expression of that commitment. Andy had been the consummate entrepreneur — bold and risk-taking, yet, unlike many entrepreneurs, he let go of control when he asked his son to move his company from its entrepreneurial-but-unstable beginnings to a viable, focused organization. He had to. Could Joe do the same when his time came?

When everything around him was in turmoil, Joe Peller found solace in his charming wife, Connie, and their six children — five boys and a girl. What mattered to him most was that each child would maintain harmony, support and love for one another while developing according to his or her own talents. Succession in the family business was not their focus in raising their family. What did each do best? What were their desires? Joe, the eldest, became a fine artist and moved to New York City; Gus opted for medicine; Jim became a farmer and landscaper; John went into law; Lori sought a career in marketing; and Jeff chose acting and teaching drama. Each had gone his or her own way, which pleased Joe. They had followed their own stars. "God bless them," he would say frequently.

In the early 1980s, after articling with a Hamilton law firm that had asked him to become a partner, John (the fourth son) realized that law was not what he really wanted to do with his life. He went to Europe for a year to gather his thoughts, study French at L'Institut de Touraine and work with DeLuze, the wine subsidiary of Rémy Martin. When he returned, he got a job in New Jersey as manager of corporate planning and development with Nabisco Brands. Then, in 1987, he was promoted to regional marketing manager for Grocery Products Division (North East Division). He was loving what he was doing, and he was in love with a girl from New Jersey with whom he was making plans for the future, when he got a call from his father, Joe.

"Sales are down, son," said Joe, now sixty-three years old, "and I'm worried about the implications of free trade. Things are getting tougher, and I'm not getting any younger." It was 1989 and the elimination of differential markups was going to present the company with severe challenges over the next five years.

Then Joe tentatively broached the subject of his call.

"Would you come back home and help out?" he asked with the same guarded hope that his father had shown when he asked him the same question twenty-five years earlier.

Although he was keen to accept, John insisted on having a family meeting with his brothers and sister to make sure they felt it was the right decision. He knew that passing a company to the next generation was one of the toughest acts in business, with only one-third of family businesses able to survive to the second, let alone the third, generation. If there were pitfalls to avoid, such as family squabbling or a lack of trust in his capacity to join the firm, he wanted any misgivings aired before he accepted the position.

Like his father before him, and with his siblings' blessings, John complied with his father's request. He had learned some of the best business practices in sales and marketing at Nabisco; perhaps he could help out. They agreed that they would take a short-term view. Joe suggested that he come for three years. "We have a great marketing guy, Dave Ringler, a first-class guy. You can work with him and try it out."

Free trade was taking its toll, and the reality of their situation finally hit, but it would turn out to be the most provocative instrument of positive change the industry could have experienced. As John later mused, "It was like someone chasing you down the alley with a knife and you fortunately discovered you could run fast." Dave Ringler and John worked well together, despite the fact that they were mirror opposites of each other — or perhaps because of it. Dave was an intellectual, analytical giant — quiet, hard-driving and detail-oriented. John was more expressive, socially engaging, intuitive and macro-minded.

John was more like his grandfather Andy — ambitious, assertive and energized by change. Change was what he could see the organization needing most. Free trade compelled it, but how could the owner's son, who would be seen as silver-spooned, spoiled and unqualified, initiate change without antagonizing a culture that was loyal to the ways things were done under his father?

John could see that too much information was held in the hands of too few — and those few controlled it, whether it was finance, marketing or sales. The company had grown beyond that traditional model. Everyone had to have access to everything, with shared accountability working with teams of other people. Instead of budgeting, he advised business planning. Rather than having a sales department and a separate marketing

Three generations of Peller: John, Andy and Joe, 1993

department fighting for turf, he suggested the two departments merge. John also realized that, if the company was to survive, it too had to move into premium, varietal, VQA-based wines. In 1991, he and Dave Ringler continued to work together to produce a new brand of premium wine under the Peller Estates label.

After two years, Joe promoted John to vice-president of sales and marketing. Dave Ringler eventually moved over to become vice-president of operations. One day Joe came into John's office. "Do you have a couple of minutes?" he asked as he took a seat across from his son. "You're doing a hell of a job, John, and I think you're the right guy to run this business. From now on all the decisions in the business will be yours. Of course, I'm going to stay on the board and you're going to get my opinion whether you want it or not, but from now on it's you. I'm stepping down." Then he walked out.

John became president and CEO of Andrés in early 1994. His father and his grandfather were both extremely proud. All three had worked alongside one another for five years and always had a good relationship, so it wasn't a big step. Working with Joe was easy. It was now time to take the business to the next stage, building on what had worked, while seeking new ways to innovate and renew. Premium wines topped John's list.

After losing their bids to buy Chateau Gai, and then Bright's, Joe and now John viewed any acquisition with caution. Hillebrand Estates had grown from a small operation originally started in 1979 by Joe Pohorly, a polymath grape grower, engineer, teacher and entrepreneur in Niagara-on-the-Lake, to a sizeable operation. It had potential.

Hillebrand's growth had been exemplary. In 1982, Pohorly had sold Newark, the winery he had opened just two years earlier, to a German firm called Scholl & Hillebrand, owned by the Underberg family, renowned for "bitters." They renamed it Hillebrand and reinvested $3.5 million in the facility. Their forward-looking general manager, John Swan, an Englishman with British wine-marketing experience, saw a profit opportunity in the retailing side of the business. He bet that trade pressures would eventually close the briefly opened window of retail-store expansion opportunities that had been available since the free trade talks began, so he embarked on an aggressive campaign to develop an unconventional network of stores, opening their first store in downtown Toronto in 1984. In 1988, he bought twelve stores from Barnes Wines when free-trade pressures shut them down. By 1990, Swan had finessed fifty additional retail stores into operation throughout the province. He might have continued to secure more retail permits, but the LCBO stopped granting them in 1993. All the existing Hillebrand outlets would be grandfathered as a result of free trade, as were Cartier's and Bright's chains of stores. Added to this was the savvy sales force of prominent wine importer and Underberg partner in the business, Peter Mielzynski Agencies, who aggressively secured listings in the LCBO stores. The result was that, between 1984 and 1990, Hillebrand's sales grew from six thousand cases annually to two hundred thousand cases annually.

By 1992, Hillebrand Estates was the winery with the most awards in Canada and the largest producer of varietal and VQA wines, but after twelve years, the German owners had decided to sell. The dissolution of the Soviet Union had opened a whole new opportunity in Eastern Europe for them, much closer to home.

In 1994, Andrés bought 100-percent interest in Hillebrand Estates for $30 million, thus inheriting a fully-fledged premium winery with a prestigious reputation as a producer of fine wine, plus the bonus of an established network of retail outlets. Newly appointed president John Peller told the *Financial Post*: "It's like Chrysler or Ford buying Lamborghini." The big-blended winery was going to be a player in VQA wines.

As John had already observed, a familial organizational culture had emerged at Andrés over the years. Andy and Joe Peller had woven the pattern and set the tone as the caring fathers whose charisma fuelled everyone's energies and inspired their loyalty. To please them and get their approval or admiration was almost as gratifying as a raise. With the integration of a very different culture at Hillebrand, the necessity for John to restructure the company became acute. Some people thrived with the changes, some resisted and left; a few were asked to leave. By 1996, the administrative organization chart had John at the head, but power was more decentralized throughout teams with specific functions. Sometimes there was a feeling that things weren't as focused or disciplined as when one captain was at the helm steering the ship. Yet, the inherent culture of family remained. Where Joe built a caring company, John was creating a learning one; employees still bent over backward to please the Pellers, John included. One of John's senior managers, who had worked both at Vincor and Andrés, would later describe the difference in the two cultures: "Vincor was well organized, but Andrés was more personally rewarding."

To outsiders, John Peller was an enigma — how could the son of Baby Duck and blended wines be a trusted proponent of the VQA? How could the grandson be qualified to run the business? John's assertiveness could be seen as bullying, his gregariousness as flighty, his high energy the resented good fortune of his affluent upbringing. He could be engaging in debate or indifferent — depending on his mood. Yet to insiders he was known to be dedicated to his wife and children, with a compassion for his people in the company that was equalled only by his father's. When a high-school friend contracted Huntington's Corea, John took responsibility for his personal care for ten years, arranging for a place for him to stay and handling his bills. Corporation insiders were aware of many other similar examples of John's humaneness.

It took longer for outsiders to get to know this other side of John, but they did. In 2001, John worked closely with chair Paul Speck and other members of the Wine Council to reconcile their competing interests. John was a known entity by the time they came together to create the "Poised for Greatness" strategic plan for the industry. He, too, loved a good time over a good brew or two, and that didn't hurt. He was president of the Canadian Vintners' Association when he urged members to join him in creating a twenty-year plan that could define where the industry was going, how they were going to get there and how everyone could improve. It was a vision to advance quality, accelerate the development of wine-country experiences and hospitality, and to consistently innovate.

The Andrés contribution to that end has taken several paths. To advance quality, in 2001 the company opened Peller Estates, a $20-million winery in Niagara-on-the-Lake, with a grand tasting room and gift shop, a fine-dining restaurant, a barrel cellar and meeting rooms, all surrounded by twenty hectares (fifty-five acres) of vineyards. To accelerate the development of wine-country experiences and hospitality, they initiated such events as a series of summer jazz and blues concerts that annually drew thousands of music and wine lovers to the commons behind Hillebrand Estates. In a major overhaul in 2004, they renewed the dining facilities in the Hillebrand restaurant, grounds and cellars. In 2005, they acquired the assets of Thirty Bench, the prestigious vineyard and winery of three once-amateur winemakers from Hamilton, a doctor, Thomas Muckle, a professor, Yorgos Papageorgio, and a Hamilton businessman, Frank Zeritsch. To enhance their presence in British Columbia, in 2005 they acquired 100 percent of Cascadia Brands, which included Calona Wines, one of the province's oldest and most prestigious wineries; Sandhill Winery, a super-premium VQA brand; and a craft-beer company, Granville Island Beer. A spirits company included in the deal was later sold. That same year they acquired another smaller operation, Red Rooster, which sat on the sought-after Naramata Bench. Although Andy Peller had died in June 1994, he would have been thrilled at the prospects of a beer company once again in the family business.

With all this investment in domestic wineries aimed at the premium side of the domestic market, between 1996 and 2008 they also bought into the wine-kit business, acquiring Vineco in Niagara, Brew King, Winexpert in Calgary and World Vintners. John had discovered that the kit business was a lucrative source of profit. The kits, although not as sexy as building a benchmark property in wine country, were another way to get the consumer involved with wine. Their research showed that the people buying wine kits were also some of the same people who went to restaurants and who spent the most money on ultra-premium wine. With sales in the blended-wine

John Peller, President and CEO, Andrew Peller Ltd., 2009

category virtually flat, kits could help sustain the year-to-year vagaries in the domestic wine industry.

When consumers left the fluffy little duckling behind to move on to more "sophisticated" table wines, they left forever. But for Andrés, the legacy of the fowl's less-than-premium feathers was hard to flick away. In 2006, they left the Andrés name behind them and, in a tribute to its founder, they renamed the company Andrew Peller Ltd.

In 2007, John Peller spearheaded the Niagara Wine Auction, a glittering Napa-style charity gala designed to bring Toronto's elite to Niagara to celebrate the success of Niagara's modern industry and to share its ambition for the future. It was a powerful idea whose time seemed premature to many. His grandfather dared to bring table wine to the Canadian table; his father recognized the potential of low-alcohol sparkling wine in a population on the cusp of wine maturity. Both were powerful ideas whose time had come. John's powerful idea may be in helping those maturing wine lovers and their children to recognize Ontario's wine and wine country as "their wine industry," and thereby to carry the torch for the continuing transformation of the Ontario wine industry. The success of John's powerful idea will be measured by the next generation, but as a third-generation winemaker with a long view in the business, he's prepared for that — and anxious to take on the challenge.

9 LINDA FRANKLIN'S NAVIGATION

"Anyone can hold the helm when the sea is calm."
—*Publilius Syrus*

Linda Franklin had been on the job as the executive director of the Wine Council of Ontario for two weeks when scientists from Agriculture Canada called an urgent meeting with the growers and wineries. They had weathered the frigid January drive from Ottawa to deliver an urgent warning. Serious infections had been discovered in vines imported from Europe and, until the source of the infection was under control, they were putting a ban on all imported vines coming into Canada.

The mood in the room was not cordial. Many of the growers had spent the last two years pulling out their Concords and Niagaras and had just begun the process of replacing them with imported *vinifera* stock from France and Germany. The wineries were anxiously awaiting the time when the harvest of the new varieties could meet the growing demands for their quality wines. Now, suddenly, they were being told "No more vines." The news was hard to take in. There was confusion as to what exactly was being asked of them. All the audience heard was *We need this form filled out, and this warranty, and this bill of sale, and, oh yes, this background on your farm, and we need it all a week from today.* They sat stunned, not grasping what was being asked of them. It wasn't a matter, at this stage, of contesting the scientists' findings, although eventually Hermann Weis and John Howard from Vineland Estates would do so — and win. At this time, it was a matter of accommodating their requests. But what were they?

"Can we get this in writing from you folks?" Linda said, sensing the uncertainty in the room. It didn't seem like a lot to ask for such a major move.

"Oh, I don't think so," the feds replied, asserting their authority over her and the people she represented.

"I don't understand what you just said to me," said Linda. "You're going to give us a week to comply with a request we don't fully understand. If we don't understand, we can't comply." Linda could see they were annoyed at her boldness. Unflinching, she added: "None of us is going to leave this room until we know exactly what's required."

Not letting her newcomer status restrain her, she simply did her job. She wasn't gong to let the industry be pushed around. Over the next fourteen years, she would be equally brave, persuasive, conciliatory and patient, enabling this nascent industry, still fresh from the upheavals of free trade, to create a workable unity of purpose and, while doing so, to quadruple its size.

That January of 1994, government funding was running out, the wine industry had no friends at the liquor board and winery growth had plateaued at around thirty properties. Between government inhibitory policies, high taxes and consumer uncertainty, it was becoming painfully clear that there was little chance to make a successful business out of a small winery. This is why the members of the Wine Council of Ontario had hired Linda Franklin to help navigate their way.

* * *

Although Linda Franklin had been born in Toronto in 1956, she had lived her entire life in Oakville, Ontario. She completed both her undergraduate degree and masters at the University of Western Ontario, in English and history, with a specialization in journalism. After graduation she worked at Global Television just long enough to know that journalism wasn't for her. When an old friend who was working for the Progressive Conservative

Linda Franklin, President of the Wine Council of Ontario, 1993–2006

caucus at Queen's Park casually mentioned that they were looking for people with skills in journalism, she applied and ended up working at Queen's Park for the next ten years, from 1981 to 1987.

She started out writing for the northern members of parliament, then soon managed the department. Ontario Premier Bill Davis had won a huge majority and had brought in Mike Harris, Ernie Eves and Andy Brandt. Harris and Eves would both go on to become premiers of the province (1995–2002; 2002–2003), and Andy Brandt would become the CEO of the LCBO, responsible for a massive transformation in retailing (1991–2006), having the longest tenure of any previous CEO in the history of the Crown corporation. Andy's office was across from Linda's in the provincial legislature, and Mike Harris and Ernie Eves were down the hall.

When Bill Davis retired, Frank Miller won the leadership of the Progressive Conservative Party in January 1985. On February 8, 1985, Miller became premier. As part of his cabinet, he appointed Ernie Eves as provincial secretary for resources development. Eves soon asked Linda to be his chief of staff. A month later, in a cabinet shuffle, Eves was moved to become the minister of skills development, and Linda came along as well. Two months into the job, Eves was moved again to become minister of community and social services and, once again, Linda came along as his chief of staff. After only a few months in office, Miller called an election and was defeated by Liberal leader David Peterson, who became premier in June 1985. Over the course of those four months, Linda had been briefed in each of her minister's portfolios, becoming the best-briefed and least-used chief of staff in the history of the Ontario government.

Linda stayed with Eves for about a year in Opposition, but there was only so much she could do without repeating herself. When the opportunity came to work with the College of Physicians for a five-year term, she left Queen's Park after almost a decade of learning the subtle inner workings of government. After the College of Physicians, she had been working as a consultant for a year when a friend called and mentioned a senior staff opening. This was also for an association, doing similar work to what she had done for the physicians, only this time it would be with winemakers.

"I don't know anything about wine," she told her friend. But, then again, she hadn't known anything about medicine either. She had never even been to a winery, but she liked to drink wine and knew what it felt like to have roots in a place. At her interview, the hiring committee dismissed her concerns about her lack of knowledge about wine. "We know about wine," they said. "We're looking for someone who knows about government relations." About that, she was confident.

Government relations was the key. For the past six years, as the free trade talks unfolded, the members of the Wine Council had realized that more than at any other time in their association's history, they needed someone on staff who really knew how government worked, someone who understood what kind of policy issue should go to the civil service or directly to cabinet. They needed someone with deep links to the political system.

They also needed someone who could cut through the thicket of their emerging competing interests. Up until this time, leadership had rotated among the old boys of the large wineries, whose interests were relatively consonant. Now that there were several new players, much smaller enterprises, with interests competing with the larger operations, they needed someone dedicated to the task of helping them find common ground. Consensus-building proved to be Linda's forte. Along with her organizational skills, her masterful ability to put into words her members' feelings opened space for agreement and action.

The Wine Council of Ontario had adapted its mandate a number of times since it was first incorporated in 1940 as the Canadian Wine Institute, a non-profit trade association of Ontario wineries. Their first mandate was to change the anti-alcohol sentiment that still pervaded Ontario society, the result of Prohibition. Governments had to be convinced that legalized drinking could be done responsibly. The wineries felt there was strength in numbers to better negotiate with their wartime suppliers, the grape growers, and their regulators, the LCBO and the Liquor Licensing Board of Ontario (LLBO). In 1965, because of the growth of the local wine industry in other provinces, all Canadian wineries were invited to join, which changed the association's mandate to reflect a much broader national interest. That proved too unwieldy to resolve provincial matters, so the wineries from Ontario and British Columbia resumed their original structure as separate provincial associations.

In July 1974, the Ontario organization incorporated and changed its name from the Wine Producers Association to the Wine Council of Ontario. Membership was open to all producers of wine, with the proviso that a member be a resident of Ontario and his affiliation with the industry had to be located in the province. Jeff Ward, president of Barnes Wines, explained to a seminar held at Brock University in 1982 that the role of the council had been "to develop and maintain a working relationship with the Ontario government, to be the face and voice of the wine industry in Ontario and to meet the administrative needs of the industry."

Both Ontario and B.C. associations continued to be members of the national association, the Canadian Wine Institute, which later became the present Canadian Vintners' Association. Its mandate was, and continues to be, focused on issues of national and mutual concerns to the wine industries of Canada, including those in Quebec and Nova Scotia, on such issues as national wine standards, interprovincial and international trade, promotion and taxation.

By 1993, the year before Linda Franklin was hired, the council had completed a strategic analysis of their industry, which had been prompted by tremendous turmoil between the Wine Council and the VQA. One organization was weighted by the interests of the large wineries and the other with those of the smaller wineries. Even within some of the larger organizations, this dynamic was playing out as a result of mergers and amalgamations.

The emerging leaders of the smaller properties — Paul Speck, Allan Schmidt, Len Pennachetti — hadn't had much conversation with the "big guys," so part of Linda's challenge was pulling them all in to talk with one another. By the time Linda arrived, they had already made the decision that they were either going to fight and win together or lose separately. Although Linda inherited an organization in which there wasn't much experience dealing with government, there was a lot of heart among them for the fight they all knew lay ahead.

Their first priority was to increase market share from 36.9 percent to 44.4 percent in five years, which would require an annual growth of 2 percent. Second, they wanted to expand exports to sixty thousand cases: thirty thousand to other provinces and the balance to the United States and United Kingdom. These targets were set against several threats to their viability, not the least of which was that the final markup advantages at the LCBO were going to disappear within two years because of the Free Trade Agreement. They were also worried that the recessionary economy would cause an increase in taxes on "sin," with beverage alcohol at the top of the list.

For her first five years, Linda's agenda to grow or die was clear: negotiate a Wine Content Act that would enable winery sustainability until new grape varieties were available, secure equitable markups once parity with imported wines was achieved and develop joint projects with growers to allocate available government funds designated to improve cool-climate viticultural practices. In addition, she was charged with promotion, fundraising and development of export markets, and with evolving a more workable organizational structure for the association.

In March 1993, the industry got hit with a destructive freeze that resulted in the worst devastation of vines since the winter of 1981. The NDP government under Bob Rae, in office since 1990, had proved responsive by way of a one-year amendment to the Wine Content Act to allow a minimum of 10 percent Ontario-grown product and up to 90 percent imported wine in a blend. That was more than reasonable for the larger wineries, whose portfolio was more heavily based on import-blended wine, but much more was at stake for the smaller companies.

During the course of her negotiations with the government on the legislative changes to the Wine Content Act, Linda learned that the NDP government had some money to give the industry, but they hadn't agreed on how best to disperse it. When she heard that Rae was scheduled to come to Vineland Estates to present the industry with a plaque of recognition, she immediately contacted Rae's staff and said, "If he's coming, we want to talk to him about additional impacts of the crop failure."

"Twenty minutes," they replied. "No more."

Vineland Estates from the very beginning was one of the most beautiful properties in the entire peninsula. Located high on the Bench overlooking Lake Ontario, with vines undulating around the rolling periphery of the winery and tasting room, it could have be set in any major wine region in the world. It was a perfect spot for a photo op. When Premier Rae arrived, his assistants thought a picture of him pruning a vine, as any man of the soil might do that time of year, would be appropriate. What they didn't realize was he didn't know pruning from prunes. Rae took the shears and snipped at the vine. Linda was standing next to Allan Schmidt, winemaker and general manager of Vineland Estates, and could see him grow visibly faint. Rae had obviously done something he shouldn't.

"Do we need another shot?" asked Rae. And he did it again. Linda knew that a third snip and Schmidt might not have been able to restrain himself. She took this as her cue and grabbed Donald Ziraldo to speak to Rae privately. They hustled him into the little cottage that was adjacent to the winery retail room. For twenty minutes she and Donald hammered Rae on the impact of the 1993 crop failure. The result of that twenty minutes was a little more than a half a million dollars Rae put on the table to compensate the wineries for their loss of sales. It would not be the last successful strategic conversation Linda would have on behalf of her members.

She never sought the limelight or made a case alone, carefully choosing her negotiating partners. Donald Ziraldo's merger with Vincor had caused some angst in the industry, but had also increased his leverage as an industry advocate. Asking him to accompany her that day helped relieve anxiety and gave her a strong representative for both large and small wineries. She concisely presented an airtight case, getting quickly to the core of her message, asking only for what she knew was practical and defensible from Rae's point of view.

With Ziraldo's role changing, new leaders were starting to emerge. Len Pennachetti, Allan Schmidt and Paul Speck were beginning to realize that it wasn't going to be enough to simply focus on growing their own businesses. They had to focus on the industry as a whole — and eventually something happened to underscore that necessity. A serious lawsuit against the VQA and two members would galvanize them. If lost, the case could set a precedent, undermining the future of the VQA.

Over the course of the next few years, the case would occupy much of Linda's time and cost endless hours of personal strain in testifying, attending depositions and working with lawyers. Because it was before the courts, the real extent of the work Linda did on behalf of the members was never known. Not even the members themselves were aware of her work; the nature of the suit precluded any sharing of evidence. She had not been named in the suit, but she had been deposed — on Christmas Eve — as a representative of the Wine Council and the VQA.

Eventually the suit was settled, but the real outcome was the clarity they developed around the VQA. Their position had to be robust enough to defend in court. Although the Wine Council had insurance to cover the case as it moved through the courts, the VQA did not. Everyone understood that this might not be the first time they would be sued. New wineries might not uphold the voluntary standards that a group of friends were willing to adhere to. The lawsuit ended up costing the industry more than a million dollars, yet nobody denied access to their funds. Every winery contributed to the defence. The realization of potential future challenges to the enforcement of the VQA also sped up their incentive to make the VQA a legal, legislated authority with the force of the government behind it in the same way that other appellation systems in the world were legitimized.

To do this, the wineries needed the ear of the government, and this proved to be one of Linda's most lasting contributions. She taught the members what it took to get a hearing, and, once the government was paying attention, how to get the policies, such as the VQA regulations, passed.

She knew that a powerful message was one that was delivered simply, by everyone, at the same time, in the same way. To make her point, she hired Mike Gourley, the former secretary to the cabinet for the Ontario government, to take them through an exercise on how to proceed when dealing with government.

He began by calling up three members.

"You, you and you, come up here and talk to me about the problems in the health-care system as if we were at a cocktail party." The first person started talking about waiting lists, the next complained about the lack of cancer care and the third spoke to the need for long-term care. At the end of the exercise, Gourley asked, "What do you think I heard?" He continued, "I have no clear idea and no sense of solutions." Ah, point made.

"We were cowboys," recalled Len Pennachetti, "loose individualists with a scatter-shot approach." Linda soon taught them how to go to a meeting and say the same thing in the same way, elevating them to a professional level when appearing before a government official or committee. Most heads of trade associations would avoid putting their members in front of an official, but Linda taught her members how to best present themselves. In the early days she would coach them, saying, "Paul, you're asking this question; Len, you're asking this; Allan, follow up with this." Linda would facilitate annual meetings, at which they identified the key points they wanted to accomplish that year. It would be much easier to cut through everything else the government was hearing if the membership had that sense of purpose.

And they were quick studies. Every member had a seat on the board, but it was a handful of leaders who committed the time. That commitment resulted in continuity that built relationships with cabinet ministers and the civil service. Len, Paul, Bruce Walker, Allan Schmidt, Jim Clarke and later Norm Beal became well-known faces, and they got used to working together. They knew each other's rhythms and operated with the camaraderie of a winning football team, each knowing the playbook by heart, knowing who was going to throw the opening gambit and who would tackle any anticipated points of resistance. Linda was blessed with these good thinkers who strove to have the industry work together. The cowboys went to school with Linda. After a few years, so well schooled had they become in government relations, all Linda had to say was, "Okay, the premier's coming. We have a half an hour. We want to speak to X, Y and Z in the meeting room.

Everybody okay?" Nothing more than that. Len Pennachetti believed this training was Linda's greatest gift to all of them.

She never became the face of the industry, as many trade association leaders tend to do. She was explicit about that and stepped back to put her committee forward. She was so seldom profiled that staff at the Wine Council office often had difficulty locating photos of her. The only time she took the limelight was to speak on the industry's behalf in adversarial situations. To be willing to take on that role was one of her strengths. The smaller wineries, with only one retail outlet other than their own wineries available to them, didn't particularly want to go nose to nose with Bob Downey or Bob Peter or any of the LCBO players. They were their clients. As a small winery owner herself, Susan O'Dell explained, "We paid Linda a lot of money to go and do the confrontational piece of supplier/merchant negotiations." The same thing was true when wineries had to confront the growers on sensitive issues, such as price negotiations.

By June 1995, Linda's old friend Mike Harris was sworn in as premier of Ontario, and Ernie Eves became treasurer. Though she had fewer connections with the NDP and Liberals, she had garnered their trust, but having the Progressive Conservatives back in office made life that much easier. Ernie Eves asked her to return to Queen's Park as his chief of staff, an offer that was hard to refuse, but she felt she couldn't leave the Wine Council, which by now had invested so much in her. And she in them.

High on their list of priorities was getting the VQA legislation passed, as well as changing an unfair law that related to wine deliveries to restaurants and bars. Each program was inextricably connected to the other.

Bruce Walker had been with the newly formed Vincor since 1994, the only manager from the Bright's side who had survived the cut when the management team from Cartier took over. Previous to his role as vice-president of marketing, then vice-president and general manager, Ontario and export, Bruce had been director of sales and marketing for Calona Wines in the Okanagan Valley. He had joined Bright's in 1991 as vice-president and general manager for western Canada until the Bright's, Cartier and Inniskillin merger. With the exception of a two-year stint with Adidas Canada and Labatt Breweries, his extensive background in the wine business was uninterrupted.

When they were ready, the foursome of Len Pennachetti, Paul Speck,

Bruce Walker and Linda Franklin approached the minister of commercial and consumer relations in charge of beverage alcohol, David Tsubouchi, with their proposal on why and how the VQA might be legislated. This time Linda took the lead. The minister listened attentively to Linda as she logically laid out their key points. To Tsubouchi, it was a no-brainer. A provincially regulated VQA would help Ontario wines be more competitive by giving a compelling reason worldwide for people to buy them; it would be an easy sell to his colleagues in the cabinet. Bruce, Len and Paul hadn't simply asked for something. They had laid things out and given Tsubouchi a reason to say yes, providing him with a roadmap for how government might accomplish the legislative change. Civil servants, such as Luisa Tmej, who was the policy adviser for the ministry, worked closely with Linda and Len, familiarizing them with a administrative authority framework that could serve as a model to expedite legislative passage. For two years they worked to convert the voluntary VQA Rules and Regulations into the language and format that was required for a legal act of government. Linda had to absent herself from this writing process; a lobbyist for a trade association writing a pubic document could have been seen as a conflict of interest. Consequently, all of the work fell to Len Pennachetti, who felt as if his right arm had been cut off when he learned that Linda couldn't assist. But he did it himself because it had to be done. She remained in the background, working with her new chair, Bruce Walker, to get it through the legislature.

When completed, it was a win-win for everyone. No political party would oppose a measure that assured quality standards were met, with the administrative authority to enforce infractions with penalties, such as a fine of up to $100,000 for non-compliance, revocation of approval if a product had been misrepresented, or complete loss of VQA status. On June 1, 1999, after ten years of voluntary compliance, Tsubouchi signed the regulations into law. It was a monumental legal and marketing advancement for the industry. But there was another issue, with immediate economic significance, that was much more difficult to wrestle through government.

The industry had reached a period of stasis, at a total of only thirty wineries. It was not growing because the profit margins were so meagre. With this in mind, the members were constantly looking for ways to increase those profit margins. One day, at a Wine Council meeting, Walter Schmorantz from Pelee Island winery asked, "When are we going to get direct delivery?"

"They've had it in B.C.," repeated former B.C. native Allan Schmidt for the umpteenth time. "I know it's possible to get it here too."

Everyone was tentative at first. Getting direct delivery could involve the arduous task of changing the Liquor Control Act, which dated back to 1927. This gave the LCBO the same markup of 58 percent per bottle on wine delivered by the winery to a restaurant or bar as one sold through the LCBO retail-store distribution channel. That meant the LCBO kept $6 out of every $10 of wine sold. The injustice was that the LCBO was raking in millions of dollars a year for performing no service whatsoever — millions of dollars that should have been going to the wineries. It simply made no sense.

It became a vicious circle. The smaller wineries could not afford to hire sales representatives or delivery services because the benefits just didn't justify the costs. The restaurants didn't carry the wines of Ontario because they didn't have sufficient access to many products that weren't carried through the LCBO because the volume wasn't sufficient to meet LCBO demand, and so it went. Consumers assumed that the wines of Ontario were still not good enough to appear on wine lists. And the wineries lost out on a fundamental sales and a significant marketing channel through the restaurants. The members of the Wine Council wanted to be able to deliver directly to the restaurants and not pay the LCBO the 58-percent tax.

As one might have expected, the LCBO resisted on a number of counts. It could be seen as a non-conforming trade measure, according to their international trade obligations, plus their revenues to the province would diminish significantly. Allan Schmidt, "the numbers guy," ran the spread-sheets, figuring out formulas that might minimize LCBO revenue losses, initially thought to be around $2 million annually. When Linda Franklin and chair Bruce Walker approached MPP Tsubouchi and Finance Minister Ernie Eves, they explained how the prevailing system was inequitable. Their timing was right, since the Progressive Conservative government was in the process of reducing taxes and fundamentally believed that people should not be taxed for non-service.

On the other hand, the LCBO was undergoing a mammoth transforma-tion under CEO Andy Brandt. It was becoming more retail-friendly, so giving up $2 million in revenue was not on the table. In fact, the LCBO estimated the loss at closer to $5 million. Eves said to Linda, as well as his staff, "Let's look at this in a different way." To him, if the government allowed wineries to do direct delivery, they would still have to pay the tax on sales. If they increased sales because of this allowance, they also increased the tax the government would make. If they hired more people to handle sales and marketing, there were going to be more personal taxes raised by more people working in the industry.

Linda, with Allan Schmidt's help, went away and ran more numbers with some creative, albeit speculative, accounting in mind, which demonstrated that the long-term benefit to the provincial economy would be substantial. That drive to incremental economic activity was later substantiated by the Canadian auditing firm KPMG, which prepared two economic reports. In 2002, for every litre of Ontario wine sold at the LCBO, $3.88 was returned to the economy, while foreign purchases added only $0.46. By 2008, that figure had risen to $11.50 returned to the economy for every litre sold. Foreign purchases added a meager $0.67 to the economy. In addition to this increase in the value-add there was a significant growth in the number of wineries, from forty-two to eighty Wine Council members and more than thirty non-members. The amount of grapes purchased increased from $21.9 million to $64.4 million, and the increased volume sales from 39.4 million litres to 62.4 million litres.

In spite of the trade sensitivities, Ernie Eves made a political decision as Treasurer to allow direct delivery, and in doing so to accept the financial hit to the province through reduced LCBO revenues. The LCBO put it through as a board of directors' resolution rather than a change in legislation, which might have made it more vulnerable to a trade challenge. They called it a "way to facilitate sales for VQA-only wines to restaurants and bars," regardless of whether a wine was listed with the LCBO. Imported blends, by now called Cellared in Canada (CIC), made under the Wine Content Act, were not part of the deal. This was a significant concession made by the larger wineries and a welcomed gain by the LCBO. The CIC wines represented a sizeable source of restaurant and bar revenue.

David Tsubouchi and his staff drove to Niagara on April 30, 1999, to deliver the double-barrelled good news to the industry in person. All the members had gathered in the stately upstairs tasting room at Château des Charmes. When Tsubouchi announced the fact that the VQA Act had received the government's seal of approval and direct delivery had been achieved, everyone rose in unison and clapped. There wasn't boisterous cheering, but an unfolding acceleration of applause that reflected their profound awareness that they were witnessing an immense turning point in their lives. For Linda Franklin it was exhilarating — the best moment of her entire career.

The VQA Act had passed, and within a year the industry would have in place an independent, delegated authority to administer and enforce the act and its regulations. Laurie Macdonald would be the first VQA of Ontario regulator. And direct delivery meant that smaller wineries could now afford to hire sales representatives to drive sales in restaurants and bars.

There was, of course, a cost. When it came to direct delivery, the pragmatic among the vintners had their eyes wide open. They could see the additional work that offering a premium service was going to entail, the high expectations that restaurants would have, the deadbeats who wouldn't pay, the delivery vans they'd have to buy, the delivery service fees they'd have to absorb, since they couldn't charge, nor could they consolidate an order among them and hire a service to do it for them. Weighing all that, the members still felt it was a monumental victory. The cost to the province was also greater than anticipated. Wineries did so well in the first year of direct delivery, that the cost to the LCBO was closer to $12 million than the highest initial estimate of $5 million.

Tsubouchi hadn't registered the real impact the act would have as he was going through the steps. It was the right thing to do, and together his ministry and the Wine Council had found a way to make it happen. But that day, standing in front of the people whose lives would change dramatically and seeing on their faces how important it was for them, turned it into one of his most gratifying moments in government.

The industry was riding high in the late 1990s. The 1998 vintage was stellar, and both the VQA and direct delivery had been achieved by 1999. With Linda's help they had accomplished what they had set out to do in their 1993 plan. After securing funds to continue their marketing program, the next big thing was to update their strategic plan. They were at the end of a phase around the Free Trade Agreement, so it was an appropriate time to look to their future development. They, along with the grape growers, the liquor board and several stakeholder ministries, such as Agriculture, Tourism, Economic Development and Consumer and

Business Services, took more than a year and a half to develop the strategic plan, "Poised for Greatness."

What industry targets would they set in the intervening years? What would be the Vintages targets? How were they going to get there? Once the strategic framework was agreed upon, Linda and her board, with new chair Paul Speck and member John Peller taking the lead, produced a tactical plan for the liquor board. Their number-one priority was to increase a market share that was hovering at the 42-percent mark. Between 1990 and 2000, foreign wine sales sold through the LCBO had increased by 74.4 percent. Domestic wine sales had increased by only 33 percent. By 2020, they targeted an eight-point rise in market share, to 50 percent.

A 50-percent market share by 2020 would be no mean feat, but the members felt that, even if they didn't get there, they wanted to set something bold, just to see just how far they could grow. As they were wrapping up a meeting with the LCBO, the corporation's chief operating officer, Bob Peter, quietly said, "No way. It's not going to work. I'm not signing onto that." Linda had anticipated his resistance, but despite her best efforts she could not find a meeting of the minds. It was time to get the government involved.

Linda had been working on the strategy with Sandy Lang, a supportive deputy minister of consumer and business services, and with Sue Corke, the assistant deputy minister (later deputy minister). These targets were not unfamiliar to them. When Linda's old boss Ernie Eves became Ontario's twenty-third premier in 2002, he moved the young minister of tourism, culture and recreation, Tim Hudak, to consumer and business services, with the LCBO as part of his responsibilities. Hudak had been born and raised in Niagara, and had strong intellectual and emotional ties to the domestic wine industry — a fact, no doubt, not lost on Eves.

To mediate between the Wine Council and the LCBO on the issue of market share, Hudak had sent Sue Corke, a person already familiar with the case, who was also a no-nonsense professional mediator with a reputation for calling a spade a spade. Although Sue brought her own style to the table, she was bolstered by the fact that Hudak had given her his blessing and encouragement to try to get LCBO compliance. No minister wants to micro-manage the Crown corporations in his portfolio, but neither does he want to miss an opportunity to serve an important constituency.

Another part of the dynamic was the tacit support Sue Corke sensed from board chair Andy Brandt. She thought she noticed a perceptible conspiratorial twinkle in Andy's eye. She was not aware that, a year before, at the opening of Colio Estates' new barrel cellar, he had endorsed the 50-percent target. In a conversation with David Tsubouchi, who was still minister, and Bruce Walker, Andy Brandt had said to Bruce, "I don't see why we can't count on 50 percent by 2020. What do you think, David?" Tsubouchi nodded in concurrence and smiled.

That, in fact, was where the 50-percent figure had originated. It didn't seem unreasonable, then, that the home producers should have at least 50 percent of the home market. The California wine industry enjoyed 80 percent of their market, the French and Italian nearly 95 percent. Whether Andy had spoken to Bob Peter on the matter was moot, however. It was Peter's call, and as the LCBO senior leader, Peter felt there were too many factors that were out of his control. He could control, to some degree, how many promotions he gave, but he couldn't control every winery's marketing plan or marketing spend, so he couldn't commit to a specific percentage growth. The two sides had reached a stalemate.

When they finally came together, they met in the boardroom of the Wine Council, on local turf in St. Catharines, which might have given the wineries a psychological edge. The LCBO men in suits sat on one side of the table, with their backs to the bank of windows, in the alpha position; the winery "dudes," dressed in more relaxed country casuals sat across from them. No-nonsense Sue had to make a breakthrough to move Bob Peter away from his strong position, but she would do it in a principled way. As in any dispute resolution, she put all the interests on the table, trying to get to the bottom of everything. Andy Brandt was first to speak and did so in his inimitable, amusing way, which eased some of the tension. Then Bob Peter weighed in, repeating why it was not going to work. "I'm not going to put the liquor board in a place where we're gong to set targets we know we can't possibly meet."

One can understand why he would take this position. For Bob Peter to position himself any differently could have been seen as negligent for a private-sector company. But the LCBO also had a public mandate to support the wine industry of Ontario. Sue stepped in at that point and the Showdown at the OK Corral continued. Leaning forward, looking directly at Peter, she said, "You are going to make this work. We are going to find a way to make this happen." With that she put some targets on the board and said, "We're not leaving this room until we've made these decisions."

It was a governmental act of support displayed on many occasions during Linda Franklin's tenure, and for which she was grateful. "The industry's story," she commented much later, "has been about the great people and wonderful moments where Cabinet people and civil servants have liked the industry enough and have been dedicated enough to want to help it along." Linda didn't limit her appreciation to the government. There were many people at the LCBO as well, such as Bob Downey, senior vice-president for sales and marketing, who fought many battles for the industry because he thought it made a difference. Another who had a lot of heart for the industry and worked energetically on its behalf was the vice-president of marketing and customer insights, Nancy Cardinal.

When Bruce Walker was chair, the Wine Council, in partnership with the LCBO, accomplished some important advances. The Craft Program was one. It gave a place in stores for emerging and small wineries that otherwise wouldn't have had sufficient supply for the immense LCBO network. Under the program, fifty-seven key LCBO stores would carry their selected wines. Another successful program was the WOW initiative, introduced in 2002 to promote "Wonderful Ontario Wines." Selected staff, throughout the LCBO system, were educated about the industry's wines, wineries and winemakers.

One of the most positive outcomes of 2003 was the finalization of an agreement with the European Union (EU) to open its doors to icewines from Ontario and British Columbia. The actual negotiations, however, had begun two years earlier, when a delegation from Ontario, weary of the lack of progress being made by the federal government to get access to the Union, took the initiative into their own hands. VQA chair Len Pennachetti was fed up. In a CBC interview, he said he was "no longer prepared to accept non-tariff barriers that were clearly fabricated by the EU when rejecting case after case of Canadian icewine at the European borders."

Linda Franklin and Council chair Bruce Walker took the case to the provincial Progressive Conservative minister of consumer and commercial relations, Bob Runciman, and explained the inequity of the existing trade imbalance. More than $600 million of EU wine was imported into Canada, but only $500,000 of Canadian wine was accepted into the EU. "How can we move this forward?" asked Linda.

Runciman replied without hesitation: "We'll go there ourselves on an Ontario mission. Let's just organize it."

Their entourage included LCBO CEO Andy Brandt and his right hand, Barry O'Brien; VQA of Ontario executive director Laurie Macdonald; Runciman and his deputy minister, Sandy Lang; Linda Franklin and Bruce Walker from the Wine Council; plus Runciman's executive assistant Justin Brown and ministry of consumer and business services analyst Nancy Kennedy, who organized the entire mission. Over the course of five days, with a gruelling schedule of twenty meetings in five different cities, the members of the delegation presented their case. They felt they weren't asking for the moon. It was largely a matter of principle. European wines were being well served in our market; why shouldn't we have the same access to theirs?

At first the officials in Brussels were indifferent to the point of being dismissive, almost rude. While they regarded the Ontario entourage as backwoods hillbillies with little sense of protocol, the Canadians viewed the Europeans as stiff and arrogant. Not until Brandt and Runciman started to balance the Europeans' sense of entitlement to the wine world with the leverage that Ontario had as an importer of European wine did they start to pay attention. Brandt and Runciman reminded the EU officials that Ontario was a very large market, and the LCBO was the largest purchaser of wine in the world, which could at any one time either increase shipments or cut them back severely. Only the Burgundian producers fully understood what was at stake. The worldwide market share for French wine was just starting to show a decline. The loss of yet another substantial market could be a blow.

Despite a more reasonable reception in Dijon, the exhausted and disap- pointed delegation came home with no agreement in place. In retaliation, the Wine Council, along with the LCBO, prepared to mount a campaign, funded by the Ontario government, to tell consumers that the French were resisting their overtures for access. Therefore, they stated, Ontario was going to be less interested in theirs. "The Europeans were being bloody- minded with their rules," Linda Franklin reminded the media. "Maybe they wouldn't be so restrictive if we applied the same rules to them." The hillbillies were not going to be bullied. When it looked as if they had some momentum, at the eleventh hour, just before the campaign hit the streets, Runciman got a call that the EU had changed its mind. It would allow unfettered access for Canadian icewines that passed VQA requirements and protocols. It was a milestone for the industry, not only in terms of access but in terms of the credibility on the international stage it provided for Canadian icewine.

As glorious as their recent victories had been, Linda was all too aware of the defeats. She, along with many others, had been working for nearly a decade to achieve national standards for wine production. Initially, the motivation was to get British Columbia to legislate its own VQA standards. The framework was in place, but there were no specifics about its enforcement. There were so many anomalies among maverick producers in British Columbia that only the force of a national body could have any effect. For ten years they had debated.

Nova Scotia wanted to include a New York Muscat on the list of accepted VQA grape varieties, despite the fact that it was an American hybrid with noticeable *labrusca* parentage, and was not on the list of accepted varieties. Then estimates came out that compliance with the standards would cost producers up to $70,000 each, a figure later shown to be blown way out of proportion.

The tipping point came when the federal regulators said that hairnets must be worn by everyone when tours were been taken through wineries. That was the psychological point of no return, which eventually led to the abandonment of national standards.

Linda could see that coming, but what she and others couldn't have predicted was Mother Nature's change of heart. After shinning brightly on the industry for nearly twenty years, she let her force be known. The effects of the 2001 Asian lady beetle invasion on the finished wines in 2002 resulted in the dumping millions of litres of tainted wine; then two severe crop failures, one in 2003 and another in 2005, crippled many producers. The developmental arc of the industry was changing, as Susan O'Dell, marketing analyst and co-founder of Eastdell Estates, explained. Prior to 2000, everyone had the same "enemy," someone or something other than themselves, which made collaboration easy. From 2001 to 2005, the enemy was still a common one, Mother Nature, but not an enemy anyone could do much about. The continuous losses started to fray everyone's nerves.

Then the enemy changed. The industry had tripled in size when it started to think the unthinkable: Was there a cap on how much consumers would drink? Spend? Or on how much the market could grow? How unfair, then, were the grossly unequal privileges that Vincor and Andrés enjoyed through their combined 368 additional retail stores?

Ontario's Byzantine regulations and a difficult trade agreement, which had been badly negotiated by the feds, affected everyone. The industry had become tired of bandage solutions. The problems were deep, entrenched, systemic and structural. The Wine Council had spent eight agonizing months creating recommendations for the Beverage Alcohol System Review (BASR), a review panel called to examine ways to transform Ontario's beverage-alcohol system, only to have the report dismissed within minutes of its final submission. The Liberals were now in office, and structural change to the beverage-alcohol system in Ontario was not part of their agenda.

It was difficult for everyone to hear. So many had given of their time and dedication. Industry morale was at a breaking point. With the report's dismissal, everyone felt disillusioned and forsaken, blaming one another, Linda, the government and Mother Nature. Each was frantically busy with his and her own businesses, yet had spent so much time with Linda moving the industry forward, where could they next fight for change? And, more important, did they have the reserves left for the battle?

In 2005, Norm Beal, proprietor of Peninsula Ridge Estates, became chair of the Wine Council in a rough period. He, too, spent much time on industry matters and was surprised how much it demanded of him, but he stepped in and did a yeoman's job. Beal represented the change in the momentum that was to usher in a new phase.

Linda and Norm worked together for two years, and she earned from him the same professional respect she had garnered in previous years from other chairs. She never felt that she had to restrain her opinions with any of them. The chairs and members expected her to speak her mind, to fight and argue with them in a dialogue that, in the end, made their core argument more cogent. As senior staff, she was their employee, hired to do their bidding, but over the years she had earned such respect that she became a leader in her own right. If they got off course, she would find a way to get the members going in the right direction again. She was extremely bright, personable, quick on her feet and engaging, with a contagious laugh and a disarming sense of humour. She also possessed a steel rod of integrity that no one could refute, one they witnessed in many telling encounters. Once, she had been given a confidential document by the LCBO; she read it and immediately gave it back. When the members discovered that she had had the document, everyone knew that she hadn't even considered making a photocopy of it, so they never asked.

Then there was the time that an employee had not been doing her job. The situation had started to accelerate to the point where there could have been heavy financial losses to the Wine Council. The members wanted to blame the person and fire her. But Linda said, "Look, folks, you're right. This is a job not well done. And I need to say, 'This happened on my watch. Should I have been paying attention and noticed it?' I think this person deserves the opportunity to be shown how to fix it and then, if it ever happens again, she's gone." The employee continued to give loyalty to the organization for several very productive years after that.

Linda Franklin earned her members' respect by harnessing their passion for their businesses and putting it to work for the industry, but she also brought a sense of reality to their efforts. During deliberations around an issue, she would go around the table and listen to their ideas. If they were impractical, she would say, "Okay, I can do that, but I can tell you, folks, the government's not going to go for it. Or do you want me to write up something that will pass?" If she thought a project could advance the mutual interests of the members of the Wine Council, yet there was disagreement among them, she would get around to each of the individuals who were resisting and have a conversation to find out how far that person might come to the centre. Everyone usually had some room to move. She would know where she could give or get something that was more important to one person and his or her objectives than the issue on which she was trying to get agreement.

She had critics within the organization. Some were angry because they thought she didn't fight hard enough for VQA stores, or for the acceptance of every VQA wine offered to the LCBO. Some thought she bent too often to the will of the larger wineries, even though they compromised on many, many issues at the expense of their own interests for the good of the indus- try. She had her external adversaries who knew she was formidable in a negotiation, such as the Grape Growers of Ontario, who once announced at an annual meeting that they should hire a "shark" like Linda.

Toward the end of her tenure, Linda could sense that the industry was approaching a new place. There were more than one hundred members, several of whom were wealthy entrepreneurs with their own ideas on where the industry should head. Stage, screen and sport celebrities were lending their names to brands, and vineyard real estate was nearing the six-figure mark. The new Green Belt was starting to set environmentalists against entrepreneurs, and a new wine producers' association, dedicated to VQA-only wines, had emerged, resulting in a bifurcation of the industry. As winery proprietor Susan O'Dell commented, "The members now needed explaining and consoling, skills that didn't play to Linda's strength. She was a fixer and a doer." The vintage of 2007 was recognized as "the best vintage the wine industry had ever known," and on that positive note, after fourteen years at the helm, Linda Franklin took herself out.

10 NORM BEAL'S PEAL

"I think we're going to see in the next five years a massive transformation, and I'll tell you why."
—*Norm Beal, proprietor, Peninsula Ridge Estates*

The first issue Norm Beal took on as chair of the Wine Council of Ontario in 2005 was to tackle an oppressive excise tax that the federal government had levied on wine. For every litre of wine produced, the manufacturer was charged fifty-one cents for the privilege of doing so. Even the tightly wound Bureau of Alcohol, Tobacco and Firearms (ATF) in the United States, which made no bones about clustering its social "sins" into one federal regulatory agency, gave its producers an exemption on the first 500,000 litres (110,000 gallons) sold. The Canadian tax was one among many significant competitive disadvantages that Canadian producers had to overcome.

For every conversation Norm and his predecessors had had about changing tax regulations, the reply was always a perfunctory, "We can't do that. We have to be trade legal." It was getting to the point where it felt as if this free-trade mantra could be safely invoked whenever the government chose to stall on anything, and it precluded any reasonable discussion about the matter. The domestic wine industry protested. If Canada's trading partners did not invoke an excise tax on their producers, why should the Canadian government levy one on its own?

The Canadian Vintners Association (CVA), under the leadership of Bruce Walker from Vincor, had tried for years to penetrate the federal Liberal government's intransigence with well-reasoned appeals for change. As a member of the CVA board of directors, Norm knew the frustrations Bruce had experienced, but he also knew that sometimes success had more to do with timing, perseverance and a new party in office.

As the proprietor of Peninsula Ridge Estates, Norm had taken a personal interest in changing the excise law. He, like other producers his size, was shelling out hundreds of thousands of dollars annually to the federal government. For many, the issue was one of survival.

Norm Beal had grown up in Niagara in the 1970s and 1980s. After graduating from school, he went into the oil business, first with Shell Canada in Calgary and then with Glencore, a Stamford, Connecticut–based commodity-trading company. For fifteen years he was a high flyer, becoming well known in aviation circles as the Jet-Fuel King. For fifteen years, the planet's planes flew on jet fuel that Norm had sold to their airlines. He learned how to negotiate and persuade, when to buy and when to sell, and how to manoeuvre his way through the intricacies of government relations. The fast-paced international life was starting to wear him out when, on a trip to Vancouver, he decided to fly to the Okanagan Valley for a breather. A solitary walk through a vineyard convinced him — "What a wonderful career this could be someday."

From then on, on every trip he made — whether to Australia, Chile, Argentina, Europe or the United States — he would no longer just take a limo from the airport, go to his meeting and fly home. He started to tack on extra days to visit wine country and plan his dream. Gradually he got to know people in the business, particularly people in California's renegade Sonoma Valley. Sam Sabastiani had split from his bulk-producing winemaking family to make quality wines and, after several discussions with Sam, the hook had been set. Norm now had to decide where he would set up shop.

Niagara in 1997 wasn't even part of his equation until Norm's sister Teresa e-mailed him and said, "Come back to Niagara." Norm remembered Niagara's wine from his days at Fonthill High in the 1970s. Making Baby Duck or port-styled wines wasn't exactly what he had in mind, but could things have changed that much in the decade and a half he had been away? His sister convinced him to take a look around. When he arrived, he spent time with a very patient Roman Prydatkewcyz, a serious grape grower as well as a farm real-estate sales representative. In their travels to look at potential land on which to plant a vineyard, Norm bought wines — from Château des Charmes, Cave Spring Cellars, Henry of Pelham, Vineland Estates, Strewn and Reif — and brought them back to Connecticut to see what his friends thought. They were stunned by the quality.

On his next trip to Niagara, he and Roman took another week looking around but, once again, found nothing. The last day, just before heading back to Connecticut, he went for a drive. It was one of those magnificent November days — bright and crisp, with skies so blue they seemed iridescent. As he approached the curve on the old No. 8 Highway between Beamsville and Grimsby, he noticed a stately two-storey Victorian home, with gingerbread trim and welcoming front and side verandas, nestled in the foothills of the Escarpment. He rolled up the long drive and knocked on the door. An old gentleman answered.

"Would you mind if I looked around?" Norm asked. "I love old architecture."

"Not at all," said the old man. "I was just about to go for a walk. Would you like to join me?"

They ended up walking the entire property line. From one high point, Norm could see the Toronto skyline etched on the horizon like a long and sturdy laker raising its hull on the northern shore of Lake Ontario. After a conversation over a glass of the old man's wine, perhaps the worst wine Norm had ever tasted, he learned that the man had taken his home off the market a couple of years before. He even showed Norm the old listing.

"Would you still be willing to sell it for that price?" said Norm.

"Yes," said the man.

Norm wrote him a cheque for the deposit. He had fallen in love with the property.

"Hold on to this," said Norm. "I want a little time to think about it and do some due diligence."

Norm Beal

Within two days, Norm's lawyer drafted a purchase of sale. Norm, a man accustomed to balancing deliberate and instinctive thinking, confessed to his wife: "I just bought sixty acres of vineyards on the Escarpment." This purchase would begin a trend toward a new kind of investor in Niagara's vineyards — the well-heeled wine lover. Exhilarated by these first steps toward a new life, Norm hadn't fully anticipated the implications of his land being part of the highly regulated Niagara Escarpment, which UNESCO had named a biosphere reserve in February 1990 — one of only fifteen biosphere reserves in Canada and part of a network of 531 reserves in 105 countries. Had he known the mire of regulations that would accompany this distinction, he might have asked, "Do I really want to get into this?" But by then he had leapt off the dock. That was also before he realized the myriad regulations that were involved in making and distributing alcohol in

Ontario. It was baptism by fire, and it didn't get any better as he moved on.

Yet this was an opportunity to come home. He was thirty-nine years old. If he was going to do something in the wine business, he recognized very early that he would not be doing it for his generation but for future generations. He also knew the millions of dollars he was about to invest was not going to make more millions. If it had been money that motivated him, he would have stayed in oil trading. There were very few businesses in the world where he could take a product to market that was so deeply tied to the soil and so vertically integrated. To do the same in the oil business, he would have had to explore for oil, refine it, market it and have his own gas station. He had also looked at the Ontario market and believed there was a demand that wasn't being filled. Or he thought that was the case. If he didn't act soon, he reasoned, it would fill up quickly. Being on the leading edge was the key to being successful. He would later discover that, at that time, most Ontario consumers hadn't even known of the existence of the wines he had tasted from the newer Ontario producers.

When he decided to break ground for his new winery, Peninsula Ridge, he learned just how complicated the Ontario government had made getting into the wine business and understood why other entrepreneurs weren't doing so at a faster pace. Layers of regulations, licences to secure, town, regional, provincial and federal zoning laws to abide by, VQA regulations with which to comply and taxes upon taxes to pay. One layer seemed to veil the next, even more complicated, set of restrictions. Never one to sit back and whine, however, Norm dove in to learn first-hand how the system operated. He joined the Wine Council and soon became its treasurer; he joined the Canadian Vintners Association and became a board member. He was appointed as a commissioner of the Ontario Farm Products Marketing Commission, treasurer of the Twenty Valley Tourism Association and board member of the West Lincoln Memorial Hospital Foundation. After only six years in the industry, in June 2005, he was elected chair of the Wine Council, succeeding Paul Speck from Henry of Pelham.

On the roster of goals that he saw as top priorities for his and the Wine Council's five-year agenda, he listed the "elimination of the excise tax on all VQA wines sold annually for volumes up to 500,000 litres." Wasting no time, only four months into his term, he, together with the CEO of the Grape Growers of Ontario (formerly the Grape Growers Marketing Board),

Debbie Zimmerman, and Linda Franklin, president of the Wine Council, made a unified pitch to the federal government: Zimmerman asked for a boost to the fortunes of grape growers who wanted to replant their farms from juice grapes or tree-fruit orchards to vineyards, and Norm and Linda presented their case for excise-tax reform.

The groundwork had been laid in 2004 with Bruce Walker, then CVA chair, who had worked tirelessly with his CVA executive director, Bill Ross. However, by the end of November 2005, within two weeks from the time Norm made his pitch, two Niagara Conservative MPs tabled a private members' bill on tax reform; then an election was called, and excise-tax relief soon became an election issue. Political change seemed to move with the speed of a glacier, until a tipping point, then an avalanche of change started things moving.

Paul Bosc Jr. from Château des Charmes, never at a loss for words, explained the unreasonable nature of the tax to a journalist covering the election: "If I moved six kilometres east, just across the river, I could save $400,000 a year." Not having to pay that tax gave a definite advantage for wineries operating in the United States and selling in Canada. Dean Allison, Conservative MP from Norm's West Lincoln riding, did a good job pressing the issue with Finance and became Norm's natural ally. Norm had worked on Allison's election campaign and co-chaired a fundraising campaign for the West Lincoln Hospital, a campaign that Allison had also supported. When the federal Liberal government under Paul Martin fell, Allison continued to lobby strenuously for tax reform among his colleagues, but Norm and his cohorts still had to make a personal appeal to the finance minister in Stephen Harper's new Conservative government, Jim Flaherty.

On April 4 Dean Allison had tabled a private member's bill entitled "An Act to Amend the Excise Act, 2004 (wine exemption)," and Norm knew it was necessary to schedule a meeting with the finance minister in advance of the 2006 Budget. By that time, however, Flaherty was in budget lockdown. Norm took the notion out of his mind; he simply wouldn't get to meet with the finance minister.

On April 18 he received an unanticipated call from Dean Allison, saying that Flaherty's office had called him. "You can meet with Mr. Flaherty, if you can be in Ottawa today. He will see you between 5 and 6 p.m." Norm and Dean, plus the executive director from the Canadian Vintners Association,

Dan Paszkowski, were astounded by this almost unprecedented invitation, but nevertheless were on afternoon planes heading for the capital.

Dan Paszkowski had worked hard on the departments of Agriculture and Finance, where he was well known and respected by the senior bureaucrats from his six years with the Mining Association. He had built a solid file that realigned their figures, making it even clearer just why reforming excise tax was important for the wine industry and how it would level the playing field with industry competitors. The threesome rolled into Flaherty's office just as the governor of the Bank of Canada, David Dodge, was leaving, ideally having just offered clarity on the financial wiggle room the government would have with the potential loss in revenue if the excise tax law was modified but, more realistically, having just briefed Flaherty on the IMF meeting they were attending in Washington the following day.

Jim Flaherty had been finance minister under Premier Mike Harris in Ontario. Under Premier Ernie Eves, Flaherty had been minister of enterprise, opportunity and innovation. In both capacities, Flaherty had known Dean Allison well, as Dean had worked on Flaherty's prior provincial leadership bid and had visited Niagara often. He had even visited Norm's winery several times. When the group entered Flaherty's office, their greetings were cordial.

The meeting lasted an hour, with Flaherty listening while each of his guests took turns on various aspects of their pitch. Norm's role was to show how the Wine Council's vision was aligned with the strategic goals of Flaherty's new government. As he spoke, he could see that Flaherty was responsive. Flaherty had made similar moves for the Craft Breweries when he was provincial finance minister. Norm's hunch was that Flaherty wanted to make a mark for his new government. Although mindful that a sucker punch could come at any time, Norm nevertheless left the meeting feeling confident.

Two weeks later, on May 2, 2006, the budget came down. As was the case in the United States, Flaherty had eliminated the excise tax on the first 500,000 litres (110,000 gallons) of 100-percent Canadian wine production annually per wine licensee in the fiscal year of the licensee that began on or after July 1, 2006. The consequences were unintentionally negative, however, because that excise tax rate would increase by 21 percent from $0.5122 to $0.62 per litre to offset the impact of the 1-percent GST rate reduction, which was also in the budget. The impact of the 21-percent tax increase would have been incurred on every litre of import-blended wine produced in Canada (as well as imports) and on incremental production of 100-percent Canadian wine above 500,000 litres. The 500,000-litre exemption would not apply to every winery operation, due to associated-company-and-related-person rules. The budget proposed that companies with multiple wineries under a corporate banner would benefit from only a 500,000-litre exemption across the business entity. The maximum savings per winery from the exemption, no matter what the size, was set at $310,000 (500,000 litres). Because of these negative implications, the CVA immediately prepared analyses to address the concerns related to the 21-percent tax increase.

In Ottawa, on May 29, 2006, on the eve of the CVA's first annual "Canadian Wine Experience" reception on Parliament Hill, a meeting was being held at the CVA offices to discuss Budget 2006 and other policy issues. In attendance were Norm Beal, Linda Franklin, Bruce Walker, Dan Paszkowski, Len Pennachetti and a few other CVA members. During the meeting Dan Paszkowski received a call from Flaherty's office to discuss a possible solution to CVA concerns with the budget. The call was the direct result of significant CVA lobbying and the reception the CVA had planned the following day on Parliament Hill and would see complete elimination of the excise tax for 100-percent Canadian wine, effective July 1, 2006, with no associated-company-and-related-person rules, allowing every estate winery to benefit from the full exemption. The offer was discussed and accepted at the CVA board meeting on May 30 with the total support of Norm Beal.

The minister of finance announced the 100-percent excise exemption on June 23, at Peninsula Ridge Estate Winery in the presence of representatives from numerous Ontario wineries and Ontario MPPs. The value of the excise exemption was $11 million annually, with a $0.62 savings on every litre of wine sold. B.C. producers also benefited. In Norm's first year as chair, he had helped to negotiate one of the most significant tax-relief reforms the Canadian wine industry had ever known. Small wineries saw a windfall of more than $100,000 annually, which they could now reinvest in other aspects of their businesses.

But there were some unpleasant consequences. The exemption caused the materialization of the government's worst fears. By the fall of 2005, the

European Union had set the stage for a showdown challenge to the ruling, claiming that, under the General Agreement on Tariffs and Trade (GATT), the measure was an unfair trade advantage given to domestic products and would violate the principle of national treatment. The Europeans wanted the same break as Canadian producers.

By January 2007, unable to resolve their differences, France formally initiated a legal challenge against Canada. That was when the Canadian Vintners Association, together with the Wine Council of Ontario, fuming, started the campaign mentioned in Chapter 9, urging Canadians to boycott European wines. On March 9, they launched a website, www.supportcanadianwines. com. Thousands of willing replies came in supporting the move. On March 24, the EU issued a formal communiqué to the Canadian government that they would drop their World Trade Organization (WTO) Dispute Settlement Panel request. Their request for WTO consultations would remain on record, but inactive. At a time when European market share was dwindling at a serious rate, this boycott leverage had forced the EU to pull back.

But it wasn't over. On September 26, the EU circled back, issuing a letter to the Canadian government advising that, unless Canada demonstrated that it was considering concrete steps to revise the excise-tax emption for 100-percent Canadian wine, the EU would commence actions for a WTO Dispute Settlement Panel challenge. This launched a year-long process of discussions between the EU, the federal government and the CVA. In October 2008, Canada and the EU agreed to disagree, with Canada requesting that the EU pull the challenge off the roster by December 19, 2008, which, as we have seen, they did.

Next on Norm Beal's list of priorities to advance the interests of the wine industry was to secure "improved margins for VQA wines sold through all retail and wholesale channels, similar to the British Columbia Quality Enhancement Program."

The initiative that he and Linda Franklin negotiated for the industry in Ontario was called the VQA Wine Support Program, which enabled smaller wineries to offer wines into the LCBO distribution channel. It delivered a 30-percent rebate on the LCBO FOB value returned to wineries that listed their products with the LCBO for the first 13,000 litres (2,860 gallons) of production. Despite the fact that in British Columbia there was no cap, this served as an important boost for small wineries that could not afford to

offer the LCBO their wines because of the LCBO's arduous markup policies. Its success, together with the excise-tax relief, proved to be an immea-
surable boost for smaller producers. As Allan Schmidt, now president of
Vineland Estates, commented, "It allowed me and many others like me to
hire salespeople and reinvest in the winery." (Unfortunately, the Budget of
2009 would cancel the program, forcing Norm to redouble his efforts to get
it reinstated before his term was up in June.)

Individual winemakers and growers never stopped helping one another.
If a winemaker needed advice on how to make sparkling wine using the
traditional method, there was another winemaker there to help him out. If
equipment broke, growers continued to call upon their neighbours for assistance. But at the political level, after a few years as chair of the Wine Council, it was becoming increasingly clear to Norm that the collaboration and
the unified voice with which the industry once spoke was starting to sound
hoarse and cracked. Most of the serious-but-amenable issues of mutual concern had been addressed. What remained were much more fundamental
issues, so systemic and so structurally divisive they pitted producer against
producer. One crucial issue was the distribution system and the inequities that existed between the haves and the have-nots — those companies
that had off-site retail stores and those who did not, or rather, could not.
This had always divided the industry, but now the have-nots could ignore
it no longer.

For Norm, the distribution of beverage alcohol in Ontario was unfairly
controlled by a trio of exclusive interests. The first interest was the monopoly the government maintained through the LCBO; the second was the
monopoly of the private, foreign beer companies that owned The Beer
Store, a privilege not given to the private general sale of wine; and the third
was the private monopoly that controlled 80 percent of the sales of wine in
Ontario — the private wine stores that had been grandfathered as a result
of free trade. After 1993, any newcomer to the industry had only three sales
channels: his on-site wine shop, bars and restaurants, and, if he was lucky to
get a listing, the LCBO. On the other hand, Vincor and Andrés had more
than three hundred additional outlets across the province in which to sell
their products. Other pre-FTA producers, Colio, Château des Charmes or
Pelee Island among them, shared a total of around twenty retail outlets.
Colio, with fourteen, had the most.

Another irritation for smaller producers was the privilege larger producers had of being able to draw from several manufacturing licences they had
inherited from previous acquisitions, licences they could transfer from one
location to another. This annoyed award-winning premium VQA producer
Harald Thiel, wealthy proprietor and co-winemaker at Hidden Bench in
Niagara, who had no such privilege when he opened in 2005. "The big
guys can do what the small guys can't," says Thiel, who witnessed large
companies squeezing the regulations for selling wine.

The regulation stated that a retail licence could be given only to a
winery that was manufacturing on the same site as at least five acres
(two hectares) of planted contiguous grapes. Vincor and Andrew Peller
(Andrés) could trump this regulation by simply transferring one of its
inherited wine retail licences to the new site. Even more absurd to Thiel
was the fact that, at the Wine Council, any of the larger wineries could
single-handedly veto a decision driven by a majority of members based
simply on the amount of literage they produced. It was a privilege they
had never used, but was nevertheless entrenched in the bylaws of the
Wine Council. "The industry will only have an effective trade organization that speaks with one voice," argued Thiel, "when all members are
treated equally in terms of access to market and when the 'literage vote,' or
threat thereof, is removed from the bylaws of the WCO." He also believed
that it made no sense to have a trade organization co-promote "Cellared
in Canada" products made from 70-percent imported wine along with
VQA products, which were 100-percent domestic. "They are effectively
competing products with frequently opposing interests," said Thiel.

The blending program that sustained 80 percent of the businesses of
Vincor and Andrew Peller, and 80 percent of the sales of Ontario wine,
and was derived from 70-percent offshore wine blended with 30-percent
domestic product, was an advantage that producers who started after the
free trade agreement did not enjoy. Even if newer entrants chose not to
blend their wines with imports, what rankled Thiel was the fact the program
sustained lesser-quality grape production. Whereas two decades before, the
dynamic of the industry was changed because of the small players, now,
believed Thiel, "the dynamic of the industry had changed because of the
big players."

When premium VQA producer Moray Tawse, a wine connoisseur and co-partner in First National Financial Corporation, opened his state-of-the-art winery in 2004, he criticized the narrow vision he discovered that many other producers were willing to accept. Setting out to make great wine, he could afford to cut no corners. "I'm going to have to spend a lot of money that I won't recoup for a long time," said Tawse, "but that's the only way to raise the bar." Larger wineries made their profits from commercial wines. He defined these as wines that were pumped out annually, and that tasted the same year after year. More interesting and authentic wines, he contended, were the *terroir*-based wines that depended on the soil, the weather and the grapes.

Ed Madronich came on the scene in 2004 with his and his father's new winery, Flat Rock Cellars. He acknowledged the inequities in the system as real and divisive; his solution was to give everyone the same rights to additional retail stores and let everyone blend. "Done," said Madronich. Yet quality was also his concern. What bothered him more than retail access was the disservice the LCBO had seemed to do to the industry when it accepted VQA wines that were below par. "One bottle is all it takes for a consumer to turn off VQA wine. I want to be measured according to the same sensory criteria of quality as any wine in the world."

In 2006, John Howard, former magnate from Canon, and previous owner of Vineland Estates, opened his new winery, John Howard Cellars, with Megalomaniac, an irreverent brand that captivated the market and sustained its share. Howard had always been on the periphery of industry governance, believing, as did Tawse, that the pursuits of the Wine Council could slip into pettiness with the intermittent haranguing of more vociferous members. He had no time for what he saw as a perversion of his and everyone else's interests. As one-third owner of a château in Bordeaux, Howard could see the differences between Ontario and Bordeaux in stark relief.

"If the Bordelais have an issue, they lock themselves in a room, argue, but as soon as they walk out they are completely united." In Ontario, he found the resentments often simmered and corroded effective collaboration. One reason was temporal. "The Bordelais are very future-oriented," explained Howard, "tradition, family and evolving the family's reputation are very important to them. In Ontario, it's all about the here and now and me, me, me."

Such outspoken differences contributed to a bifurcation in the industry that led some of its most talented producers, such as Thiel, Tawse and John Howard, to turn away from participation in its governance. This absence of some of the most successful entrepreneurial minds in Canada was a major disappointment to Norm Beal, who also came from a background of personal wealth and business acumen. There would have been nothing he would have liked better than to reflect their interests in terms of change, but reflecting everyone's interests turned out to be a near impossibility. When he seemed to be expressing the interests of the larger players, he would be called an "Uncle Tom." For the smaller players, anything less than eliminating import blending was a failure of leadership. However, neither personal slights, a broken distribution system, dysfunctional membership or the lack of participation in industry governance by some of the industry's most brilliant business minds could compare to the third challenge he set out to accomplish as chair of the Wine Council: "to vastly improve grower/industry relations so that we can lobby government with one voice."

* * *

The Grape Growers of Ontario had begun its life as a marketing board in 1947 "to serve the needs and represent the interests of grape growers in their dealings with processors." It joined the ranks of other marketing boards after the war to help farmers market their products, conduct research and determine the price processors would pay for such agricultural commodities as asparagus, beans, pork, potatoes, sheep, tender fruit, chicken, eggs and tobacco. Commodities, by definition, were considered to have no qualitative differentiation across a market. Rather, they possessed uniform quality and were produced in large quantities considered equivalent, and usually sold to large conglomerates that could easily overpower a small farmer in a take-it-or-leave-it negotiation over price.

When the Grape Growers Marketing Board was formed, the wineries in Ontario were very large and had immense leverage over growers. For a farmer, to have access to the negotiating skills of a third party speaking on his behalf, with every farmer getting the same price for the same grapes, was deliverance. The more grapes they could harvest, the more money they would get paid. In 2008, these were the same assumptions on which the marketing board (its name changed to Grape Growers of Ontario in 2002) still operated, despite the fact that grapes did have qualitative differences across a market and did not possess uniform quality — and despite the fact that, when they are grown in large quantities, their quality decreases. The premise for the Grape Growers Marketing Board in 1947 was based on the nature of growing *labrusca* vines, where yield made minimal difference to wine quality. Growing *vinifera* was vastly more complex than growing *labrusca*, yet the marketing board hadn't changed these basic assumptions in sixty-two years.

Every year the representatives from the Wine Council and the representatives from the grape growers sat across from one another in confrontation to negotiate the prices that the "processors" would pay for grapes that reached minimum levels of ripeness. The system had alienated the parties, and this became a major source of irritation when the issues were discussed that related to driving up the quality of grapes. There was no other system in the world that did not allow the people making the wine to speak about price with the growers from whom they bought their grapes. It was a system that fundamentally rewarded quantity over quality. Come grape-negotiation time, tempers invariably flared. Neither side was immune to using power plays to achieve its ends.

These unenviable conditions forced wineries to plant their own vineyards and tend their own vines to get the levels of quality they sought. As their supplies of grapes increased, they bought less and less from independent growers. Having their own grapes, however, didn't exempt them from paying processing fees required by the marketing board. These fees had to be paid by all growers to the Grape Growers of Ontario, and would be used to support negotiations against the wineries' own interests. Of course, it was more complex than that, because the Grape Growers also used those fees to sponsor research from which all wineries also benefited. But come annual price-setting time, those benefits were forgotten and tempers still flared.

In 2005 the pent-up anger and feelings of powerlessness that had built up in the growers over the years, coalesced. A group of growers decided to form a type of co-operative and open a winery of their own. The purpose? To outsmart their "enemies" — Vincor and Andrés — whom they felt had held them hostage long enough. They were through with the uncertainty of having their grapes rejected with what they believed was impunity. They would deprive the big guys of the source of most of the grapes for their Cellared in Canada wines. Within two years, the project would become a cautionary tale of devastating humiliation and monumental financial loss. It would serve as proof that no project built on a negative vision is likely to succeed.

The same year that Norm Beal became chair of the Wine Council, Helmut Klassen was hired as CEO and chair of the board of the newly established wine company called Niagara Vintners. After several years working for the Ford Motor Company in Canada, the United States and China, he had come back home to Niagara and, in 1998, bought one of the vineyards near his parent's property that he had worked on in his teens for T.G. Bright. He was then working for one of Ford's suppliers, Visteon, which required its employees to make a contribution of value to their respective communities. Klassen chose the Grape Growers Marketing Board to fulfil his community obligation. It would be an effective way to become immersed, once again, in the industry with which he felt such close affinity.

The members of the Grape Growers saw in Klassen an articulate man whose commitment to growers' interests was deep and strong. In 2000 some growers came to him and asked if he would become a committee member; shortly after, they asked him to run for director. The organization was experiencing internal strife caused by internal colliding interests, and they looked to Klassen to help keep them intact. After witnessing the adversarial relationship between the growers and the wineries, he told the growers that what they needed was a reliable customer who returned every year.

Talk of a co-operative had been on the growers' minds since the mid-1990s, and Helmut Klassen seemed to be the man to guide them through this process. He had a knack for facilitation that encouraged them to define their values in a meaningful way and to become more conscious of their own needs. This skill enabled the growers to move to action. Klassen was experienced in mass customization and commercialization, business development and production supervision. True, the experience was in the automotive industry, but could the wine business be so different?

Klassen's motive was to strengthen the growers' conviction that they could stand on their own, build strategy, create a business and successfully market their wines. "Let's prove to the government that we are an intrinsically valuable entity within the province," stated Klassen.

He accepted the challenge to build a grower-owned winery, and asked a lawyer to form the structure around which shares would be created and financing raised. Ontario's first co-operative was formed "to ensure a sustainable viticultural supply base as [they become] the premier producer of Ontario-grown and processed value-priced wines." The goal was to eventually produce one million cases of wine a year, using the more than 4,400 acres (1,780 hectares) of grapes available from its shareholders. But the co-operative wasn't exactly a co-op. Since there were twenty shareholders, and each shareholder had one vote, it was a hybrid between a co-op and a shareholder-held operation. A minimum share was $100,000, but most of the shareholders who stayed invested hundreds of thousands more, eventually raising $19 million. One grower invested more than $2.5 million. The growers had an obligation to bring their grapes from their farms to their new venture, but the winemaker and Klassen would decide whether the grapes would be purchased. A shareholder could not insist that the company buy his grapes if the grapes were not up to par, a detail not clearly understood by the shareholders. According to Klassen, when he started enforcing these rules, things began to fray.

In 2004, just before his full-time employment with Niagara Vintners, Klassen had scouted around for a firm to help him prepare a business plan and develop a brand. He chose the Toronto communications agency Davis+Gilbert, where the partners found Klassen fascinating. "He was not just engaging; he was passionate about the new business venture," stated managing partner Michael Gilbert. Klassen and Davis+Gilbert worked together for the next eighteen months preparing the company's business plan, branding, packaging, advertising and marketing plans, plus the bank financing and sales forecasts. The plan called for four sales channels: bulk juice, bulk wine, private label and retail sales of Niagara Vintners' new 20 Bees wine to the LCBO.

Klassen and the Niagara Vintners' winemaker at the time, Rob Sommers (who subsequently accepted an offer to be winemaker at Hester Creek in British Columbia), were the only ones responsible for all the operational and administrative aspects of building the new winery. Klassen seemed quite capable of handling everything. Reinforcing his regard for Klassen, Gilbert wrote on November 26, 2006: "At every turn, Helmut impressed our staff with his ability to listen and grasp new concepts. He showed an ability to be consumer-focused and to think laterally in addition to his plentiful analytical skills. His dedication, leadership and decision-making skills were often tested, especially given the nature of the winery's structure, with an inexperienced Board and eighteen other shareholders to be accountable to."

Perhaps the eventual clash between Klassen and his board had more to do with a clash of values. Against Klassen's advice, the board rescinded the plan to sell bulk juice and private-label production other than to Creekside Winery. These decisions, according to Klassen, threw the business plan off, resulting in eventual imbalances in the winery's finances. Perhaps it was a conflicting model of governance. For the growers, their project was based on their understanding of autonomous principles of democratic member-control, in which each actively participated in setting policies and making decisions. The assumed purpose of the enterprise was to meet worker and community needs. Perhaps Klassen's mental model was one of a corporation such as Ford, where the CEO directed the ship, and top-down leadership determined the means to accomplish the ends toward which the organization strives. A corporation is based on the values of performance, continuous improvement, customer satisfaction, innovation and return on investment. A co-op, on the other hand, is based on the values of self-help, self-responsibility, democracy, equality, equity and solidarity. Whatever the source of their clash, however, the one thing Klassen and the co-op members had in common was the need to produce wealth, and at first it seemed as if their dreams were coming true.

The LCBO welcomed their new brand. 20 Bees would be different from their other "critter" brands, such as Yellow Tail, Little Penguin and Twin Fin. Besides being a VQA product, which would help them fulfil their mandate to promote Ontario-grown brands, 20 Bees had an intriguing story behind it — a story of twenty hard-working growers who tended their vines as stewards of the land. Bees were also the symbol of fecundity and the fertilization of their vineyards. The growers also liked the analogy of the bees, which, like them, once perturbed had a mighty sting. Vincor and Andrés had perturbed them, and they were set to sting them in the marketplace with more VQA wine than both companies combined. This marketing goal also pleased the LCBO.

To better define their brand and be market-driven rather than product-driven, Klassen had gone to the LCBO and asked what the LCBO most wanted in a brand — "fruit forward, crisp, clean, defect free and sulphur stable," said COO Bob Peter. According to Klassen, Peter added, "If you can do that, we'll give you as many listings as you want." Even LCBO CEO Andy Brandt phoned the Vintners' bank and stated: "We're behind these guys and think this is a good idea." Eventually the Bank of Nova Scotia lent Niagara Vintners $22 million, which gave them priority in getting paid back when the receiver was divvying up proceeds of the sale.

The prospect of having an Ontario wine on General List, selling at low prices and in great volume, was music to the LCBO's ears. The catchy name and colourful label and box would also make sales easier. So impressed was the LCBO that 20 Bees won the LCBO's annual Elsie Award for Ontario's best product launch. *Grower Magazine* hailed it as an exemplary story of entrepreneurship in farming and awarded Niagara Vintners an Agri-Food Innovation Award. The 20 Bees website featured the nineteen growers (the twentieth was the winemaker), clad in sneakers and blue jeans, engaged in conversation on bales of hay in a country building. The message was, "We're simple folks, not wine snobs." They boasted of controlling 40 percent of Niagara's grape production, which they were going to turn into unpretentious, value-priced, everyday drinking wines. When winemaker Rob Sommers left for British Columbia, the growers pulled off a coup in attracting Sue-Ann Staff from Pillitteri Estates Winery to replace him. She was named one of the world's top women in wine with a five-generation pedigree in grape-growing and winemaking behind her. Yet even Sue-Ann wouldn't be able to stop the bleeding once it started.

Their agent from Churchill Cellars vouched for Klassen's character, saying in a letter that "he pursued his objectives with rectitude" and was always "professional, straight-forward and supportive." On September 27, 2006, a director from the Agricultural Business Banking division of the Bank of Nova Scotia wrote to Klassen saying, "Your understanding of the numerous risks involved with managing this new entity through the critical first 12–18 months, and your dogged determination to keep the project on schedule, regardless of the obstacles thrown in front of you, is a major reason we decided that we would step out of the box a bit and proceed with the company's financing request."

Just before Klassen was fired one month later, on October 20, 2006, Niagara Vintners had sold almost sixteen thousand cases of wine through the LCBO channel alone. Klassen was dismissed by the board of directors for just cause; the board claimed breach of trust, lack of judgment and actions that compromised the financial interests of the company. From Klassen's point of view the board had been micromanaging him, making sure any purchase over $500 went through the board. He now believed that he had been hired primarily to represent them publicly, build the winery, develop a brand and get that brand into the LCBO, not to act as a CEO in the way he understood a CEO ordinarily operates. Klassen had got word that board members were complaining about him to shareholders, contractors and to the public, effectually undermining his authority and influence. For every claim, Klassen claimed otherwise, and sued for wrongful dismissal. So many questions remained. Klassen had never before been a CEO for so large an operation. Was he simply in over his head? When he acquired a position of power and authority did he lose a sense of boundaries or equilibrium? Were the shareholders bamboozled, or did their quest for vengeance and wealth mesmerize them to the extent that it distorted their perception of the events spinning around them?

Before the case for wrongful dismissal could come before the courts, the company went into receivership, with Deloitte in Canada named as receivers. What had gone so horribly wrong?

According to Deloitte, the company became insolvent due to the following reasons: extensive equipment and capital construction costs principally financed by debt; inadequate financing to fund working capital and marketing expenditures necessary to launch a new brand; fractured and ineffective governance structure, with numerous shareholders participating in varying degrees of the management and no apparent controlling party providing direction; overproduction of wine and related wine purchases; and a lack of management depth and experience in construction project management, sales and marketing, and finance.

Some observers felt that the shareholders believed Klassen for too long and only too late started asking the hard questions, that they were naive and slow to react. They owed their creditors $12 million. The board should have declared bankruptcy a year earlier but skirted it. Rumour said they had erected a $20-million facility and had paid for only $2 million. Should the tradespeople have let their invoices go unpaid so long? Should the bank have stopped the train sooner? Did the members of the board, who were also significant shareholders and desperate to be liberated from the tyranny of the larger wineries, ignore the need for checks and balances, choosing instead to micromanage for personal gain? Was this desire so powerful it elimated any caution?

In 2006, the winery turned 3,800 tonnes of grapes into wine, selling 30,000 cases of it to the LCBO. The remaining 200,000 litres (44,000 gallons) was sold as bulk, leaving an inventory of approximately 2.8 million litres (616,000 gallons). This meant they were going into the 2007 harvest needing only 300 tonnes of grapes to supply to existing sales channels. They had a capacity to hold 2,000 additional tonnes of grapes and yet they brought in (but didn't pay for) 2,700 tonnes of grapes. The board of directors let that happen. Despite this surplus, when Klassen refused to accept a load of poor-quality Sauvignon Blanc from a shareholder, the shareholder threw his jacket on the ground and said, "You're out of your mind. You're costing me $30,000. You're an %$# @!#%." According to Klassen, that guaranteed his departure.

They had many contracts for private labelling, some with Creekside Estates, who produced the Mike Weir and Wayne Gretzy brands. Creekside partner Peter Jensen had become a "Bee" and took over as CEO for a brief period when Klassen was asked to leave. Niagara Vintners also had a co-packing agreement with Pillitteri for icewine, until the Vintners discovered the money that Pillitteri Estates would make through icewine sales in Asia and ended the deal. The shareholders believed they could do it themselves and make their own profits, forgetting the years that Charlie Pillitteri had spent in developing relationships and building markets in Asia.

The receivers discovered a significant shortage of case goods and bulk wines. Shareholders claimed it was their property, and they had stored it in private warehouses and tanks. Deloitte thought differently, and reported the shortage to the police. Desperate times provoked irrational measures. One could understand the growers' desperation, no matter who was to blame for the outcome. None of the growers ever got paid a dollar for their grapes. They had gone two full vintages, some of them a third, with no pay. The saddest part was the vintage of 2008. Thousands of grapes ended up with no home because the shareholders had burnt their bridges with Vincor and Andrés. Emotions were high and extreme. A bomb had gone off in the grower community, and a year later the shock waves were still being felt.

The losses that resulted from this reign of error multiplied exponentially. Some of the smaller investors lost their farms, others lost millions of dollars but were able to remain solvent because of other holdings. They all suffered the disgrace of public failure. The community lost thousands of dollars in unpaid bills. Helmut Klassen lost his reputation and became a pariah in the wine industry. Only Diamond Estates, the enterprise that wine industry veteran Murray Marshall and his partners formed in 2000, took anything positive out of the deal when it purchased Niagara Vintners.

As president and CEO, Marshall had nearly thirty years of experience in the beverage alcohol trade and at one time had sold more wine than any individual in Canada. He had held senior positions at Bright's, Colio and Andrés. His partners brought extensive business experience: Andrew Green in corporate banking and international trade law, where he had a background in mergers and acquisitions, and Murray Watson in strategic leadership and extensive capital-raising. Combined with Marshall's wine-business savvy, they were unlikely to make the mistakes of their predecessors. The broader industry was happy that, unlike Vincor, which was now American-owned, the company stayed in domestic hands rather than selling to offshore interests.

Diamond Estates wine and spirits distribution and marketing agency had become one of the largest in Canada, and its Ontario winery portfolio included Birchwood Estate, Eastdell Estates, Lakeview Cellars, De Sousa Estates and Dan Ackroyd wines. The $17 million they paid for Niagara Vintners included a $32.8-million facility, which included equipment classified by some as the Ferrari of the winemaking cellars. The deal also included 3.6-million litres (792,000 gallons) of bulk wine and 21,000 cases of bottled wine. They validated the 20 Bees brand by maintaining it and keeping it as part of their portfolio.

Diamond Estates wasn't the highest bidder, but theirs was the cleanest bid. They worked hard to eliminate another $2.5 million in security that the bank held over those former individual investors who had personally secured the loan. "Even though the shareholders have lost their investment," said Marshall, "they wouldn't be chased after [for] it again. There has been enough damage. These guys have already taken a hit." This purchase made Diamond Estates, now producing 135,000 cases of wine annually, the fifth-largest producer in Ontario. Six months after the deal was finalized, 20 Bees Chardonnay and Cabernet-Merlot became the new house wines for Niagara Falls Casino and Casino Niagara. Diamond Estates was finding its market.

"Inevitable surprises," according to visionary Peter Schwartz, are inevitable because they are composed of predetermined elements or forces that we can anticipate with certainty because we already see their early stages. "They surprise us," states Schwartz, "because, while the events are pre-determined, the timing, results and consequences are not. We do not know how they will play out or when they will occur." Wine industry observers were predicting the demise of 20 Bees months before it actually fell.

Schwartz suggests that a more effective strategy of preparing for future possibilities is to balance short-term reactions with long-term vision. Put in place the necessary preparations to rapidly change direction if need be.

The wine industry would do well to heed this advice. There is a predetermined force on the horizon that, if ignored, could create turmoil in the wine industry. People's livelihoods will be seriously affected. Norm Beal had tried to reassure an uncertain public that the demise of such a monumental project as 20 Bees was not a reflection on the stability of the industry at large. The event had, nevertheless, accelerated the collision of several elements. A perfect storm in the grape and wine industry was brewing.

The grape growers felt it too. When Debbie Zimmerman, CEO of the Grape Growers of Ontario, and her chair, grower Bill George, went to the government after the disappointing harvest of 2008 to ask for assistance for the thousands of tonnes of grapes that had no buyer, included in their request was support for necessary structural changes to the way in which things operate in Ontario. They, too, were predicting the perfect storm.

The pressures building up to the collision included several factors. The first was increasing supply. Fruit-processing plants had closed, forcing fruit growers to look for other means of sustaining their farms. Being in the Green Belt precluded selling lucrative land to hungry developers; consequently, many growers, with the help of government assistance, planted vineyards. The quality of grapes available from independent growers forced further vertical integration by many wineries, so they could have better control of their raw material. In 2006, a vineyard inventory revealed that there were more than one million vines in the ground that had not yet come to market but, within three years, would flood the market with product. The second predetermined force was demand. In 2008, growers harvested 54,129 tonnes of grapes; wineries needed only 38,000 tonnes. The third force was the consumer, who simply was not buying VQA wine at the rate the producers had hoped. Sales have flatlined.

It is being forecast that these forces, combined with the retail challenges of the LCBO and Green Belt pressures to stay agricultural, will collide within two to five years. When the growers made this clear to the provincial government, the government gave the Grape Growers of Ontario $4 million to compensate them for their 2008 losses, and the next day, November 20, 2008, issued an ultimatum to the grape and wine industry, in the tone of an exasperated parent: "The industry must find solutions to its structural problems by February 2009, or the province will impose changes of its own." The date came and went with little progress.

Norm Beal and many of his members acknowledged the friction between the two organizations, but they also believed that the role the government played in setting the stage for their differences couldn't be ignored. Len Pennachetti, president of Cave Spring Cellars and former CEO of the VQA, stated: "It's disingenuous for the government to blame our two organizations for the problems between us, because the government has created the friction that we live with every day by the way they have structured the industry. They control the supply side through the marketing board. They control the demand side through the LCBO. The government holds all the cards. For them to scold us for not getting along and say go away and figure out how you're going to be nice to each other is outrageous." As one editorial in the *St. Catharines Standard* suggested: "If the province wants a long term solution to the woes of the grape and wine industry, it has to be prepared to do its part."

Author V.S. Naipaul reminds us in his novel *A Bend in the River* that "we make ourselves according to the ideas we have of our own possibilities." In such conditions of disequilibria that characterize today's Ontario wine industry, one can only hope that its entrepreneurial men and women will have the creativity, the confidence and the willingness to gamble on their imaginations as their predecessors did when they were on a threshold of transformation.

Stay tuned.

ACKNOWLEDGEMENTS

Chapter 1: Sublime Madness
Thanks go to Julie Dixon from the Grape Growers of Ontario and Lisa Murray from the Alcohol and Gaming Commission for their up-to-date figures on grapes and wineries. Books by Andrew Sharp (*Vineland 1000: A Canadian View of Wine*, 1977); Tony Aspler (*Vintage Canada*, 1983); and William Rannie *(Wines of Ontario: An Industry Comes of Age*, 1976) were helpful. A paper delivered to a symposium on the evolution of the Niagara grape industry held at Brock University in 1982, "The Niagara Grape Industry — Evolution to World Status," by Ronald C. Moyer, was also very helpful. Dr. Tony Shaw's paper "The Niagara Peninsula Viticultural Area: A Climatic Analysis of Canada's Largest Wine Region" provided helpful climatic data. Thanks also goes to Arden Phair at the St. Catharines Museum for his invaluable help on historical records; Jim Clark, president of Colio Estate Winery, for his overview of Lake Erie North Shore and Colio Estates and Laurie Macdonald, executive director of the Vintners Quality Alliance of Ontario. Credit must be given to Malcolm Anderson, Quebec wine writer, from whom I first heard the phrase "sublime madness." Forgive me, Malcolm.

Chapter 2: Harry Hatch's Bright Ambition
I found John Ghetti, the fieldman for Bright's wines, at his home in Niagara, where he and his wife, Gloria, graciously offered me a glass of President's Port, 1965, after admonishing me for being one of those journalists who had only bad things to say about old Ontario wines. The wine was beautifully mellowed and had no trace of foxiness. I was chagrined. Sadly, he died just a few months before the book was published. Dorie Browning from Vincor retrieved scores of old scrapbooks and annual reports from their archives in the old Bright's building in Niagara Falls. Dr. Helen Fisher, scientist with the HRIO, gave me background on its

activities during this period, and research scientist John Paroschy shared stories of some of the research activities at Bright's when he was there as a young scientist. The books that filled in the background for me were many, but the most important were Craig Heron's *Booze: A Distilled History* (2003); C.W. Hunt's fascinating stories about Canadian's involvement in bootlegging, *Booze, Boats and Billions* (1988); Tony Aspler's *Vintage Canada* (1999); Percy Rowe's seminal *The Wines of Canada* (1970); and William Rannie's *Wines of Ontario* (1978). For insight into Prohibition in Ontario I turned to Gerald A. Hallowell (1972), Reginald G. Smart/Alan C. Ogborne (1986) and Georges Masson (1979), and reports from the Ontario Grape Growers Marketing Board. I am also indebted to the tireless help of Arden Phair from the St. Catharines Museum and his assistant, Linda, for helping me access files on the industry, plus pulling down scores of boxes of data, donations from Mr. George Hostetter, where I found numerous old reports and papers that proved absolutely fascinating. Dave Evans, the LCBO archivist, also directed me to information I might have otherwise overlooked. I also spent a fascinating afternoon chatting with Mrs. Clifford Hatch, Harry Hatch Sr.'s daughter-in-law, now in her eighties. Great-grandchildren Mary Hatch and her brother Carr Hatch kindly lent me original photos of their great-grandfather.

Chapter 3: Donald Ziraldo's Zap

Appreciation goes to the following individuals for their recollections of those early days: former product consultants for the LCBO Claudius Fehr and John Tait; Frank Faigaux, once food and beverge manager for the Windsor Arms; David Sherman, in charge of Special Collections at Brock University; Terry Nagagowa from the Alcohol and Gaming Commission of Ontario; Luisa Tmej, with the provincial government; George C.C. Kitching, Major General Kitching's son; archival videos from the CBC, David Sharron Collections, Brock University; Debi Pratt from Inniskillin; Gerry Schwartz, CEO, Onex Corporation; and, of course, Karl Kaiser and Donald Ziraldo.

Chapter 4: Len Pennachetti's High-School Report

Lloyd Carmichael, former fieldman for Jordan & Ste-Michelle winery; Andy Dabrowsky, former winemaker, Jordan & Ste-Michelle winery; Alex Karumanchiri, former chemist with the LCBO lab; Gerry Schwartz, CEO,

Onex Corporation; Valerie Gibbons, former deputy minister of consumer and commercial affairs; Joyce Feinberg, former director of policy for the ministry of consumer and commercial affairs; Jack Corbett, executive director of the Wine Council of Ontario; Jim Rainforth, former executive director of the Grape Growers Marketing Board of Ontario; Brian Nash, former chair of the Grape Growers Marketing Board of Ontario; Jan Wesctott, former president of the Canadian Wine Institute; Leonard Franssen, LCBO; Allan Schmidt, Vineland Estates; Paul Speck, Henry of Pelham; Brian Leyden, Grape Growers Marketing Board; Millard Roth, whose father owned Parkdale Wines, which became Cartier; Linda Lowery; Donald Ziraldo; Peter Gamble, former executive director of the VQA; the business librarian at Brock University; and Len Pennachetti, president of Cave Spring Cellars.

Chapter 5: Paul Bosc's Journey

Mira Ananicz, former assistant winemaker to Paul at Chateau Gai; Dorothy Turcott and the Grimsby Library; Tony Aspler for lending his file on the "Champagne" case; Ezio Di Emanuele, Agriculture Canada; Paul Bosc Jr.; Steve Murzda, grower; Thomas Bachelder, author of "Leaving Labrusca Behind," *Wine Tidings*, October, 1978; and Paul Bosc Sr.

Chapter 6: Paul Speck's Challenge

Thanks go to Allan Schmidt, president of Vineland Estates, along with Len Pennachetti, president of Cave Spring Cellars; Bobbi Speck, Linda Franklin, Brian Leyden, former communications directors for the Grape Growers Marketing Board; Brian Nash; Sandra Marynissen, Marynissen Estates; and Paul Speck.

Chapter 7: Don Triggs and the Rise of Vincor

Bob Luba, Allan Jackson, Roger Provost, Bruce Walker, Richard Jones, Debi Pratt, Donald Ziraldo and Gerry Schwartz all gave considerably of their time and attention. This chapter was one of the most difficult to write, because of the intricacies of the details. I was surprised to discover how clear they remained in these key players' minds. When there was an occasional difference in how an event unfolded, a quick e-mail clarified the sequence.

Chapter 8: Pellers' Cellars

Don Campbell, former senior executive for Andrès; Ed Arnold, former winemaker; Dave Ringler, former VP of Marketing, then Operations; Dr. Joe Peller, director and former president; Andy Peller, through the miracles of television. I found an interview in the McMaster library archives of Pierre Berton interviewing Andy (Nov. 1988) on his show *Country Canada*. That, plus Andy's autobiography (*The Winemaker*) gave me insight into his character and the events of his life. Peter Pachette, CFO; Newman Smith, former DFO; and a book by Peter Mielzynski-Sychlinski, *The Story of Hillebrand Estate Winery* (Key Porter Books, 2001) were extremely helpful. Evan Crandall, the creative person behind the Baby Duck label and advertising campaigns, was fun and helped me to learn the behind-the-scenes work that produced the pretty duckling. And, of course, John Peller, president and CEO of Andrew Peller, Ltd.

Chapter 9: Linda Franklin's Navigation

Thank you to Len Pennachetti, chair of the VQA and president of Cave Spring Cellars; Allan Schmidt, president of Vineland Estates; Bruce Walker, vice-president for government relations for Vincor Canada, and former chair of the Wine Council of Ontario. Luisa Tmej, Mary Shenstone, Alex Aguzzi and Sue Corke all worked for the provincial government in various senior capacities and were very helpful. Thanks too go to Joanna Romano, marketing director of the Wine Council of Ontario; David Tsubouchi, former Ontario minister of consumer and commercial relations; Pat Ford, policy analyst for the LCBO; Hillary Dawson, president of the Wine Council of Ontario; Susan O'Dell, former president of EastDell Estates and business consultant; MPP for Niagara-West Glanbrook Tim Hudak; Walter Sendzik, executive vice-president and general manager of the St. Catharines–Thorold Chamber of Commerce; and to Linda Franklin, president of Colleges Ontario.

Chapter 10: Norm Beal's Peal

Thank you to Debbie Zimmerman, chair of the GGO; Linda Franklin, former president of the Wine Council of Ontario; Dan Paszkowski, executive director of the Canadian Vintners Association; Bruce Walker, in his capacity as chair of the Canadian Vintners Association; Harald Thiel, proprietor of Hidden Bench winery; Moray Tawse, proprietor of Tawse Winery; Ed Madronich, proprietor of Flat Rock Cellars; John Howard, proprietor of John Howard Cellars; Helmut Klassen, former CEO of Niagara Vintners; David Churchill, Churchill Cellars; Rick Davis from Gilbert+Davis; Murray Marshall, CEO of Diamond Estates; Jim Clark, president of Colio wines; Barry Katzman, president of Mike Weir Estate Winery; Len Pennachetti, president of Cave Spring Cellars and, of course, Norm Beal.